D0900430

James Joyce's
*Ulysses*

# James Joyce's
# *Ulysses*

*A Reference Guide*

## BERNARD McKENNA

Greenwood Guides to Fiction

**GREENWOOD PRESS**
Westport, Connecticut • London

**Library of Congress Cataloging-in-Publication Data**

McKenna, Bernard, 1966–
    James Joyce's Ulysses : a reference guide / Bernard McKenna.
       p.  cm.—(Greenwood guides to fiction, ISSN 1535–8577)
    Includes bibliographical references and index.
    ISBN 0–313–31625–2 (alk. paper)
    1. Joyce, James, 1882–1941. Ulysses—Handbooks, manuals, etc.  I. Title.  II. Series.
PR6019.09U68367   2002
823′.912—dc21      2001042329

British Library Cataloguing in Publication Data is available.

Library of Congress Catalog Card Number: 2001042329
ISBN: 0–313–31625–2
ISSN: 1535–8577

First published in 2002

Greenwood Press, 88 Post Road West, Westport, CT 06881
An imprint of Greenwood Publishing Group, Inc.
www.greenwood.com

Printed in the United States of America

The paper used in this book complies with the
Permanent Paper Standard issued by the National
Information Standards Organization (Z39.48–1984).

10 9 8 7 6 5 4 3 2 1

Dedicated to Patricia and Bernard McKenna

# Contents

# Preface

James Joyce's name and even his image are quite familiar to contemporary readers. The neighborhood bookseller or the bookshop in the local mall most likely carries his picture or likeness on its wall. Most bookstores carry copies of his works, and most college and high school English classes require reading some of his writings. Moreover, most students find the stories in the *Dubliners* collection enjoyable and accessible. However, readers coming to James Joyce's *Ulysses* for the first time face a challenging yet, potentially, rewarding experience. Unfortunately, most people who try to read *Ulysses* find the text, in whole or in part, inaccessible. Consequently, *James Joyce's* Ulysses: *A Reference Guide* seeks to introduce initial readers to Joyce and to *Ulysses*, to remove some of the obstacles initial readers face when approaching the text, to provide background information in order to facilitate understanding of the nuances of the book, and to introduce readers to the critical dialogue surrounding the text. As a result, readers can come to *Ulysses* with the same level of confidence they have when they approach Joyce's other, more accessible writings. Moreover, initial readers will, hopefully, discover the rewards of reading the book and find that they outweigh the potential obstacles to understanding *Ulysses*.

In order to introduce readers to Joyce and *Ulysses*, Chapter 1 offers a brief biography of Joyce and a survey of the importance and cultural impact of *Ulysses*. Chapter 2 provides a detailed summary of the narrative, with an aim toward eliminating the major obstacle to understanding *Ulysses*. Most initial readers find it difficult to follow Joyce's plot line. Consequently, they abandon the text in frustration. A summary of the narrative should enable readers to overcome their frustration with the novel's plot and enable them to open themselves up to the text's rich and revolutionary qualities. Chapter 3 reviews the genesis of the text and its publication history. Chapters 4 and 5 offer some useful background information. The fourth chapter explores *Ulysses'* historical and cultural context, providing background information on late nineteenth- and early twentieth-century political and social trends and ideas, the First World War, Modernism, and Irish history and literature. Chapter 5 considers the novel's major themes and issues. Chapter 6 explores Joyce's narrative art: his character development, language, images, and style. Chapters 7 and 8 introduce readers to the academic and critical responses to *Ulysses.* Chapter 7 offers a summary of various theoretical responses to the text, and Chapter 8 surveys the more traditional critical response to the novel.

In preparing *James Joyce's* Ulysses: *A Reference Guide*, I attempt to include the best qualities of the various teachers and students with whom I have had the pleasure of working. I first read Joyce as a student in a Jesuit secondary school, and the priests and scholastics at Loyola-Blakefield not only infused in me a love for his work but a respect for his artistic epistemology, even if that excluded many Catholic teachings. Father Joseph Cocucci deserves my special thanks. I next came across Joyce's texts as an undergraduate at the University of Delaware. The late Robert Hogan revealed the less serious side of Joyce's works, opening up new possibilities for understanding his writings. As a graduate student at the University of Delaware and later at the University of Miami, Bonnie Scott, Zack Bowen, and Patrick McCarthy introduced me to the rigors of Joycean scholarship. The voices of these teachers and scholars can be heard in the following pages. I also owe a tremendous debt to my fellow students and my own students with whom I have had the pleasure of reading Joyce and *Ulysses.* I owe a particular debt to the Wesley College students from the Spring 1998 seminar on *Ulysses.* They made me aware of what they needed in order to come to terms with Joyce's sometimes difficult text. Their suggestions contributed to the chapters devoted to the context of Joyce's works and to the narrative summary. I also owe a debt of thanks to my colleagues at Wesley, particularly Linda Pelzer, for their support and assistance. In addition, friends and family have offered insights into chapters in the text and have responded with incalculable patience to my devotion to Joyce's works. Peter Campbell and Dr. Charles Campbell offered encouragement and advice. My family—Thomas, Shannon, Michael, Joan, Gabriel, and Grace—

all had to live with me at various times during the composition of this text. I would also like to thank Susanna Garcia, Victoria Courmes, Liz, Marvin, and Tania for their support during the process of revising the text. Finally, a special lady deserves my gratitude for her charity and kindness. The good that is in this book is theirs. The faults are mine.

James Joyce's
*Ulysses*

# 1 Introduction

## BIOGRAPHY

James Joyce was born on February 2, 1882, in Dublin, Ireland. Joyce's family history is colorful. His father, John Stanislaus Joyce (1849–1931), was born and raised in the city of Cork, in the southern part of Ireland. John Joyce's life was one of promise, potential, advantage, and, ultimately, disappointment.[1] He studied medicine, unsuccessfully, at University College Cork, excelled in sports, and took an interest in amateur dramatics. He also inherited a small fortune, receiving a bequest from his grandfather's estate and an annual income from his father's estate. When he was twenty-five, John and his mother moved to Dalkey, just south of Dublin, where John lived a life of leisure, sailing, singing, and taking an interest in politics. After he helped two Liberal candidates win the parliamentary election in 1880, the new Lord Lieutenant of Dublin appointed him Rates Collector. Consequently, John Joyce had income from both a job and an inheritance, money from another inheritance, a position, and an abundance of talent, all of which attracted the attention of Mary Murray.[2] James Joyce's mother's family came from County Longford. She was an educated woman, studying privately at a school situated in a home on Usher's Island, located along the southern bank of the Liffey in Dublin and the setting for Joyce's long short story "The Dead." Against the objections of both John Joyce's and Mary Murray's family, James Joyce's parents married and settled in Rathmines for what promised to be a comfortable life. Unfortunately, John Joyce's drinking habits, his improvidence with money, and the expense of supporting a large family ruined his fortune.[3]

However, James, the first of ten children, four boys and six girls, received some of the benefits of his father's income and position. His father sent him to Clongowes Wood College. Clongowes, run by the Jesuits, accepted the young James six months earlier than they usually accepted pupils and at a reduced fee. Jesuit education helped the young Joyce develop his intellectual capabilities,[4] even though he, on the whole, rejected their theological teachings. While at Clongowes, Joyce found some academic success and enjoyed swimming, although he disliked many other sports, such as rugby. Clongowes also provided a strict daily religious discipline, including times for Mass, the taking of the sacraments, and chapel services. Moreover, the Jesuits stressed virtues and standards of behavior, including accepting personal responsibility for one's actions and gentlemanly behavior. Joyce succeeded at Clongowes. After only three years of study, his father's financial circumstances deteriorated, because his job was eliminated, and John Joyce not only withdrew his sons from Clongowes, he moved numerous times to stay ahead of the rent collectors.

James Joyce studied at home, reading independently, and eventually enrolled in the Christian Brothers' school on North Richmond Street; Joyce's short story "Araby" and the "Wandering Rocks" episode of *Ulysses* reference the school. The Christian Brothers had a good academic reputation but nothing that rivaled the Jesuits' strict academic discipline. After only a few months with the Christian Brothers, Joyce and his younger brother Stanislaus received free tuition at the Jesuit school in Dublin, Belvedere College, located on Great Denmark Street. Father John Conmee, who also appears as a character in both *A Portrait of the Artist as a Young Man* and *Ulysses*, played an instrumental role in Joyce's free admission.[5] Belvedere College specialized in preparing students to enter the university ranks and, subsequently, professional careers. Like Clongowes, Belvedere's schedule and curriculum emphasized religious and intellectual discipline. James Joyce excelled at both, initially. He was especially strong in languages, studying Latin, French, and Italian. In addition, he won numerous examination and composition prizes, many carrying with them a monetary reward. He also kept a strict religious devotion, becoming a member of the Sodality of the Blessed Virgin Mary, a initial step for many young boys who feel a religious vocation. However, Joyce, falling victim to the physical urges of his maturing body, abandoned his religious devotions and began to explore his sexuality with prostitutes. Like Stephen Dedalus of *A Portrait*,

Joyce attempted to reform his ways and briefly returned to his religious devotions but, ultimately, rebelled against them, refusing to write the catechetical examination. Joyce was allowed to write his other exams only through the intervention of his French teacher. Joyce's social life at Belvedere was a bit less bleak than Stephen Dedalus's fictional experiences. Specifically, the young Joyce made a number of close friends, many of whom would become influential figures in the Irish political and literary scene. Notably, Joyce met Richard Sheehy, a future circuit court judge, who remembered Joyce as a moody young man fond of practical jokes.[6] Rejecting a vocation for the religious life, Joyce went on to University College Dublin.

University College Dublin, at the turn of the last century, was under the trusteeship of the Jesuit order. Consequently, certain aspects of the curriculum would have been familiar to the young Joyce. He continued his study of languages, adding German and Norwegian to his Latin, French, and Italian. Joyce also made several friends who would figure prominently in his later fiction, including George Clancy, the model for A *Portrait*'s Davin, and John Francis Byrne, the model for Cranly. Byrne also lived at 7 Eccles Street, Leopold Bloom's residence. Joyce delivered papers and articles for the college and other organizations, including a review of an Ibsen play for the *Fortnightly Review*. Ibsen sent him a note about the piece. Joyce also wrote a rather scathing review of the fledgling Irish Literary Theatre, which the college newspaper declined to print. Joyce, however, paid to have it printed and distributed privately. He also wrote a play, whose structure and plot confused the editor of the *Fortnightly Review*. In addition, he delivered a lecture about James Clarence Mangan, a nineteenth-century Irish poet. After taking his degree in 1902, Joyce tried to study medicine in Dublin, but he decided instead to travel to Paris. He wrote to, among others, Lady Gregory, informing her of his imminent departure. Gregory responded with great kindness and deference to a young man who, at that time, showed some promise as a critic but had demonstrated little literary ability. She used her connections to help him earn extra money by reviewing books for the *Daily Express*. Moreover, she convinced Yeats to meet with him in London,[7] after which Joyce traveled to Paris. While in Paris, Joyce again took up the study of medicine. Joyce, despondent and lonely, returned home for Christmas after only a few weeks of work. Joyce returned to Paris, and his family sent him money and supplies. While in Paris, Joyce met John Millington Synge, with whom he disagreed about Ireland and writing. Joyce began to establish himself in Paris when he received news, via a telegram, that his mother was dying and that he should return home.

Joyce did return, borrowing the money for the ticket, and found his mother gravely ill. Joyce and his brother Stanislaus, much to the family's disappointment and anger, declined to pray at her bedside. Stephen Dedalus, in *Ulysses*, also refuses to pray at his mother's deathbed.

After his mother's death, the Joyce family household fell into disarray. Joyce, however, continued to pursue his literary studies, submitting an essay titled "A Portrait of the Artist as a Young Man" to a new literary journal. Although the journal turned down the essay, Joyce expanded and revised it into his first novel. Joyce also tried singing, entering the Feis Ceoil in 1904; winning the competition brought with it a year's study in Italy. Joyce impressed the judges but withdrew after being asked to sight-read a piece. In addition, Joyce worked as a teacher at a local private school, experiences he would utilize for scenes in *Ulysses*.

However, the most significant experience of Joyce's life in Dublin in 1904 involved meeting Nora Barnacle, his lifelong companion and future wife. Nora worked at Finn's Hotel, a location that would figure prominently in *Finnegans Wake*. They met when a rather bold Joyce struck up a conversation with her one day on Nassau Street. A few days later, on June 16, 1904, they had their first date. It is also the date of the events in *Ulysses*. Nora Barnacle was born and raised in County Galway, in the Irish West, like Gretta Conroy in "The Dead". Also, like Gretta, she was romantic and independent. However, unlike Gabriel Conroy, Joyce, after meeting his wife, began more actively to pursue his literary aspirations, publishing and writing poetry and short stories and a novel titled *Stephen Hero*, later revised as *A Portrait of the Artist*. One of the stories he wrote at this time, titled "The Sisters" and published in the *Irish Homestead* under the pseudonym Stephen Dedalus, was later included in the *Dubliners* volume.

In late summer and early autumn of 1904, Joyce and Nora decided to move to Zurich. Joyce, in early September, had lost his apartment in Dublin and wandered from friends' to relatives' homes, ultimately taking up residence in a Martello tower with a young medical student named Oliver St. John Gogarty and a neurotic young man, Samuel Trench. Joyce left the tower after only a short time because of Trench's nightmares and Gogarty's behavior. The tower, Gogarty, and Trench did become models for characters and situations in *Ulysses*. In October, Joyce and Nora left Ireland for Switzerland and a teaching job at the Berlitz School in Zurich. Arriving in Zurich, Joyce discovered that a job did not await him. He traveled on to the Berlitz School in Trieste, with another promise of a position, only to be disappointed again. Ultimately, he did find work at a school in Pola. However,

Joyce and Nora ultimately returned to Trieste for a more secure and comfortable teaching position.

About this time, Joyce and Nora started a family and began to build a household. A son, Giorgio, was born on July 27, 1905. In addition, Joyce's younger brother Stanislaus came to live with them, also teaching at the Berlitz School. In the next few years, Joyce lived briefly in Rome,[8] working for a summer as a clerk in a bank. He and Nora also had a daughter, Lucia, born on July 26, 1907. He wrote articles about Ireland for several local Italian-language newspapers. Unfortunately, eye troubles began to plague him, as they would for the remainder of his life. In the course of the next thirty or more years, Joyce suffered several painful operations, intermittent periods of intense eye pain, and periods of blindness.

In 1909, Joyce and his son traveled to Ireland, visiting his family in Dublin and Nora's family in Galway. He also checked in on old friends, one of who, Cosgrove, confessed to an affair with Nora. Joyce, troubled and despondent,[9] roamed the streets of Dublin, finally calling on Byrne at 7 Eccles Street for advice. Byrne informed Joyce that Cosgrove's claims were lies. However, Joyce had already written several despondent letters to Nora. Byrne and Joyce's brother Stanislaus, who contacted Joyce by mail, talked sense into the dejected Joyce, who then wrote asking for Nora's forgiveness. Joyce also frequented the theater while in Dublin before preparing to return to Trieste. He said goodbye to his family. His sister Margaret left for New Zealand shortly thereafter to become a nun. Joyce took another sister, Eva, back to Europe with him. Homesick, Eva returned to Ireland a year or so later but not before planting the seed in Joyce's mind about opening a movie house in Dublin. Arranging for financial backing from local (Trieste) businessmen, Joyce returned to Ireland and made arrangements to rent a hall and open Dublin's first movie house. The theater did not succeed financially, largely because it declined to show American films. However, after an English investment group purchased it and ran American films, the movie house became an enormous success. Returning to Trieste, Joyce left the Berlitz School and began taking in private students. In 1912, Joyce returned to Ireland with Nora and his children and visited the Aran Islands. Returning once again to Trieste, Joyce began teaching in a local school. Joyce's sister Eileen also came to live with her brothers and met and married a local businessman. With the arrival of the First World War, the family, with the exception of Eileen who left for Prague, moved to neutral Switzerland. Joyce had already begun writing *Ulysses*.

After leaving Dublin and prior to focusing his complete attentions on *Ulysses*, Joyce published a volume of poetry, *Chamber Music*; wrote a collection of short stories, *Dubliners*; and finished his first novel, *A Portrait of the Artist as a Young Man*. In addition, he wrote the play *Exiles* and a long prose poem titled *Giacomo Joyce*.

Fifteen realistic short stories comprise *Dubliners*; each one focuses on an aspect of Dublin life at the close of the nineteenth century. Although one or two of the stories often appears in anthologies, studying them separately blunts their impact and force. Themes, images, minor characters, and motifs appear and reappear across stories. Moreover, the fifteen stories taken together comprise a life-cycle pattern. The first three stories cover early life. The subsequent four stories focus on young adulthood. The next four stories examine characters dealing with middle age. The next three stories deal with issues associated with public life in Dublin, including art, politics, and religion. "The Dead," the collection's final story, functions as a type of summary story. Today, critics consider *Dubliners* a work of literary genius, and many readers find it the most accessible of Joyce's works. However, over forty publishers rejected it, although a few started the publishing process before turning it down. Ultimately, *Dubliners* was published in 1914.

*Chamber Music*, published in 1907, contains a few well-crafted poems. However, none approaches the literary quality of Joyce's prose texts. William York Tindall notes that the poems trace the development of a romantic relationship between a young man and a young woman, who fall desperately in love but who eventually grow apart. A rival takes the young woman's attentions, and the young man retreats into exile.

Joyce completed *A Portrait of the Artist as a Young Man* in early 1915. The Egoist Press, formed by Harriet Weaver in order to publish the book, issued the novel in book form in 1917; it appeared in a series of installments in *The Egoist* journal from 1914 to 1915. The book traces the artistic, intellectual, and spiritual development and maturity of Stephen Dedalus. Many of the characters and themes that originally appear in *A Portrait* also appear in *Ulysses*.

*Exiles* is Joyce's only extant play. Also written just before the First World War, *Exiles* received a few productions during Joyce's lifetime. However, with the exception of a production in London in 1970, directed by Harold Pinter, the play proves difficult to stage successfully. From a theatrical standpoint, the dialogue and characterization tend toward monotony. Pinter's production relies heavily on his revisions and adaptations of Joyce's text. Thematically, the play focuses on issues associated with betrayal and lost hope, including marital infidelity. *Exiles*, despite Pinter's adaptation, remains interesting largely for the light it sheds onto Joyce's other writings.

*Giacomo Joyce* is an extended prose poem with a curious publishing history and history of composition. Joyce wrote the piece just before the First World War but never attempted to publish it. Rather, he left it with his brother Stanislaus in Trieste, where it remained unnoticed until Richard Ellmann discovered it while researching his biography of Joyce; Ellmann also edited the published edition that appeared in 1968. Even though Joyce never tried to publish his manuscript, he took careful pains to recopy it onto oversized sheets of sketch paper. The prose poem has all the hallmarks of a love poem, and critics indicate that the woman of the poem was Amalia Popper, one of Joyce's students. Indeed, the sensitive nature of a love poem written to a student may have jeopardized Joyce's relationship with Nora. The prose poem itself suggests a relationship between an older man, presumably Joyce's persona, and a young woman, who assumes the characteristics of virgin/whore/Eastern lover. *Giacomo Joyce* has received some critical attention, but it remains studied essentially for the insights it grants into Joyce's other work.

When Joyce and his family took up residence in Zurich in late spring 1915, they gave up the community to which they had grown accustomed in Trieste and gave up also friends and the comforts of a familiar language. Joyce, because of his academic training, understood German, but his wife and children did not. Consequently, Giorgio and Lucia were placed in school a few grades behind where they had been in Trieste. However, the Joyce family quickly became part of the cultural scene in Zurich. Numerous British and European artists, writers, and businessmen had also fled to neutral territory to avoid the worst effects of the war. While Joyce continued to work on *Ulysses*, he enjoyed lively social evenings that often included the theater. Joyce supplemented the small royalties on his publications by giving private English lessons, but he still did not earn enough to maintain his family. Nora received some money on a regular basis from relatives, and Yeats and Pound successfully petitioned, on Joyce's behalf, the British government for artistic grants, one which he received from the Civil List and another from the Royal Literary Fund. Joyce also received an anonymous donation from Harriet Shaw Weaver, who arranged, through a solicitor, to pay Joyce a quarterly income until the end of the war. John D. Rockefeller's daughter also gave Joyce a generous monthly stipend. However, even as his financial situation improved, his physical health began to decline. Glaucoma and operations to correct it impaired his sight and caused tremendous pain.[10]

Meanwhile, Ezra Pound and Harriet Shaw Weaver arranged to publish *Ulysses* in monthly installments in both *The Egoist* in England and in the

*Little Review* in the United States. Joyce also struck up a friendship with the English artist Frank Budgen, who worked for the British Consulate in Zurich. Joyce took time to explain the ideas and principles behind *Ulysses* to Budgen, which helped Joyce more clearly discern the overall design of the novel. Joyce shared a love of French symbolist poetry with Budgen, and they often recited selections of verse to one another. The two men also discussed numerous literary figures, including Hamlet and Telemachus. Nora expressed some concern about Joyce's evenings with Budgen.[11] She, perhaps, was motivated by jealousy and, more definitely, by a maternal instinct that wanted her husband to avoid drinking and carousing. Joyce, however, included Nora in his social and artistic life. He took an active role in organizing a theatrical group that staged English-language plays, mostly by Irish authors, in Zurich. Nora took a role in a production of J.M. Synge's *Riders to the Sea.*

After the end of the war, Joyce, Nora, and their children remained in Zurich for another year before returning to Trieste, which was now an Italian possession. Stanislaus, Eileen and her husband, and the Joyce family resumed their lives. However, the war changed Trieste. The commercial high school where Joyce had taught was now the University of Trieste and Joyce continued to teach there. Trieste, under Austrian control, had been a strategic military and commercial center; however, Italian control meant that Trieste no longer occupied a central place in its governing nation's economic or strategic plans; it had been Austria's access to the Adriatic and Mediterranean trading routes. Moreover, with the decline of commerce came the decline of the city's cultural activity. Joyce and his family moved to Paris in 1920, leaving Eileen and Stanislaus in Trieste.

The cultural activity that was centered in Paris during the period between the wars suited Joyce. He encountered, with a variety of emotions ranging from joy to annoyance, various writers and artists,[12] including Hemingway, Gertrude Stein, F. Scott Fitzgerald, T.S. Eliot, Wyndham Lewis, and others. Joyce renewed his friendship with Ezra Pound and also established a very strong friendship with Sylvia Beach, who owned and operated a bookshop in Paris called Shakespeare and Company. Joyce's children also made attempts to join the artistic and cultural establishment in Paris. Giorgio tried to begin a singing career, without much success, and Lucia attempted both singing and dancing, also with little success. She did manage to design some artistic lettering and printing but succumbed to mental illness. Joyce also met Samuel Beckett and Paul Leon, both of whom assisted Joyce in his literary work.

As the composition and serial publication of *Ulysses* proceeded, the work received critical and legal attention. A charge of obscenity halted the *Little Review*'s installment publication of the text. However, Joyce's friends, both new and old, gave him a great deal of encouragement. Moreover, the book received high praise from a number of influential critics. In October 1921, Joyce finished a draft of the text. However, because of the legal controversy surrounding its content, publishers in the United States and in Britain declined to issue an edition of *Ulysses*. Sylvia Beach, however, agreed to publish Joyce's book under the Shakespeare and Company imprint,[13] and Joyce received the first copies of the book on his fortieth birthday, February 2, 1922. The edition, with ivory-white lettering on light-blue boards, contained 732 pages, a leaf for every one of the 366 days in 1904; it was a leap year.

Joyce and his immediate family spent most of the 1920s and 1930s in Paris, with the exception of occasional vacations, including a trip by Nora, Lucia, and Giorgio to Galway. The Irish Civil War erupted while they were in Ireland, and their train came under fire. Joyce, terrified at hearing the news, determined not to return to Ireland. In the 1920s, Joyce had several more eye operations, none of which proved entirely successful. Joyce also made the acquaintance, at his brother's suggestion, of John Sullivan, a tenor born in Cork but raised in Paris since the age of twelve. Joyce championed Sullivan's cause, gaining him a wider audience. Personally, Joyce began work on his final novel, *Finnegans Wake*.

In 1927, Sylvia Beach's Shakespeare and Company published Joyce's second collection of poems, titled *Pomes Penyeach*. The collection contains thirteen works, whose composition spanned twenty years. In fact, the earliest poem, "Tilly," almost made it into the *Chamber Music* collection. The other works in the latter collection were written in Paris, Zurich, and Trieste. *Pomes Penyeach*, then, encapsulates aspects of Joyce's life dating from prior to his exile from Ireland through the publication of *Ulysses*. Many of Joyce's friends and critics found Joyce's later poetic achievement unworthy of his prose works. However, Archibald MacLeish saw merit in the poems,[14] and a few critics explore their thematic value beyond the insights they grant into Joyce's life and other works. Specifically, a number of critics recognize in the poetry commentary on maternity, spirituality, and creativity, particularly Irish poetic and dramatic achievement of the late nineteenth and early twentieth centuries.

The late twenties and early thirties brought several unpleasant circumstances. Nora had a cancer scare and needed a hysterectomy in 1929. In 1931, Joyce's father died. Also in 1931, Joyce and Nora formally married at a registry office in London; they had moved to Kensington for a few months in order to establish residence. As he approached his fiftieth birthday, Joyce became pragmatic about his marriage, realizing that a legal union would facilitate the transfer of his estate to Nora and their children. Giorgio, who now preferred to be called George, married and had a son, Stephen, in 1932. George's wife, Helen, was an older, divorced American and the initial news of their marriage disturbed Nora, although she later warmed to Helen. George divorced her after her stay at a mental institution. Apparently, although Joyce himself disputed it as a cause, George's lack of love and affection drove Helen to desperation. Lucia also had bouts with insanity, eventually succumbing to them completely. Joyce even sent her to Carl Jung for analysis,[15] but to no avail. Lucia lived with a variety of Joyce's friends and family for varying periods of time in the hope that a change of scene might enable her to regain her sanity. Lucia traveled to London where Harriet Shaw Weaver took her in as a favor to Joyce. However, after Lucia proved too difficult to handle, she went to stay with Eileen (Joyce's sister) in the lovely seaside town of Bray just south of Dublin. Lucia ran away, and Eileen feared that she had died. However, the police in Dublin found her after six days. Subsequently, Lucia left Ireland and again stayed with Harriet Shaw Weaver in London. After undergoing more psychiatric exams and tests, Lucia was ultimately committed to an asylum in France. She stayed in various French institutions until the early 1950s before being transferred to a hospital in England, where she remained until her death in 1982.

In May 1939, Joyce published his final work, *Finnegans Wake*. He began work on it about a year after the publication of *Ulysses* and continued revising and updating it even after its initial publication, submitting thirty-one pages of corrections to his publishers in 1939. In the seventeen or more years Joyce worked on the text, he revised and updated his designs for the book and the particular structure of individual sections. Consequently, early published versions often vary widely from their final form. Six episodes form the foundation of the book, and Joyce's unused notes from *Ulysses* form the subject matter for many of these episodes. Joyce published parts of individual chapters and episodes from 1924 through the mid thirties, and critical attention focused on their genius and, often times, inscrutability. Joyce became so concerned with the early reception of his text that he orchestrated a critical volume explaining *Finnegans Wake*'s basic design and structure; Shakespeare and Company published the collection of critical essays titled *Our Exagmination round His Factification for Incamination of "Work in Progress"* in 1929; "Work in Progress" was Joyce's public working title of *Finnegans Wake*. In 1936, Joyce finished a complete draft of the text and began preparing it for publication. Viking Press issued the volume in the United States and Faber and Faber brought it out in Britain. Joyce received an advance copy of the first edition on his fifty-seventh birthday.

Thematically and stylistically, the volume suggests a circular pattern of thought and human life and human civilization and culture. The style recalls dream narratives, in which words find crosslingustic meanings and connections. Overall, a mythic pattern emerges from the text, tracing the development of human civilization. However, the volume also traces the happenings of a single family and a single individual. Moreover, Irish geography, folk tales, popular songs, history, and myth provide another framework for understanding the text. Readers coming to the *Wake* would do well to consult the various critical volumes devoted to its content and meanings.

After publishing *Finnegans Wake*, the Second World War occupied much of Joyce's thoughts and daily activities. He struggled to secure the safety of his family from Nazi persecution, relocating Lucia to another asylum, finding a safe home for his grandson, and moving his family first to a small village in Vichy, France, and then back to Zurich. However, the tragedy of the war found Joyce's inner circle. The Nazis arrested Paul Leon, who returned to Joyce's apartment in Paris to rescue some of his notebooks. Leon, a Jew, died while under Nazi control. He did, however, succeed in retrieving Joyce's notebooks, giving them to the Irish embassy in Paris with the instructions that they were to remain under seal until 1990. Joyce spent Christmas 1940 with friends and family in Zurich, sang a few songs, and played records. He felt ill, however, and did not join in Christmas dinner. A few weeks later, Joyce, overcome by stomach pains, was rushed to a nearby hospital. Doctors diagnosed a perforated duodenal ulcer and performed emergency surgery. Joyce rallied briefly after the operation but soon lapsed into unconsciousness. The hospital advised Nora and George to return home, reassuring them that they would be called as soon as Joyce recovered consciousness. Joyce did wake up and asked for his wife and son but died before they could return. His family buried him in Fluntern cemetery in Zurich. Nora continued living in Zurich until her death in 1951. She returned to practicing her Catholic faith, often attending daily Mass and taking the sacraments. George moved from city to city in Europe and died in Germany in 1976. Joyce's grandson, Stephen, currently lives in Europe, heroically defending his grandfather's literary reputation and the family's rights to royalties associated with Joyce's works. Other than *Giacomo Joyce* and numerous volumes of letters and notebooks, Joyce left no unpublished major works. Richard Ellmann, however, cites Joyce's plans to follow *Finnegans Wake* with a short and easy-to-understand prose work, reminiscent of waking after a dream.[16] Joyce's literary reputation continues to grow, nearly sixty years after his death. A recent edition of *Ulysses*, published in Dublin, proved to be a bestseller, and The Modern Library cited three of Joyce's books for inclusion in their best 100 books of the century. *A Portrait of the Artist as a Young Man* is third on their list, and *Ulysses* occupies the number one position.

## *ULYSSES*

Recently, in New York City on June 16, Bloomsday, Le Chantilly restaurant served kidneys and other inner organs of beasts and fowl. Simultaneously, actors associated with the Daedalus Theatre Company roamed about, entertaining guests by reading from *Ulysses* or by playing characters from the book. In addition, singers and musicians entertained the restaurant's patrons with songs that were featured in *Ulysses* or that were popular in Ireland at the turn of the century. Moreover, the General Consul of Ireland opened the proceedings with a speech, organizers read more recent Irish poetry, and popular musicians, including Susan McKeown, sang contemporary songs. Robert Trenthan also sang. He gave a stirring rendition of Arthur Heller's musical settings of *Chamber Music*.[17] Across town, the Symphony Space staged its annual reading of portions of *Ulysses*. Simulcast on local radio, the twelve-hour event drew an interested and relatively large audience. The Symphony Space event included extended readings of the text, shortened samplings, readings of material by other Irish writers (less popular than *Ulysses* with audience members), and dramatizations of certain scenes from the text. The people in attendance usually conducted themselves in an appropriate manner. Many even followed along with their copies of Joyce's work. Others sat and absorbed the theatrical experience of a recitation, watching as characters came to life on stage before them. Of the actors that read and performed *Ulysses*, Malachy McCourt and Fionnula Flanagan participated. Throughout the city, an extended audience in coffee houses, apartments, and homes listened to the festivities on radio. Likewise, audiences in Dublin, London, and other cities across the world attended to their community's Bloomsday celebrations. Performances in Dublin often include a reading at the James Joyce Centre, which features the door from 7 Eccles Street, rescued from the wrecking ball and the closing of the pub where it lived for decades.

Newcomers to Joyce's text, especially students frustrated at a first reading, might well wonder what significance *Ulysses* carries within its pages that warrants such massive popular attention. Indeed, what lies behind the sometimes seemingly inscrutable text that commands such devotion from such a diverse worldwide audience? Essentially, the text cherishes and values the ordinary thoughts of ordinary men and women, making their lives extraordinary by placing them not so much in the context of the *Odyssey* but in the context of the significance of ordinary people and things. *Ulysses* elevates ordinary, everyday experience to an importance often ignored by the powerful and influential and the wealthy, accustomed to finding their inner thoughts and lives the subject of popular and literary attention. Audiences who come to the text make a personal connection with the characters and events as they unfold before readers and hearers. People see their own thoughts and problems reflected in the variety of lives depicted within the pages of *Ulysses*. Indeed, Joyce made an effort to reveal the inner self of his characters to his readers, including, within *Ulysses*, even the passing and random, and seemingly random, reflections of a variety of individuals. Joyce gave respect to what some might call the mundane that the individuals living within the "mundane" give their lives and thoughts.

When *Ulysses* found publication, first in serial form and later in book form, it revolutionized novel writing. Other writers, among them Dorothy Richardson, Sherwood Anderson, and even the Joyce of *A Portrait of the Artist as a Young Man* used the stream-of-consciousness narrative technique. Other writers also focused on ordinary people and events; however, no one employed the narrative focus and technique to the extent that Joyce used them in *Ulysses*. In just the same way that Picasso took artistic thought and trends to their logical and extreme conclusions, Joyce's novel revolutionized prose narrative. Moreover, Joyce's stylistic innovations and experimentations were never used to the extent that he used them. *Ulysses* stands as a mark of innovation and revolution in art alongside the painting of Picasso, and, just as no artist painting after Picasso can afford to avoid his work and cannot help but be influenced by it, all writers after Joyce must come to terms with *Ulysses*.

*Ulysses* presents an exhaustive review of life in turn-of-the-century Dublin, a city near the heart of the British Empire but very much on its periphery. Its citizens helped extend colonial power and influence across the world as soldiers and clerks, but at home their religion, language, and lifestyle were lampooned, degraded and devalued by the Imperial authorities. In this sense, Joyce's text and his other works anticipate the late twentieth-century's explosions of literature from colonized and formerly colonized societies; readers of Salmon Rushdie's works, Cristina Garcia's writings, and Naipaul's books hear in them and in numerous other writers' works echoes of *Ulysses*. Novas's *Mangoes, Bananas, and Coconuts* even includes in the lives of Cuban immigrants an explicit reference to and the presence of a Joycean character. Joyce's text also comically deflates many of the anti-imperial institutions of Irish society, including the Catholic church, Irish nationalism, and journalism. Joyce systematically strips away the pretenses of society revealing the essence and substance present in the lives of seemingly unimportant people, or at least the people "great" powers and institutions might consider unimportant or unimpressive. Moreover, there is great significance and even tragic anticipation in Joyce's choice to feature a Jew as the hero of a story and a book that in part presents the turmoil of life at the beginning of the twentieth century.

*Ulysses* also parallels the beginnings and the development of psychoanalytic thought and theory, another intellectual marker of the twentieth century. Joyce features not only the inner lives of his characters but also the trauma that results from the dislocation of emotional, physical, and intellectual experience. He explores depression and guilt in the person of Stephen Dedalus, infidelity and revenge in the person of Molly Bloom, homosocial behavior, and even transsexual tendencies in Leopold Bloom. Joyce knew the theories of the early psychoanalysts, and, even though he did not entirely agree with Freud and Jung, he sent his daughter to Jung for treatment. Moreover, psychoanalytic theorists devote a considerable amount of criticism to characters and themes in Joyce's text.[18]

*Ulysses* even impacts the legal world. The dispute over publication of the text in the United States has helped to clarify issues associated with government censorship and control of the arts. As the *Little Review* published portions of *Ulysses* in installments, many morally conservative organizations attempted to have the chapters banned. After the July–August 1920 issue of the *Little Review*, which contained a version of the "Nausicaa" episode, a three-judge panel agreed with those who considered *Ulysses* obscene and fined the editors of *The Little Review*. The American publisher who had agreed to come out with the American edition of *Ulysses* asked Joyce to make alterations to the text, hoping that changes would quiet the book's moral critics. Joyce refused. Consequently, more than a decade passed before *Ulysses* was published in America and before it could legally be brought into the country. Throughout the twenties, returning Americans smuggled disguised and hidden copies of Joyce's text into the United States. The book became an object of literary daring and curiosity for tourists. However, in the early 1930s, a reader turned himself and the text in to

United States customs officials, hoping for a favorable court ruling. In 1933, Judge John M. Woolsey read the book and in a lengthy and learned opinion declared it not obscene but rather a brilliant artistic achievement. Many editions of the book carry the judge's opinion. Random House published *Ulysses* shortly thereafter, in January 1934.

*Ulysses* focuses on the lives of numerous characters but concentrates on three in particular: Stephen Dedalus, the now twenty-two-year-old protagonist of Joyce's earlier novel *A Portrait of the Artist as a Young Man*; Leopold Bloom, an advertising salesman in his late thirties and a Jew; and Molly Bloom, Leopold's wife and a singer in her early thirties. The action of the story takes place in and around the city of Dublin and begins at about eight o'clock on the morning of June 16, 1904, and ends in the early hours of June 17. As the book's title suggests, the characters' lives and actions roughly parallel certain characters and events from Homer's *The Odyssey*. Leopold Bloom corresponds to Odysseus, or Ulysses in the Latin spelling. Molly corresponds to Odysseus's wife, Penelope, and Stephen roughly corresponds to Telemachus, Odysseus's son. Essentially, *Ulysses* condenses Odysseus's journey of many years and to many places into the confines of a single twenty-four hour period of time and within Dublin's city limits. Joyce's technique does invite comic comparisons between the ancient Greek hero, who some critics call the central hero in Western culture, and Bloom. However, *Ulysses* is not only a comic text. Bloom's life unfolds before the reader, who observes his tragedies, his unfortunate circumstances, his hopes and ambitions, and his heartbreak and attempts at recovery. Bloom, at the end of the story, does not exist as a buffoon but as a new type of hero, an ordinary human being coming to terms in heroic ways with ordinary events. Moreover, *Ulysses* tells the story of many more people and lives than Bloom, his wife, and Stephen. Joyce's book lays out, in extraordinary detail, the city of Dublin as it existed in 1904. Joyce's letters to friends and family members still living in Ireland reveal requests for detailed information regarding the precise layout of scenes and places in the city. In addition, Joyce placed within the text some of Dublin's more eccentric characters, including one individual who walks only on the outside of lampposts on the street.

In terms of *Ulysses'* revolutionary character as a novel (indeed, some critics question whether Joyce's text can be called a novel, so revolutionary is its technique), the book contains no traditional plot or theme development. Rather, the action of the novel "advances" itself through a series of recurring motifs and themes. The variety of themes and motifs includes the heroic journey, the return of the hero, faithfulness and domesticity, familial reunion, and paternal/filial love. The book contains eighteen episodes, divided into three sections. The first section contains three episodes that focus on Stephen Dedalus and take place between eight o'clock and about noon. The first section introduces the reader to Stephen's circumstances. He lives in a Martello tower with Buck Mulligan, a medical student, and Haines, a student of the Irish language who is an Englishman. Stephen's mother died about nine months prior to the story's opening, and he struggles with his guilt and depression consequent of her death. He works in a small private school run by an Ulster Presbyterian, who has firm but not always factual notions about politics and history.

The second section contains twelve episodes, focusing primarily on Bloom but also on Stephen and some other characters. Bloom reveals himself to be a practical man, with an eye for women, a love for food, and romantic tendencies. He sells advertisements for a local paper, but not very successfully. His acquaintances and colleagues treat him with deference, but not excessive respect and kindness. He belongs to a Masonic lodge and converted to Catholicism to marry Molly, but he understands little of Catholic doctrine and teaching. His father was a Hungarian-Jewish immigrant who committed suicide. Bloom lost a son, Rudy, about ten years before the novel begins; Rudy died when he was only eleven days old. Bloom also has a daughter, Milly. Bloom wanders about Dublin during these twelve episodes. He cannot return home because his wife has a sexual liaison with a man named Blazes Boylan. In his travels, Bloom encounters many Dubliners, including Stephen. Bloom tries to help Stephen and, at the end of the second section, they do come together.

The third section contains the final three episodes and focuses on Bloom's and Stephen's relationship and on Molly. The first two episodes reveal that Stephen and Bloom could benefit from a closer relationship. Bloom feels the want of a son, and Stephen finds his father inadequate and pathetic; however, Stephen responds to Bloom's kindness with ridicule and derision. They part company, but their future relations remain ambiguous. Molly, the daughter of a British soldier, was born in Gibraltar, a British military outpost in Spain. She has a reputation as a good singer but also as a flirtatious and even promiscuous woman. Although some contemporary critics reject the negative connotations associated with the word "promiscuous," many in the novel consider her only for her physical attributes, which apparently are ample. Moreover, well deserved or not, many, including Bloom, focus on her tendency to enjoy sexuality and sensual things.

The style and innovative narrative techniques also make *Ulysses* a significant text. However, these factors often present problems for readers coming to Joyce's work for the first time. One of the better strategies for reading *Ulysses* involves using a episode-by-episode guide as a map through the text for the initial reading. Subsequently, readers should try to make their own way through the text, discovering their own individual and unique interpretations. On a cautionary note, many readers abandon *Ulysses* in frustration, wanting to understand everything on an initial reading. However, readers would be better advised to approach the book the way people come to know a new city or new landscape. These places cannot be taken in in one glance but require repeated visits to grasp even their most basic parameters. Joyce spent eight years writing *Ulysses*. He emphasized the individual nuances of his characters, their subtleties; no guide or quick reading can substitute for careful individual exploration of the text. Readers are best advised to enjoy the book and come back to it repeatedly and to welcome revisions to their initial impressions and to welcome new understandings.

Indeed, even professional critics who explore the text find contradictory readings and new discoveries each time they review Joyce's work. Moreover, many skilled readers of *Ulysses* come to firm but very divergent readings of the text. Some see *Ulysses* teaching readers about true morality and humanity as opposed to prejudiced and prudish notions of ideal behavior. Other readers find no such pronouncements in the book. Some readers see Joyce's text as the triumph of the individual spirit, while others see it as the story of individuals overwhelmed by life. Doubtlessly, *Ulysses* focuses on the movements of the thoughts and circumstances of individuals, how events change around them. Critics can debate whether individual characters change or grow in response to these factors. Perhaps, Joyce's genius for writing and *Ulysses'* true significance as a work of art lies in its potential for various readings and experiences. Joyce opens possibilities for readers, lays out a variety of potential interactions with the text. In a sense, readers could re-create the Dublin of 1904 using *Ulysses* as a guide, so detailed is the book's realistic re-creation of the city. However, the text also possesses surrealistic qualities that challenge readers to formulate their own individual responses to the text and to characters. Significantly, the surrealistic qualities may also be "realistic" representations of the human mind. Consequently, *Ulysses* offers readers not only numerous challenges but also numerous rewards.

One of the challenges many readers attempt involves exploring contemporary Dublin in order to discover the remnants of the Dublin of Joyce's *Ulysses*. Readers might be surprised to discover that much of Bloom's Dublin remains intact. Writing for the *Irish Independent* in 1995, John Ryan explored Dublin for the relics of the world Joyce chronicled in his work.[19] Although Ryan laments the loss of many of *Ulysses'* landmarks, much of 1904 Dublin remains. Specifically, the Martello tower in Sandycove not only survives but also houses the James Joyce Museum. Visitors can explore the bathing pool Buck Mulligan used near the tower, still in use today. Also, Deasy's school in Dalkey has changed little. It is no longer a school but a private residence, but development has passed it by so far, and visitors can roam the hockey fields, which are now private lawns. Unfortunately, Sandymount Strand now houses industry and homes. Although observers can wander on the beach and look out toward Dublin Bay, the slightest glance westward reveals how much Dublin has changed in the last 100 years. In Bloom's part of town, many things have also changed. The house at 7 Eccles Street now serves as home to part of the Mater Hospital Private Clinic, and the bells from Saint George's Church were removed years ago when it closed its doors. However, All Hollows Church, now Saint Andrew's Church, still stands, as does the chemist shop where Bloom purchased a bar of lemon soap. Tourists and interested bathers can still buy lemon soap there. Visitors can still follow the funeral route Bloom and his companions took to Glasnevin Cemetery; however, many things along the route have changed. The Irish Republican Army bombed Nelson's Pillar years ago (not, incidentally, out of hatred for Joyceans), and Parnell's monument was also completed years ago. The office's of the *Freeman's Journal* now house the *Independent* newspapers. Ryan notes that much of the office staff and equipment survive little changed from 1904. Davy Byrne's pub still stands, as does Trinity College, the National Museum, and the National Library. The Ormond Hotel serves customers to this day, but Barney Keirnan's pub no longer exists. The National Maternity Hospital on Holles Street still exists, and rowdy visitors are still discouraged. Olhausen Butcher Shop still sells crubeen, but Bella Cohen's brothel now serves as a retreat house for the Sisters of Our Lady of Charity. The cabman's shelter is now part of an international banking center, although many of the sites Bloom and Stephen passed still stand and still service customers, including the City Morgue, the North Star Hotel, and Mullet's pub. Dublin is a living, changing, thriving modern city. For nostalgic reasons, many Joyceans and casual readers of *Ulysses* might lament the loss of so many places that once served as landmarks for the city of Dublin. However, so much survives that it would be difficult not to find a sense of joy in that Bloom and Stephen could still find their way around the city.

# NOTES

1. Richard Ellmann, *James Joyce: New and Revised Edition* (New York: Oxford University Press, 1982), pp. 11–23.

2. Ibid., p. 54.

3. Ibid., p. 123.

4. Kevin Sullivan, *Joyce Among the Jesuits* (New York: Columbia University Press, 1958).

5. Ellmann, *James Joyce*, p. 35.

6. Ibid., p. 51.

7. James Joyce, *Letters of James Joyce*, Vol. II, ed. by Richard Ellmann (New York: Viking Press, 1966), pp. 4, 15–16, 17.

8. Ellmann, *James Joyce*, pp. 224–26.

9. James Joyce, *Letters*, Vol. II, pp. 231–59.

10. Ellmann, *James Joyce*, pp. 536, 538, 543, 566, 568–69.

11. Ibid., pp. 429–39.

12. Ibid., pp. 515–35.

13. Edmund Epstein, "James Augustine Aloysius Joyce," *A Companion to Joyce Studies*, ed. Zack Bowen and James F. Carens (Westport, CT: Greenwood Press, 1984), pp. 21–23.

14. Ellmann, *James Joyce*, p. 591.

15. Ibid., p. 659.

16. Ibid., p. 603.

17. Joseph Hurley, "Novel Celebration: As Usual, Joyce's 'Ulysses' Blooms on Broadway," *Irish Echo* 19–25 (June 1966):29.

18. Alan Roughley, *James Joyce and Critical Theory: An Introduction* (Ann Arbor: University of Michigan Press, 1991), pp. 175–216.

19. John Ryan, "Final Chapter for Joyce's Dublin?" *Sunday Independent*, January 29, 1995, p. 11.

# 2   Content

The events detailed in James Joyce's *Ulysses* take place in less than twenty-four hours, beginning on Thursday morning June 16, 1904, at about eight o'clock, and ending sometime before dawn on Friday June 17. Various locations around the city of Dublin provide the story's setting. The story itself contains eighteen unnamed and unnumbered episodes. However, the novel does provide divisions between episodes and three numbered sections. The first section, made up of the first three episodes, focuses on Stephen Dedalus, the protagonist of *A Portrait of the Artist*. The second section, comprising the twelve subsequent episodes, focuses mostly on Leopold Bloom, although certain episodes and sections of chapters focus on Stephen Dedalus and some other characters. The novel's third section, comprising the final three episodes, focuses on Stephen's and Bloom's first substantive interaction and also concentrates on Bloom's wife, Molly.

In order to facilitate an understanding of the novel, I provide a summary of the activities of each chapter and have organized the summaries under both chapter and episode headings. The episodes are numbered from one to eighteen, whereas the chapters are numbered within each of the three major sections of the text.

## PART I

### Chapter One (Episode I)

The first episode has three major sections, which take place on top of, inside, or just outside of a Martello tower, a stone turret built by the British in the early nineteenth century to guard against French invasion. The first section begins at about 8:00 A.M. and introduces Buck Mulligan and reintroduces Stephen Dedalus, the protagonist of *A Portrait of the Artist*. The opening establishes Mulligan's comic and irreverent character, his rivalry with Stephen, the themes of art and money, and Stephen's guilt regarding his mother's death. The chapter begins as Buck Mulligan parodies the Catholic Mass on top of the tower in which he lives with Stephen and an Englishman named Haines. A shaving bowl, mirror, and razor function as comic substitutes for the chalice, paten, and crucifix. With Stephen watching, Mulligan jokes about an electrical current transforming the lather and water into the body and blood of Christ. Subsequently, Mulligan and Stephen begin a conversation about their names, Haines's nightmares, water, Stephen's mother, art, and Ireland. Stephen also privately reflects on his mother's death and his personal guilt. Ultimately, Stephen's conversation with Mulligan takes a less cordial tone as Stephen confronts Mulligan about his insensitive behavior regarding Stephen's mother's death and as Mulligan takes a callous attitude toward death in general. The opening section ends with Mulligan luring Stephen inside the tower with promises of Haines's money for Stephen's thoughts and sayings.

The second section includes sequences that focus on eating; a milk woman; discussions of washing, money, and art; and Stephen's guilty associations. It begins as Stephen carries Mulligan's shaving gear into the tower and discovers that the breakfast is burning, covering them all in clouds of smoke and grease. After some fumbling to find the key, they open the door, airing out the room, and the three settle down to eat. The arrival of a milk woman interrupts their breakfast. As the milk woman speaks with a patronizing and arrogant Mulligan and Haines, Stephen reflects on her as a symbol of Ireland, as a symbol of a woman, and as a witch. She deferentially gives Haines and Mulligan their milk, essentially ignoring Stephen. Ultimately, they send her on her way without paying her in full. Afterward, the conversation turns to money and bathing. Haines suggests making a collection of Stephen's sayings and responds dismissively when Stephen asks about payment for them. Mulligan chides Stephen for mentioning money, and Stephen discusses compensation for artistic productivity. In addition, Mulligan teases Stephen about his hesitancy to bathe regularly, which prompts Stephen to muse about the sea as mother and his guilt surrounding his mother's death. The section ends as Mulligan prepares to leave the tower to bathe.

The third section begins with Mulligan's comic antics and ends with Stephen's exile. As Mulligan, Stephen, and Haines leave the tower and begin walking to the beach, Haines asks Stephen about his theory regarding Hamlet and Shakespeare. A hesitant Stephen pleads tiredness, avoiding conversation, while a garrulous Mulligan makes a joke of Stephen's theory. However, the joke does reveal some truth about Stephen's search for a father figure. Mulligan continues joking, chanting the "Ballad of Joking Jesus" and charging the water with arms flapping like wings, an obviously humorous reference to Stephen's name and his artistic/spiritual vocations. Left alone, Stephen and Haines begin to discuss faith and religion. Stephen reveals that, although he fancies himself a practitioner of "free thought," he serves three masters: the British, the Catholic hierarchy, and a master not specifically mentioned that most likely refers to Ireland or, at least, Irish artistic identity. Stephen then muses on the church's relationship with heresy and heretics before, once again, considering the sea. The section and the chapter end with the sight of a priest emerging from the water, talk of a friend who will join the army, and Stephen turning over money and the tower's key to Mulligan. As Stephen walks away resolving not to return to the tower, he turns to the water, catching a glimpse of Mulligan's head, comparing the sight to a seal.

### Chapter Two (Episode II)

The second chapter has two major sections and takes place in a private school in Dalkey. The first section begins at 10:00 A.M. and focuses on Stephen's work as an instructor, while the second section explores Stephen's interaction with Mr. Deasy, the school's owner and headmaster. The first section opens with a Roman history lesson. As a teacher, Stephen cannot focus on the lesson. He lets his personal thoughts and the students' interruptions break his concentration. Stephen tests the students on facts while he muses about history and forms of telling, about Blake and the innocent private thoughts and lives of his students. Stephen at one point amuses himself with the clever thought that a pier is a "disappointed bridge" and thinks it suitable for Haines's notebook. Stephen then considers that he, like one of his students, is a court clown who puts amusing facts together for a master. Stephen then continues the lesson only to have the students distract him with requests for stories and riddles. Indulging them, he recites sections of Milton's *Lycidas*, a poem about a young man who dies at sea, and tells them a riddle whose answer involves a fox digging up a body. Stephen also privately considers Aristotle and the soul and the biblical parable of the talents. The class ends with a call to a hockey game. All the students, save for one, leave. He comes to Stephen to check sums he has copied, revealing that Mr. Deasy's only concern is for the correct answers and not necessarily for understanding. Working with the boy, Stephen recalls his own boyhood and, once again, considers his mother and his guilt, revealing the interconnectedness between his unrealized artistic and priestly vocations and his remorse and self-blame connected with his mother's death.

The second section considers Stephen's interaction with Deasy. As Stephen focuses on getting paid, Deasy lectures Stephen about debt, money, women, and the Jews, revealing a deep and abiding anti-Semitism. Deasy's thoughts cause Stephen to reflect privately on the relative poverty and disadvantages of the Catholic working class, especially compared with the Protestant merchant class. Deasy also lectures Stephen about history, reciting sometimes inaccurate facts about Ireland's politics and history, further revealing his prejudices. Deasy is an Ulster Protestant, and his anti-Semitic comments coupled with his thoughts about the Irish cause link, in Stephen's mind, the Jewish and Irish peoples. Most significantly, Deasy asks Stephen to use his literary connections to publish Deasy's thoughts on a solution to a disease infecting Ireland's cattle. Deasy suggests that Ireland adopt a solution implemented in Hungary. The suggestion has a historical counterpart. Arthur Griffith argued in a series of articles, titled "The Resurrection of Hungary" and published in *The United Irishman*, that Ireland follow Hungary's model to achieve independence.[1] Deasy also suggests that Stephen is, perhaps, not suited for work as a teacher in his school and concludes the chapter by chasing Stephen down to tell him yet another anti-Semitic joke. The chapter's final interior monologue casts Deasy in the stereotypical, anti-Semitic image of the money-grubber.

### Chapter Three (Episode III)

The third chapter finds Stephen Dedalus focusing on the essential nature or identity of things and people. He speculates about perception, imagination, and mutability; death, decay, and rebirth; and the impact and effect that these processes have on each other and how they inform reality. The chapter begins with a series of philosophical speculations and then considers Stephen's thoughts, musings, and experiences with the people and things that occupy and are in the vicinity of the seashore on

Sandymount Strand, a beach on the south side of Dublin Bay, at about eleven o'clock in the morning. For Stephen, the beach, with its changing tides and constant erosive forces, serves as an ideal metaphor for the essential nature or identity of things and people.

The chapter's opening passage records Stephen's musings about the nature of reality and its relation to individual conscious and unconscious interpretation, to an individual's sensory perceptions, and to an individual's relation of that reality to others and to himself. More specifically, the chapter begins with Stephen's speculations about the "ineluctable modality of the visible,"[2] which can be read as the undeniable mutability of things perceived. Stephen then speculates on his personal interpretation of reality—"thought through my eyes." Indeed, Stephen's perceptions change the nature of reality, and least for him and anyone, such as a reader, who hears his interpretation. Subsequently, Stephen returns his thoughts to the reality that stimulates his personal interpretation—"Signatures of all things"[3] that he is "here to read." He then lists some of the items on or near the beach, all of which have a relation to the mutability, death, and decay that occur to both mammals and natural items when exposed to the change agents of sea, wind, and tide. "Seaspawn" indicates the expanse and life of the sea and symbolizes birth and regeneration. "Seawrack" is the seaweed cast up on shore and symbolizes death and decay but also sustenance for those who gather it. The "nearing tide" is the primary agent for mutability on the shore. As a force of nature, it possesses no will or intent; its perception does not change or alter reality. Rather, its force produces changes in reality. The "rusty boot" is a man-made item decaying, because of the forces of the natural world, back into nature, symbolizing both the conscious change agents of man, who made the boot, and the unconscious change agents of nature. Stephen then considers the colors of the objects. At first, he named the objects and now he names a description of them. The terms he uses suggest a combination of human and natural forces. "Snotgreen" links decay to the unconscious processes of the natural world to those same forces in the world of the human body. "Bluesilver" suggests the sea but also quicksilver. "Rust" again references decay and regeneration, the transformation of an object and, again, a man-made object. Stephen then uses the term "coloured signs"[4] to indicate the limits of his perceptions. He sees the objects not for what they are but rather through the necessarily limited lens of his or anyone's life experiences, education, and understanding. Essentially, "coloured signs" represents the change agents of Stephen's perception and reflection. The word "diaphane"[5] reinforces this interpretation. Literally, it means transparent and light (illumination, understanding, sight) shining through; Stephen's perceptions illuminate the inanimate and animate objects in the world around him, but, still, his vision or the light of understanding finds its limits in his expansive but still limited perceptions, represented later in the paragraph by the word "adiaphane."[6] Stephen then considers Aristotle's theory of color ("he [Aristotle] adds") that is the visible or "diaphane" of bodies. Color is the external light of objects and both the limit and prime agent of perception. It allows an individual to identify an object, but color is only an external trait of the object and not the object. Stephen then playfully asks himself how Aristotle "was aware" of objects before he could perceive their color and answers the question by speculating that Aristotle must have "knock[ed]" his "sconce,"[7] or candlestick, against the objects. The image indicates that Aristotle, because of the limits of the candle, did not see the objects he ran into and also alludes to Dr. Johnson's proof of a reality independent of perception; he kicked a rock with his foot. Stephen then makes reference to some popular myths about Aristotle, that he was "bald" and "a millionaire."[8] Further, Stephen references Dante's description of Aristotle as the "master of those who know."[9] Both descriptions have replaced the reality of who and what Aristotle was for many.

Next, Stephen offers a humorous definition of reality through touch; it functions as a satire of Dr. Johnson's manner of definition in his dictionary. Rather than rely on the obvious differences between a door and a gate, touch becomes necessary to distinguish between them. Stephen's final parody reinforces the paragraph's themes of the limited nature of sensory perception and the judgments made based on its inputs and also how perception can change the reality of an object for an individual but also functions as the only way someone can come to know the reality of a thing.

The next paragraph finds Stephen focusing on sound as an agent of perception[10] and, therefore, an agent of change. Linked to sound through Stephen's stream-of-consciousness associations are concepts of time and space. Specifically, the paragraph begins as Stephen walks along the strand trampling "wrack and shells." He knows them through the sounds they make under his feet; they also represent the limits of his knowledge. Significantly, his movement through the debris on the shore changes the nature of the debris, just as time and movement (through space) are also change agents. Stephen's random thoughts pour into his mind. He considers "nacheinder,"[11] time, and associates it as Lessing did with literature and the audible—sound. Stephen then reconsiders the visible as "nebeneinder,"[12] which literally means "space." The two words together suggest a movement past the random associations of ideas and into the intentional/volitional reassociation of words and images into works of the creative imagination.

Three references to fathers and to creativity, to art and to paternity as creative forces, reinforce this movement. The first reference is to Shakespeare's *Hamlet*. "If I fell over a cliff" alludes to Horatio's warning that Hamlet's father's ghost might change Hamlet's sanity or perceptions so as to cause his death. The second reference, to "Los Demiurgos," refers to the father/creator in Blake's poetry. The final reference, to the remembered association between shells and money, is to Deasy, compared with God the father. The first two allusions build up an expectation that Stephen's thoughts might create art that at least attempts to rival the creative transformations of Blake and Shakespeare. Certainly, Stephen has the intellectual background and training; however, the third reference suggests Deasy's letter and flawed creative production.

The remaining sections of the chapter's opening passages fall into self-parody, references to the rhythm and not the meaning of poetry, to philosophical self-mockery and, finally, the remnants of a Catholic prayer.[13] These gathered associations suggest that Stephen cannot move from intellectual reflection and stream-of-consciousness associations into imaginative creative regeneration.[14] The remaining sections in the chapter reinforce this theme, offering different perspectives on creativity, creation, and artistic representation.

After his initial philosophical contemplations, Stephen's thoughts turn toward other figures on the shore and to associations with life and creative transformation. He sees two women; later, he understands that these women are cockle pickers. However, he, on the moment, creates a fiction about them as midwives, invents their pasts, and imagines them carrying a misbirth with navel cord. His thoughts wander from these women to a contemplation of birth, parentage, creation, and God. Stephen then considers his parents and the act of his conception and, in his mind, creates an association between his birth, the birth of mankind, Christ, the priesthood, and artistic creation. He even considers the transformative powers of Mananaan,[15] the Irish god of the sea. Ultimately, he remembers that he must deliver Deasy's letter, as his (Stephen's) thoughts turn toward the practical consideration of money and away from artistic and sublime transformations.

Subsequently, Stephen considers dropping in to see his Aunt Sarah, and his thoughts turn toward his father, his (Stephen's) family, and his youthful artistic and intellectual ambitions and pretensions. At first he imagines his father's opinions of his considered visit to his aunt's house. Stephen's thoughts reveal an image of his father as someone with contempt for his dead wife's family and for his son's artistic vocation. Stephen then imagines the greeting he would receive at his aunt's house and imagines his uncle welcoming him with offers of food and drink, while Aunt Sarah bathes one of her children; this is a significant image, considering that Stephen declines to wash regularly and because of the chapter's focus on the transformative powers of the sea as mother. Stephen's thoughts then turn toward memories of his life at Clongowes and how he lied about his family, partly out of shame and partly to impress his schoolmates. Stephen recalls more of his life as a young man, thinking of his pious efforts at stringent Catholic devotions and of his sexual temptations. He also considers his youthful intellectual and artistic ambitions, as the sinking sand at his feet recalls him from his memories. The sand also reminds him of the sunken ambitions of others who now lie at his feet, their bodies transformed through decay and degeneration into grains of sand.

Stephen subsequently confronts his life in Paris and his now seemingly pathetic and futile youthful aspirations for himself as artist and artistic savior for his country. He begins by recalling a parody of the annunciation,[16] revealing a subtle contempt for himself as an artistic messiah. As Stephen thinks of his life in Paris, he reveals that it was a period of great artistic ambitions and youthful pretensions; he tried to dress as a young artist with an affected walk and manners. He reveals his desire to do great things and his more compelling desires for risqué magazines. Subsequently, Stephen thinks about the telegram he received in Paris from his father, announcing his mother's grave illness. Stephen then considers Kevin Egan, a figure of the apparently forgotten Irish revolution who futilely labors in exile to liberate his indifferent countrymen. Ultimately, the sinking sand underneath his feet recalls Stephen to the present after his thoughts of his failed artistic and creative ambitions.

Stephen then confronts life on the shore. He sees things more realistically and less through an imaginative and artistic filter. Stephen begins with thoughts of his current predicament and determines not to return to the tower and life with Mulligan and Haines. After he sees a dog's carcass, he considers some of the tragedies of Irish history—the Viking invasions, various famines, failed wars and revolts, and dead heroes. Stephen then considers, in very realistic terms, a dog running around the beach, as it enthusiastically sniffs the dead carcass, urinates, and then runs away from his master. Stephen also recognizes the women that he thought were midwives as cockle pickers, as they move in and out of the tide, sinking in the wet sand, and filling their bags. Stephen concludes his contemplations by giving them a romantic identity as gypsies, bringing to an end his realistic contemplations with an imaginative transformation.

The chapter's final section finds Stephen ready for artistic and creative expression and communion. He begins with a more serious consideration of the annunciation, moves into an imagined physical/sexual embrace, and searches for paper on which to record his thoughts. He, significantly, tears away the blank portion of Deasy's letter and writes down words. Stephen then contemplates the utility of his own artistic impulse, wonders who will read his work, and then falls back into the philosophical musings that began the chapter. Stephen then considers various women in his life—his sexual preoccupations and his mother. He thinks of his loneliness, of Kevin Egan, and of futility. Stephen then urinates into the sea and the sand, leaves snot on the rocks, and contemplates drowned fathers from Shakespeare. Stephen also considers life, death, creation, and rebellion. As he leans on his staff, sinking into the sand, he observes the masts of a ship, which allegorically suggest Christ crucified[17]—an emblem of triumph over death.

Ultimately, Stephen seems to come through his philosophical musings with a sense of oneness and a creative response to death. He writes, seemingly overcoming the practical ghost of Deasy and also overcoming his father, his fears of futility, and his guilt. He seems at one with the sea and sand, unifying the natural product of his bodily transformations with the sea and shore, the symbols of nature's decay and transformative regenerations. However, Stephen never reveals his poem. Unlike a similar scene in *A Portrait of the Artist*, where Stephen's completed creative works stand as a symbol of artistic promise and as a gesture of communication, Stephen's creative work in this episode remains silent, implying a private revelation but also suggesting public silence. As a silent artist, Stephen's work resembles that of Kevin Egan, laboring in forgotten and unheard futility in Paris. Stephen's silence also recalls his philosophical musings at the beginning of the chapter. If no one perceives Stephen's creative transformations/representations, they then have no impact on the constant mutability that informs everyday existence. In essence, Stephen, however illuminated, cannot communicate his artistic/philosophical vision, which raises questions concerning the value of his artistic vocation.

## PART II

### Chapter One (Episode IV)

The fourth episode focuses on Leopold Bloom, a practical counterpart to Stephen Dedalus. Bloom is a middle-aged man of Jewish heritage and the son of an immigrant. As the focus of the book turns toward Bloom, it also returns to the beginning of the day. The chapter starts at about eight in the morning and takes place in and around Bloom's house at 7 Eccles Street, located a few blocks north of the Liffey at about the midpoint between Phoenix Park and Dublin Bay. The chapter establishes, in a series of scenes, the essential qualities of Bloom's nature. He is a man who enjoys his pleasures: eating, defecating, watching women. He also enjoys human contact and is intellectually curious, although he does not share Stephen's education and philosophical background. Indeed, he occasionally confuses ideas.

The chapter's opening section finds Bloom preparing breakfast for his wife, Molly, and his cat. The first paragraph describes Bloom's taste for the inner organs of animals and his hungry reaction to the morning's light and air. Bloom then takes great care to prepare his wife's breakfast just as she likes it, engages the cat in conversation while giving her milk, thinks admiringly of the cat's intelligence and abilities, but then teases her about her stupidity and cruelty, and calls to his wife to see if he can pick her up something special for breakfast. Her reply, a short verbalization standing for the word "no," is reminiscent of the cat's verbalizations. As Bloom leaves the house, he thinks of his wife's past and their bed, which Molly brought with her from Gibraltar, where it was purchased at auction by her father.

As Bloom leaves the house, he discovers that he has forgotten his key but decides not to return for it; he does not want to disturb his wife. While crossing the street, on his way to the butcher's shop, his thoughts range from the heat of the day to the imagined Orient to money and commerce. Significantly, even though he indulges in deeply romantic thoughts, he catches himself, realizing that the East is probably not like his fantasy version of it. Bloom also very practically assesses the viability of selling advertisement space to various individuals; thinks of cattle, of Arthur Griffith, the clergy; and overhears a school lesson, all of which create interesting parallels with Stephen Dedalus's thoughts, occupation, and circumstances.

As Bloom arrives at Dlugacz's, the butcher's shop, he pauses for a moment to gaze into the window, admiring the various meats. Entering the shop, his attention falls on the last kidney and a girl with attractive hips. He allows his mind to wander into thoughts of the butcher's extramarital activities, cattle farms, and the girl beating a carpet—an image in which Bloom takes sadomasochistic delight. All the while, Bloom takes careful note of the butcher's activities. After the girl leaves the shop, Bloom hurries his order, hoping to follow the girl for a while, admiring her swinging hips. He also imagines her form and sexual life in some detail. As he rushes from the shop, he finds that the girl has disappeared.

On his journey home, Bloom's thoughts range from Levantine planter's propositions to a romanticized dream of the East to his early life with Molly to a bleak view of Palestine to death and desolation and finally to hope of renewal. After leaving the shop and losing sight of the girl with attractive hips, Bloom begins to read the newspaper. He catches sight of an offer for shares in orange, olive, almond, or citrus groves in the Middle East. Bloom rejects the idea of an actual investment but allows himself the fantasy of perfect citrons loaded on the docks awaiting shipment to Ireland. His fantasy merges with idyllic memories of his early life with Molly, prior to the loss of their son and their previously active sex life. As a cloud passes overhead, Bloom's thoughts grow bleaker. He imagines the once holy and fertile land of Palestine grown bleak and desolate. He then observes an old, bent-over woman and likens modern Palestine to her withered sexual organs. As he approaches his home, he sees further signs of desolation in an unlet house on the street and in his aging and cold body. Rousing himself, he considers taking up exercise, a home filled with smells of food, and a warm bed with a companion. To confirm his uplifted spirits, the sun reappears, and Bloom likens it to a golden-haired girl running to meet him.

After he enters the house, he finds the mail. He delivers to his wife a card from their daughter and a letter from Blazes Boylan, arranging the time later that afternoon for their romantic meeting. Bloom temporarily puts aside his own mail. Molly asks him to get her tea and berates him for his delay. Bloom returns to the kitchen but only after opening the shade for his wife, to let the light in, and after gathering her dirty laundry. Going downstairs, Bloom first prepares Molly's tea and then quickly glances at his letter from Milly, while quickly putting his kidney in the frying pan. He lets the cat have the kidney wrappings, to lick the blood and juices, while thinking that giving her too much will spoil her. Bloom then carefully checks that the tray for Molly's breakfast is complete and carries it up to her. She berates him for taking so much time. As Bloom straightens her sheets and fetches her book that has fallen to the floor, Molly tells him that Blazes Boylan will be by, ostensibly, to deliver the program for her concert tour. While on the floor, Bloom notices her soiled underwear and her chamber pot. As he gets up, Molly asks him to define the word "metempsychosis." Bloom tells her that the word means reincarnation. Satisfied, Molly asks Bloom to get her another book, one that is smutty. Bloom, however, wants to provide a more detailed explanation for the word and, noticing a picture of nymphs above her bed, proceeds to confuse metempsychosis with metamorphosis. Molly interrupts him, smelling the kidney that has started to burn. Bloom leaves the room, rushing down the stairs in an effort to save his breakfast.

The chapter ends with Bloom indulging himself in thoughts about life and death, hens and cattle, and eating. He reads Milly's letter, while taking the time to enjoy his tea and kidney, generously tossing a portion of it to the cat. Slang and jargon fill Milly's letter but also a reference to Blazes, to whom she asks that her father send her love. Bloom then speculates about her birthday; she turned fifteen the day before. As he considers her birth and the midwife that assisted it, his thoughts turn toward his son, Rudy, who died shortly after birth. Bloom's thoughts soon return to Milly. Bloom thinks about her budding sexuality with some trepidation but, more so, with nostalgia for old times with Molly. Finally, Bloom resolves to visit Milly in August. For now, he tells the cat, which persistently bothers Bloom, that she will have to wait to go outside. Bloom, meanwhile, feels the urge to defecate but delays going to the outhouse until he finds some light reading material. With an old copy of *Tidbits*, he leaves the house. Molly, in her final appearance of the chapter, calls to the cat from the bedroom. In the yard, Bloom plans a garden and considers droppings from the neighbor's hens, ashes, or cattle manure as possible fertilizers. Taking his seat in the outhouse, Bloom carefully paces his elimination for optimum satisfaction and enjoyment and also to keep pace with the story. Before he finishes, he considers writing a story of his own, a collaboration with Molly, and calculates the money they would receive from it. Ready to go, Bloom cleans his bottom with the story he had been reading and comes out into the sun. He checks his trousers to make sure they are not dirty, resolves to verify the time of the funeral, and sings a cheerful song in time to the nearby church bells with a passing thought for Paddy Dignam, who recently died.

Episode four introduces the reader to the life of Leopold Bloom. He reveals himself to be a bit henpecked by his wife and very vulnerable to the charms of women and to food. However, he also shows himself to be a practical man with a buoyant personality and a self-deprecating sense of humor. Many of his actions and thoughts parallel those of Stephen Dedalus. However, whereas Stephen intellectualizes his problems and circumstances, Bloom deals with issues practically and with common sense.

### Chapter Two (Episode V)

The fifth episode begins at about ten in the morning, or just before, and traces Bloom's thoughts as he wanders through an eastern part of Dublin, traveling from the convergence of the Royal Canal and the Liffey to just south of Trinity College. In a series of scenes, Bloom encounters various people and places who seem content using their work, faith, gambling, sports, or moments of recreation as not simply momentary distractions from or as sources of support for dealing with their problems but as ways to avoid their problems and responsibilities entirely. Bloom, although he engages in revelries of escape and puts himself in the proximity of the mechanisms of avoidance, nonetheless manages to remain apart, at most indulging in a surreptitious romantic correspondence.

While Bloom walks to an out-of-the-way post office to check on his secret romantic correspondence, his attention and thoughts wander over a variety of subjects. Specifically, he considers emotionally and physically scarred children and the hopelessness of their lives. He thinks how smoking or playing gives them the only, albeit temporary, joy they have. He then, prompted by the sight of the Belfast and Oriental Tea Company, permits himself another fanciful daydream of the East that includes visions of languid idleness, of exotic flowers, and of magical places. He reflects on the Dead Sea and recalls a picture of a man floating effortlessly on its surface. However, Bloom does not allow himself to dwell on his daydream. He tries to recall the scientific reason for the floating man and thinks of the "Law of Falling Bodies."

As Bloom picks up his mail at the post office, he focuses on various examples of betrayal and disloyalty. The letter and envelope, addressed to him from a woman named Martha whom he has never met, reveals that Bloom not only carries on a flirtatious correspondence, a subtle betrayal of his wife, but that he also has not given Martha his real name; she thinks his name is Flower. Prompted by the image of soldiers in a recruiting advertisement and also, perhaps, by a guilty conscience, Bloom thinks of his wife's father, who served in the British army and was stationed in Gibraltar. Bloom thinks also of the British military presence in Ireland, of Maud Gonne's opposition to them, of Arthur Griffith's newspaper stories about the army, and sexually transmitted diseases. Bloom's thoughts suggest an interesting correspondence between the scientific formula, recalled earlier, and Ireland. Bloom considers that an object falls at a rate of thirty-two feet per second. Ireland has thirty-two counties, which, in 1904, were still under British control.

As Bloom opens the envelope, while it is concealed in his pocket, M'Coy interrupts him, speaking to him about Paddy Dignam's death, Molly's singing, and about signing his (M'Coy's) name on the death registry. In the short story "Grace," part of the *Dubliners* collection, Joyce reveals that M'Coy also has a wife who sings and who may be disloyal to him. M'Coy felt comfortable about speaking to Bloom regarding the funeral because Bloom was wearing a black suit, a sign that he would attend the funeral. Bloom, however, does not completely focus on M'Coy. Rather, Bloom considers an attractive woman across the street, other women he has seen in his wanderings, and song lyrics associated with love and betrayal.

As Bloom continues walking, his thoughts turn toward loss and homelessness. At first, he thinks of a lost leather valise and then of things more serious—his wife's concert tour. She will be separated from him. He then thinks briefly about the play *Leah*, going up that night in Dublin, and about *Hamlet*, which ran the night before. Both plays touch on themes of loss. *Leah* involves love and identity betrayed and an eventual suicide.[18] *Hamlet*, of course, stresses infidelity and the loss of a father. Quite naturally then, Bloom thinks of his father's death, itself a suicide, before considering the gelded cab horses, an image of impotence; the wandering rootless lives of the cabmen; of solitary children; and of his lost childhood.

Bloom opens Martha's letter and, while it is concealed in a newspaper, reads it and considers issues associated with betrayal and superficiality. Martha's letter is chatty and flirtatious and hints at playful sadomasochism but also at empathy. It also contains a scentless flower. Bloom then contemplates meeting her after her Sunday rosary and thinks of the possible tryst as a type of narcotic, likening it to a cigar. He then considers the pin, which held the flower to the envelope. He thinks of its origin, as part of her wardrobe, and remembers a bawdy street rhyme about pins and women's garments. He then thinks of the empathetic nature of some women and the restful effect telling his troubles would produce. After tearing the envelope to pieces and letting it sink into the water, Bloom thinks of rivers of alcohol bringing languid forgetfulness.

After discarding the envelope, Bloom enters a Roman Catholic church. His reflections reveal his lack of understanding of the tenets and practices of his avowed religion and his opinion of religion as a type of narcotic for its devotees. Entering through the backdoor, Bloom notices a posting about a lecture on missionary activity by one of Stephen's former Jesuit masters. Bloom considers the utility of missionary work and prayers for conversion, noting that all religions must believe that they are the true faith. After a momentary thought about Molly, Bloom enters the church and notices that it is nearly empty. The priest distributes Communion. However, Bloom cannot recall the names of the sacred vessels nor the exact phrases or procedures associated with the sacrament. He does reflect on the Communion wafer as the body/corpse of Christ and thinks it a clever idea. However, he also notes the narcotic effect of Latin; the Catholic Mass was said in Latin until the early 1960s. Bloom also observes the blank, lifeless faces of the returning communicants. His mind comes to life, relating the Communion wafer to what he does know, his Jewish heritage. He likens it to matzoth. After reflecting on what he considers some mind-numbing aspects of Catholic ritual, Bloom notes a man sleeping near the confessional, misidentifies two series of initials on the priest's garments, and thinks of the hypocrisy of pious frauds who contemplate murder and betrayal while outwardly practicing their faith. Bloom then sarcastically considers the use of wine rather than Guinness for Communion, before noting the absence of music at the service. He enjoys sacred music and recalls sitting through a sermon to listen to the subsequent musical recital. Bloom, while thinking of sacred songs, recalls the castrati and what he thinks of as the worry-free state of their lives. As the Mass comes to an end, Bloom notes the intimate gestures of the priest and the congregation's corresponding motions. As the after-Mass, English-language prayers are read, Bloom considers a range of sacraments practiced without reflection for forgetfulness or with hypocritical intentions. Getting up to leave, Bloom observes that two of his waistcoat (vest) buttons have come undone and then thinks, with relish, of women's undone buttons revealing attractive bottoms. Bloom leaves the church, noting what he sees as the empty ritual of dipping hands in holy water, summing up the lifeless nature that Bloom perceives as Catholic ritual as practiced by some in Ireland.

After Mass, Bloom decides to go to the chemist's shop to have a lotion prepared for Molly. On his way, he realizes that he has forgotten both his key and the lotion's recipe. As the chemist looks up the recipe in his prescription book, Bloom considers the chemist's profession, thinking alternatively of the skill and alchemic nature of transforming herbs into useful things but also of the potential lethargy and sleeplessness produced by some of the chemicals and mixtures. Bloom then thinks of the effects of the lotion on Molly's skin, making it pale, which brings out her dark eyes and Spanish features. His thoughts turn to Martha, massages, bathing, and the glum nature of the imminent funeral. Buying a lemon soap, Bloom leaves the shop, resolving to return for the lotion after it has been prepared.

Leaving the shop, Bloom runs into Bantam Lyons, who asks to see Bloom's newspaper and for tips on one of the day's races. Giving Lyons the paper, Bloom tells him to keep it, as he was just going to throw it away. Bloom does not realize that Throwaway will run in the race; he will actually win it. Lyons, misunderstanding Bloom, thinks he has bet on that particular horse and offers the name as a tip. Bloom, meanwhile, considers the potential harm of gambling.

As Bloom approaches the Turkish baths on Leinster Street, his thoughts take a momentary practical turn as he considers a way to improve an advertisement. He then thinks about cricket and some other sports, the cycle of life and death, and his imminent warm bath. Bloom imaginatively thinks how the bath will reproduce the feeling of being inside the womb and contemplates his sexual organ floating like a flower on the warm water. Even with his final indulgent fantasy, Bloom manages to avoid more permanent escapes of gambling, religion, drugs, excessive patriotism, and sex.

### Chapter Three (Episode VI)

The sixth episode details Bloom's journey to the cemetery and his thoughts and activities in the cemetery. The episode begins with a funeral procession that originates on Newbridge Avenue in Sandymount; moves past Irishtown and Ringsend; travels over the Grand Canal and across the Liffey via the O'Connell Street Bridge; continues along Great Brunswick Street, Sackville Street, and Rutland Square past Dorset Street very near Bloom's home; and moves along the North Circular Road, around Dunphy's Corner, past Montjoy prison, and over the Royal Canal to Prospect Cemetery, Glasnevin. The chapter itself can be divided into two parts: the journey to the cemetery and the activities at the cemetery. The first part alternates through reflection, conversation, and images of despair and optimism. The second part also includes images of despair and optimism but ends on a hopeful note.

The chapter opens as Bloom joins Paddy Dignam's funeral cortege. Bloom boards a horse-drawn funeral carriage with Martin Cunningham, Jack Power, and Simon Dedalus. At the starting point in the procession, the houses have their blinds drawn, as a sign of respect for the dead. Bloom, however, notices an old woman peeking out from behind the blinds and thinks of the traditional role of women in preparing the dead. Bloom then thinks about Molly and their servant cleaning his body when he dies. The procession continues at a rapid pace with the carriage's occupants correctly noting that they are likely to pass through the center of town, an old custom that allows as many people as possible to pay their respects to the dead.

As the procession passes Ringsend, Bloom catches a glimpse of Stephen Dedalus on his way to Sandymount Strand. Stephen's father tries to see him but does not and asks if Mulligan was with him. Simon speculates that Stephen is on his way to visit his Aunt Sally Goulding and her family. Simon then voices his disapproval of Mulligan, whom Stephen's father considers a social inferior. Bloom then thinks about Rudy, his dead son, contemplating what he would be like. Bloom also considers his daughter, Milly, and how she is growing into womanhood. Bloom speculates that, although she is his heir, she is her mother's legacy.

The chapter then shifts focus to the juxtaposition between life and death. The passengers note breadcrumbs and the carriage's damp seats, the apparent remnants of lovemaking. Just before the procession passes over the Grand Canal, Bloom notes the Gasworks and the tradition that its aroma cures whooping cough. He then thinks about potentially dangerous childhood diseases and considers himself lucky that Milly managed to avoid most of them. Bloom then remembers his father's charge to care for his dog after his death and recalls how the dog pined away at the loss.

The chapter focuses on images of betrayal and vulnerability. Rain begins to fall and then, just as suddenly, stops. The sun reemerges. The men in the carriage discuss the capricious nature of Irish weather. Talk then turns to a rendition of "The Croppy Boy," a song about an Irish patriot who confessed to a British soldier disguised as a priest. Bloom then tries to remember if he tore up Martha's envelope.

Bloom thinks about issues of life and death, gain and loss. Notably, Bloom's thoughts do not dwell on the negative. Rather, he reflects on the positive consequences of death or loss that might compensate for the loss. Bloom, as the carriage passes over the railway line, notices the man (pointsman) whose job it is to manually switch the tracks. Bloom anticipates an automatic device that will cost him his job but then considers that the production of such a device will provide other jobs. As the cortege passes the Queen's Royal Theatre, Bloom's thoughts turn to music, his wife, and her appointment with Blazes Boylan, who walks by the carriage at that moment. Bloom then reflects on his hands, nails, and his aging body but then concentrates on an image of his wife's still shapely hips and bottom. Asked about Molly's concert tour, Bloom explains that a tour that travels through the major cities makes economic sense, as a loss in one town will inevitably be made up in the next town. Bloom also confesses that he will not be going on the tour. Instead, he must travel to County Clare on "private business." It is the anniversary of his father's death. Bloom then notices another death-day commemoration for Smith O'Brien, a hero of the 1848 rebellion. He was given the death penalty, but his sentence was commuted in favor of penal servitude and he was eventually pardoned. Bloom also notices a disbarred attorney selling bootlaces and makes a reference to a play titled *His Last Legs*, in which the hero, O'Callaghan, goes from one failure to the next until he, as the play closes, apparently finds fortune and happiness through marriage.[19] Bloom then reflects on Power's smile and kind words about Molly and about his apparently sexless marriage. The carriage then passes O'Connell's statue.

A negative tone once again descends on the carriage as Bloom's circumstances as a Jew living in a largely Roman Catholic country come into play; he is reminded of his sufferings. The carriage passes an elderly Jewish man, at whom and about whom Cunningham, Power, and Simon Dedalus yell and say anti-Semitic remarks. The man is a moneylender. Cunningham notes that they all, except for Bloom, have had to borrow money. Bloom then quickly begins to tell an anti-Semitic story about a Jewish solicitor who tips the man, who saved his son from drowning, a ridiculously small amount of money even though the man took ill as a consequence of jumping into the river. The group then considers Dignam's death and sudden death, which Bloom thinks is the best way to die because there is no suffering involved. The other men stare at him astonished. As Catholics, they feel that sudden death does not offer the opportunity for repentance. The carriage then passes a child's funeral procession, reminding Bloom of his son and causing the others to contemplate the sudden nature of death. Power and Dedalus then speculate that the worst form of death is suicide, saying that it is a cowardly way out that disgraces the family of the deceased. Cunningham, knowing that Bloom's father killed himself, tries to temper their comments. Bloom reflects on Cunningham's kindness, thinking him sympathetic and intelligent, comparing his face with Shakespeare's face. Bloom thinks of the intolerance of suicides, of his father's desperation, and of the details of his father's death and its aftermath, dwelling for the most part on loss.

However, Bloom soon considers the future. The group begins to notice the cortege's fast pace, which prompts them to think about motor races. As they pass Bloom's street, the carriage slows because livestock, going to slaughter, clogs the street. Bloom offers the idea of a train line that could take the cattle directly to the slaughter yards. He adds that another train line could be established to take bodies to the cemetery. The men think Bloom's proposals ingenious and add that a rail line would make scenes where coffins have fallen out of their carriages a thing of the past. Bloom then thinks about an after-the-burial drink, a toast to life. The carriage passes over the Royal Canal, and Bloom notes that the horses making the return journey from the cemetery seem relieved.

Realizing that he must still make the journey to the cemetery, Bloom becomes somewhat depressed. In fact, as the cortege nears the graveyard, everyone's mood darkens. They pass the gloomy houses and gardens of the stonecutters. They also pass the untended graves reserved for murderers. Eventually, they see the statues and markers for Prospect Cemetery.

When the cortege arrives at the cemetery, Bloom leaves the carriage. He shifts his lemon soap from his trouser pocket to one of the inner pockets of his suit coat. Bloom also notices how small Dignam's cortege really is, how routine are the rituals of the dead, and even observes a man selling cakes and fruit. Bloom looks for the child's funeral party and notices that it has already arrived. Bloom then observes the carriage horses and wonders if they are conscious of their task and takes particular note of the number of deaths per day. Bloom also notes the faces of the mourners and how they appear similar to dead faces.

Subsequently, the narrative focus shifts to the legacies of the dead and loss. Martin Cunningham tells Power that Bloom's father poisoned himself. Power, embarrassed, declares his ignorance. Meanwhile, Bloom and Kernan discuss Dignam's family. Apparently, the father borrowed against his life insurance. Consequently, the mourners consider helping the children and the wife. Bloom contemplates the widow and notes that one partner must go first. He considers Hindu tradition, where wives throw themselves on their husband's pyre. Bloom also considers Queen Victoria who survived her husband by many years. He then thinks of himself dead and away from Molly's warm bed. The focus then shifts to Simon Dedalus, who has survived his wife. Ned Lambert graciously engages him in small talk. Just before the mourners enter the chapel for the graveyard service, they discuss raising money for the Dignam family. Bloom finds himself standing behind Dignam's son.

The chapel ritual and the other rituals associated with death offer little comfort for Bloom. As the mourners enter the chapel and kneel for the service, Bloom remains in the back and kneels on a newspaper. As the priest performs the rituals and recites the Latin prayers, Bloom's mind wanders from nursery rhymes to mimetic devices. He recalls the priest's name, because Coffey sounds like coffin. Bloom's thoughts wander from the priest's physical build to Molly to the comfort people take from rituals surrounding death. Before leaving the chapel, Bloom contemplates the army of the dead, old and young, male and female. After the chapel service, the mourners consider O'Connell's memorial, Simon Dedalus's wife's grave, and the mournful emotional state of a cemetery. Kernan and Bloom discuss the service. Kernan, a Protestant from the Church of Ireland, dislikes the Latin and the speed of the service. Bloom's thoughts wander to Kernan, who may also be a Mason, before politely agreeing with his observations. As Bloom contemplates the dead and their leftover parts, two mourners, Ned Lambert and John Henry Menton, contemplate Bloom, whom Menton finds weak, and Molly, whom he finds quite attractive and above Bloom. Menton also implies that he had some type of physical involvement with Molly.

Subsequently, the narrative perspective once again shifts, focusing on Prospect Cemetery's caretaker, John O'Connell. He comes across as a sympathetic figure, who offers a few words of kindness to Simon Dedalus. O'Connell also appears to enjoy life. The narrator describes him as a portly man. He also tells the mourners a joke. Bloom favorably contemplates the caretaker, admiring his bulk and decency before thinking about an advertisement. Bloom's thoughts return to the caretaker, considering his sex life and that the graves may be an aphrodisiac.

Considering the amount of people the caretaker has buried, Bloom thinks of the dead. He reflects on various examples of plants and flowers that seem to thrive on or near graveyards, concluding that the decomposing body parts make great fertilizer. Bloom also notes that the dead body's cells keep living, even without the body. Bloom then reflects on the individual consciousness and how the dead would appreciate the latest news, fashions, or even a good joke. Bloom also reveals that he thinks coffins and other adornments are wasteful. Bloom contemplates and anticipates death and memories of the dead. He considers that Parnell's memory is already dying out, that the caretaker must be thinking about who his next customer might be, and that the living might accidentally be buried. Bloom thinks about precautions that could be taken to avoid just such a contingency. Hynes interrupts Bloom to ask questions about Dignam's funeral. He wants to make sure he records the names of the mourners, including a man no one can identify. Bloom refers to him by his macintosh, which Hynes mistakes for his name. After the grave has been filled, the mourners propose visiting Parnell's grave. Bloom contemplates many of the other markers in the cemetery, noting that rather than religious references, the gravestones would do better to note the profession or interests of the dead. Bloom reflects that an even better memory of the dead would be a recording of their voices connected to the grave or even in the family kitchen. Ultimately, Bloom confronts a reality of the dead in the form of a large gray rat, who Bloom observes would very quickly eat dead flesh. Bloom also reflects on the other creatures that take sustenance from the dead corpses.

As Bloom prepares to leave the graveyard, he gives a final thought to the dead, reflecting on Mrs. Sinico's funeral[20] and his father's burial, on ghosts, on the afterlife, and on those among the living that use the dead for sexual pleasure. On the way out of the cemetery, Bloom notices John Henry

Menton, remembering that Menton dislikes him (Bloom). However, Bloom triumphantly ends the chapter by pointing out a dent in Menton's hat. Menton becomes embarrassed while Bloom becomes invigorated.

### Chapter Four (Episode VII)

The seventh episode takes place in the eastern section of Dublin on the north side of the Liffey in and around the office of the *Evening Telegraph* and the *Freeman's Journal* on Prince Street North near O'Connell Street. Headlines punctuate the chapter's narrative, sometimes interrupting stories, sometimes complementing them, and sometimes bearing no relation to the narrative whatsoever.[21] The chapter's thematic divisions focus on two main characters. The first part of the chapter reviews the bustle of the city and the activities of Bloom. The second part focuses on the machinery of the printing room and on Bloom's job. The third part contains a juxtaposition between Bloom's reflective nature and the tendency of his companions to gossip and engage in idle chatter. The fourth part focuses on Stephen and the esteem in which the crowd holds him; he actually joins in their chatter. The chapter concludes with Bloom receiving little respect for his efforts to sell an advertisement and Stephen receiving praise.

The chapter begins by focusing on the bustle of Dublin. The narrator describes the sound of trams and conductors as they travel around Nelson's pillar, the terminus for the Dublin trains. Subsequently, the narrative surveys the activities at the General Post Office as mail cars and postmen wearing the British Royal symbols travel to and from the GPO picking up and delivering letters, cards, and packages from around the city and around the world. The narrator's attention then turns toward Bloom, who discusses some details for an advertisement with Red Murray. A delivery of Guinness interrupts their conversation. Murray then proceeds to describe the deliveryman as an obscenely fat person who has a passing resemblance to Jesus Christ. Murray's description prompts Bloom to recall an Italian singer, Giovanni Matteo Mario, who, Bloom thinks, also resembled Christ. The conversation comes to a close as Bloom moves toward Nanetti's, the master printer's, office in the printing room. Bloom moves inward toward the bustle of the newspaper office.

Bloom enters the printing room and encounters a series of people and situations in which machines talk as living characters and people become like machines. He initially likens the sound of the presses to the rotting and decomposing body of Paddy Dignam. Subsequently, a reader encounters a headline that likens the paper to an organ. In between the sound of the presses, which are thumping like a heart, Bloom considers Nannetti's Italian name and his position as insider with the paper and as a local politician. Nannetti communicates with a few words, with scribbled messages, and with gestures. Bloom tries to communicate the details of a proposed advertisement that involves crossed keys. Bloom explains the advertisement at length. Nannetti answers with a few words about the design before reviewing a galley page. The presses, Bloom notes, spit out sounds that resemble speech. As Nannetti's attention turns to the archbishop's letter, Bloom tries to leave quietly. Nannetti tells Bloom to get a three-month renewal for the advertisement. After Bloom exits, he travels through the typesetters room, noticing the "day father," the supervisor of the daytime printers, and the typesetters. They mechanically set the type, writing the paper backward. Bloom recalls his father reading his Hebrew prayers from right to left. Bloom then walks down the hallway, the walls stained with nitrate and grease, and catches the scent of his lemon soap, seeing it as a token of human life amid the mechanized sights and sounds.

The next section features idle yet bombastic chatter, portions of a bombastic speech, and a reflective Bloom. Professor MacHugh, Simon Dedalus, Bloom, Ned Lambert, and, eventually, J.J. O'Molloy humorously discuss and read portions of a melodramatic and patriotic speech by Dan Dawson. Subsequently, as the others continue their running commentary on the speech, Bloom reflects in a sympathetic way on J.J. O'Molloy and Dan Dawson. As Bloom goes into the inner room to call about the advertisement, the group outside, now joined by Miles Crawford and Lenehan, discusses the favored horse in the Gold Cup race. Bloom quickly reenters the room, running into Lenehan and declaring that he must go over to Bachelor's Walk to catch up with Keyes about the advertisement. As he leaves, to the indifferent comments of the crowd, newsboys follow him out. Lenehan then makes a derisive comment about Bloom's clumsy feet. After Bloom leaves, talk turns to the British Empire and to Rome. Joking about their contributions to civilization, Professor MacHugh observes that the Romans brought toilets to the world. In the chapter, Bloom shows himself to be focused and reflective but also the object of, for the most part, indifference and, occasionally, the derisive comment.

Shortly after Bloom leaves, Stephen Dedalus reenters the narrative. The same people that treated Bloom with polite indifference and subtle disdain give Stephen unmitigated positive attention and even paternal encouragement. As Stephen comes in, he discovers that his father left just before. Stephen submits Deasy's letter. Deasy quickly becomes the topic of conversation. Myles Crawford brings up Deasy's late wife, who apparently possessed quite a temper. Crawford scans the letter, reciting parts of it, which sparks conversation. The professor speaks about what he sees as an Irish sentiment for lost causes, about the Greeks, and about fabulous Irish failures. The conversation then turns toward creativity and creative expression, with Lenehan's limerick about Professor MacHugh and a discussion of various arts: the classics, the press, advertising (a surprising nod to Bloom), and conversation. Subsequently, they encourage Stephen's artistic vocation before discussing one of the glorious episodes in the paper's history. Ignatius Gallagher, a pressman and editor for the paper, wrote a special article for the *New York World* about the "Invincibles," a splinter group of the Fenians (an Irish rebel organization). The Invincibles were involved in an assassination in Phoenix Park. Frederick, Lord Cavendish, the Chief Secretary of Ireland, and his undersecretary, Thomas Henry Burke, were killed.[22] As a phone call from Bloom interrupts the story, the conversation turns toward history, but not serious history. Rather, the discussion takes on a tabloid feel, riddled with clichés and superficial comments. Stephen's thoughts turn inward as he thinks of lines, words, and fragments of poetry. J.J. O'Molloy, meanwhile, speaks out loud about journalism and newspapers. O'Molloy continues discussing, in melodramatic fashion, a court case and in praising Roman law and oratory. Stephen privately considers the beauty of language. The talk then turns toward the spiritualism fashionable in the Irish artistic community. The group cites George Russell, AE, as an example. Further discussion considers popular oratory, focusing on a speech by John F. Taylor that addressed Jewish exile, slavery, freedom, and the Jewish Diaspora. Stephen's thoughts consider Ireland, Irish legend, and myths of a savior. Ultimately, Stephen suggests adjourning for a drink at the pub. All enthusiastically agree. As they leave, Stephen, once again, receives praise and encouragement.

As the chapter comes to an end, Stephen and Bloom share the narrator's attention. As they leave, to the cry of newsboys declaring the racing special, Stephen tells a bawdy story about two Dublin spinsters who climb to the top of Nelson's statue to see Dublin. They pull their skirts over their heads for fear of falling and eat plums, spitting the seeds between the rails, as Nelson's statue stairs blankly on, one arm raised. Meanwhile, Bloom reappears, having failed to obtain a three-month renewal from Keyes. Meeting with angry dissatisfaction, Bloom declares that there is still hope, if he could find a copy of a previous ad and if the paper could give Keyes a favorable article. Stephen's bawdy story receives favorable attention, while Bloom's failure receives hostile attention. Indeed, the chapter's ending reinforces its overall themes. Amid the bustle of Dublin, little seems accomplished. Trams travel in circles around the city; a paragraph at the end of the chapter mirrors the opening description of them. People go to work and speak at length, but mostly about trivial subjects. Melodrama and humorous distractions receive the most respect and attention. Bloom's industry, albeit with a disappointing result, receives little respect. Moreover, the individuals in the chapter appear as servants—to their impulses, to their jobs, and to machines.

### Chapter Five (Episode VIII)

Episode eight begins at approximately one o'clock in the afternoon and ends about an hour later. As Bloom wanders through the center of Dublin, just to the south of the River Liffey, he travels in and around Trinity College, the Bank of Ireland, the Queen's Royal Theatre, the Freemason's Hall, the National Library, and the National Museum. His thoughts wander also to and from familiar topics like sex, religion, Ireland, art, justice, and advertising. However, the chapter focuses on yet another familiar topic: food and the digestive process. The chapter basically has three sections. The first centers on Bloom's prelunch wanderings and encounters. The second section focuses on Bloom's attempts to find a place to eat and on his lunch. The final section explores Bloom's experiences after lunch.

The chapter's first section begins as the narrator observes a Christian Brother buying sweets from an attractive young salesgirl. The narrative commentary wanders from the digestive process, to religion, then to sex, and even to advertising, noting the Royal seal/endorsement on certain candies in Ireland. Subsequently, a young man hands Bloom a throwaway religious flier. Reading it, Bloom initially misreads "Blood" for "Bloom" but quickly corrects his mistake. Bloom then ponders the notion of sacrifice within a religious context and the theatrical illusions of organized religion, thinks of his lost son, and, ultimately, catches sight of one of the Dedalus girls wearing a tattered dress, apparently selling furniture. Considering the amount of children in the Dedalus family, Bloom mistakenly thinks that a married Catholic woman must produce a child annually to remain in good standing within the church. Bloom then considers what he sees as the selfishness and indulgence, particularly when it comes to food, of the Catholic clergy, and doubts they could keep the Yom Kippur fast. Noticing a brewery barge on the Liffey, Bloom considers rats trapped in porter vats, bloated and drunk; the river's sewage and the amount that must have been swallowed by Reuben J's son; and, finally, the clever feeding habits of the gulls. Thinking of the gulls, Bloom attempts a poem about them and thinks about poetry, recalling some lines from *Hamlet*. Bloom's attention then turns to an apple vender, from whom he buys an apple to feed the gulls. Receiving no gestures or signs of gratitude from the gulls, he rejects an idea to buy some more food for them and considers, instead, the diseases they carry. Looking down on the water, Bloom then catches sight of a floating advertisement and speculates that it is a clever idea that probably costs the advertiser nothing, like fliers or "bills." Bloom then recalls a restriction against posting bills that was defaced into a joke about venereal disease, which prompts Bloom to seriously consider but then dismiss the possibility that Boylan has a sexually transmitted disease.

Bloom's thoughts then wander to concepts, words, and ideas. Prompted by the sight of the fallen ball at the Ballast office (the ball falls at one o'clock in the afternoon Greenwich time and at 12:35 P.M. Dunsink or Irish time), Bloom thinks of Robert Ball, the then-astronomer Royal, and the concept of parallax. Parallax involves the change, or apparent change, in the position of an object based on the change of a point of observation. Bloom considers the origins of the word, thinks of asking a passing priest, and then thinks of his conversation with Molly, transmigration, and her malapropisms. Seeing a group of five men wearing white clothes with tall white hats on which each wears a scarlet letter of the word "Hely's", Bloom likens them to the priest he saw that morning with Catholic symbols inscribed on his vestments. The five men are a walking advertisement for a local stationers, printer, and bookbinder's shop. Bloom then guesses at the advertising agent who suggested the idea, considers that it might be Boylan but then remembers that it is M'Glade. Bloom does not think the advertisement is a good idea and likes his proposal of a "transparent show" of attractive young women riding around in a cart doing the company's business. One of the walking lettermen eats a loaf of bread, which prompts Bloom to consider eating habits. Bloom then recalls his time collecting money for Hely's, remembers that convents were particularly difficult accounts, and especially remembers one nun. Bloom thinks that she entered because of a broken heart and thinks that her order's patroness, Our Lady of Mount Carmel, has a sweet name; it reminds him of caramel. Bloom then remembers his life when he started at Hely's, remembers details of his daughter and wife, the food they ate, the smells of perfumed bath water, and reflects that it was a better life than he has now. Remembering also how Bartell D'Arcy, a singer who made an appearance in Joyce's *The Dead*, gave Molly at that time a song titled "Winds That Blow from the South," Bloom begins to reflect on a cold and windy night that he romanced Molly with a warm fire, mutton, and mulled wine. He remembers her skin and the happy moments that followed.

Mrs. Breen interrupts Bloom's thoughts. After an initial exchange of pleasantries and mutual enquiries, Mrs. Breen notices Bloom's black funeral suit and asks if the deceased and Bloom were close. Bloom encourages her empathy, noticing her eyes, but then asks about her husband. Mr. Breen is upset and more than a bit obsessed, even contemplating legal action, with an anonymous note with the letters "U.P." that has been sent to him. The initials may refer to imminent death or some sexual inadequacy but are an obvious taunt. Bloom also notices that her clothes are getting old and a bit ragged and that she shows signs of age. Consciously changing the subject, Bloom asks about a mutual friend; he calls her Mrs. Beaufoy. Mrs. Breen corrects him; her name is Purefoy. Bloom, thinking to himself, acknowledges that he confused Purefoy with Philip Beaufoy, a writer for *Tidbits*, whose story Bloom read on the toilet that morning. After asking himself if he flushed the toilet, he acknowledges his mistake to Mrs. Breen, who tells him that Mrs. Purefoy has spent three days in the Holles Street hospital with complications associated with childbirth. Bloom diverts her attention from serious subjects to an eccentric man, an actual Dublin character, who walks only on the outside of the lampposts. Mrs. Breen comments that her husband will be like him one day. She catches sight of her husband leaving a confectioner's shop and rushes across the street to catch him, sending her regards to Molly in parting. Bloom watches Mrs. Breen greet her husband, a thin and bearded man, and thinks of the Yiddish word for demented, as Breen speaks excitedly and earnestly to his wife.

Bloom walks away considering a wide range of subjects, including childbirth, sexuality, elimination, art, advertisements, sight, and Ireland. Initially, he thinks the note to Mr. Breen is a joke written by some other Dublin characters. Passing the offices of the *Irish Times*, he wonders if there are any other answers to advertisements for female companionship he placed there. Bloom then thinks of women in the context of AE's female companion, upper-class women fox hunting or giving him their underwear to hold in a hotel, and Mrs. Purefoy and breast-feeding. He subsequently considers childbirth, wonders that someone has not invented something to better relieve the pain, and thinks, gratefully, of Molly's relatively easy births. Bloom then catches sight of a flock of pigeons, considering that they are thinking about who will be the target of their elimination. Shortly thereafter, Bloom looks on the public urinal under Thomas Moore's statue. Bloom also considers a troop of policemen marching after their lunch, thinking that would be the best time to ambush them. Bloom recalls being chased after an anti-British/pro-Boer rally, but he also recalls how many of the young leaders now have posts in the British colonial administration of Ireland. Bloom then considers plainclothes policemen (G Men) and informers who seduce young servants as if ordering from a menu. Bloom thinks of various Republican leaders, including James Stephens, who organized the resistance into groups of ten to limit potential damage by informers; Parnell; and Arthur Griffith, whose intelligence Bloom acknowledges but who also, according to Bloom, lacks the common touch. Bloom's mind wanders over a series of questions associated with the Republican movement, including issues involving the Irish language and economic autonomy. Bloom then thinks of examples of sex and food as lures for betrayal. As a cloud covers the sun, Bloom succumbs to feelings of depression and anxious thoughts about death, pain, failed rebellions, and the seeming uselessness of life. As the sky clears, Bloom catches sight of Parnell's brother, a Dublin city marshall. Bloom then reflects on familial dynasties, various members of the Parnell family, and wonders if John Howard Parnell is as bright as his brother. AE and Lizzie Twigg, his female companion, pass by and Bloom associates the contemporary literary movement with British rule, wondering if AE's initials stand for Albert Edward, the king's name. Bloom also thinks about the sexual lure of writers and AE's philosophies and eating habits, which Bloom considers lightweight and nonsubstantial. Rewriting his earlier poem, Bloom likens AE to a confused bird flying over dull waters. Afterward, Bloom passes a shop window and thinks of buying some binoculars, considers new glasses, thinks of claiming some lost ones at railway lost and found, and tests his eyes to see if he can see a watch on the top of the Bank of Ireland. Bloom then reflects on several scientific concepts. He blots out the sun behind his finger, notes that there will be an eclipse later in the year, remembers that the time ball at the Ballast office falls on Greenwich not Irish time, and contemplates and then dismisses the notion of a visit to the Dunsink Observatory. Bloom's thoughts then turn toward Molly and his relationship with her. He recalls her betrayal, their formerly active sex life, the decline in their relationship, and considers offering her a present; her birthday, he recalls, falls on September 8, the feast of the Virgin Mary's birth. His thoughts turn melancholy as he longs to embrace her.

The chapter's second section encompasses Bloom's efforts to eat lunch. He initially stops at The Burton, an inexpensive Dublin eatery catering to the working classes. Disgusted by the eating habits he sees there, Bloom leaves, thinking about germs and diseases, the animal-like eating habits of Burton's patrons, blood, and flesh. Bloom arrives at Davy Byrne's, a more respectable eating establishment, where Bloom once cashed a check with a proprietor who does not seem particularly talkative to Bloom. After Bloom returns another patron's, Nosey Flynn's, greeting, he considers his lunch order. Reviewing the range of food choices, Bloom recalls comic lines and puns, advertisements and slogans, kosher dietary laws, sex and death before settling on a cheese sandwich. Nosey Flynn engages Bloom in conversation regarding music. Bloom, privately reflecting that Flynn knows little about music, tells him about Molly's upcoming tour. Flynn unconsciously makes a sexual reference when he asks who is organizing the tour. Bloom diverts the question, focusing on his lunch, but Flynn presses, mentioning Boylan's name. Bloom acknowledges Boylan's role in the tour. Flynn, oblivious to Boylan's meeting with Molly, proceeds to describe his masculinity. As Flynn and Davy Byrne begin to discuss horse racing, Bloom takes refuge in his sandwich. Seeing but then rejecting an opportunity to participate in the conversation, Bloom sips his wine, which apparently raises his spirits slightly. His thoughts, subsequently, consider a range of foods, including oysters, reputedly an aphrodisiac, which Bloom speculates that Boylan may have eaten earlier in the day. Sipping more wine, Bloom recalls a picnic with Molly on Howth. He describes an Edenic setting in which she passes him seed cake from her mouth to his mouth, and they embraced each other enthusiastically. Flies interrupt Bloom's thoughts. He resolves to visit the statues of goddesses in the museum to help his digestion but actually to explore a pristine example of female beauty, although Bloom also considers their elimination.

Bloom retreats to the bathroom and the narrative focuses on Byrne's and Flynn's conversation about Bloom. After discussing Bloom's black suit and Molly's physical appearance, they speculate that Bloom cannot possibly make enough at his job to maintain his lifestyle and that it is through connections as a Freemason that he brings in a comfortable income. Ultimately, they acknowledge Bloom's decency and kindness, although they conclude that he gives anything but money and does not drink or socialize as freely as he should. Paddy Leonard, Bantam Lyons, and Tom Rochford enter the bar and, immediately, Lyons talks about the tip he received from Bloom about the horse race, as Bloom passes them, unaware of their conversation.

The chapter's third section begins as Bloom leaves Davy Byrne's; he passes a dog eating its defecation and then hums a portion of *Don Giovanni*, focusing on revenge. The wine revives Bloom's spirits. He passes a plumbing shop and thinks of intestines. He resolves to go to the library for a copy of Keyes's ad that ran in Kilkenny and calculates his earnings based on selling the Keyes advertisement, another advertisement, and collecting the money Hynes owes him. Bloom resolves that he has enough to buy Molly a present. He then thinks about that afternoon's liaison and resolves not to think about it, but he sees reminders of betrayal on the street, in book titles, and in thoughts about people who took food during the famine in exchange for converting from their faith.

Bloom then encounters a blind man and offers him assistance in crossing the street. Thinking that he must respect the man's dignity, he attempts casual conversation. The blind man does not respond. Bloom then contemplates the experience of being blind, particularly tasting food. He considers the skills the blind develop in compensation for the loss of sight, including touch, sound, and smell. He also considers their experience with sex before experimenting seeing with his hands the color and texture of his body. Bloom then reflects on the injustice of the blind man's fate and the fate of hundreds of people who died the day before on a steamer in New York. Bloom catches sight of a judge and wonders about justice and the courts and the judge's personal habits, including his favorite wine. Suddenly, Bloom catches sight of Boylan, confirming his identity by his flashy dress. Nervous and depressed, Bloom resolves not to think of him and to focus instead on the statues at the museum. Looking at them, he searches his pockets and finds, to his relief, the lemon soap he purchased earlier.

The chapter reveals Bloom to be a decent but troubled man, respected but not overly well liked by the people he meets. Bloom constantly reflects on the happiness of his past life with Molly even as thoughts of their current difficulties assail him. Bloom attempts to raise his spirits repeatedly and devises schemes to accomplish this, ranging from eating to wine drinking to statue watching. Bloom also reveals a broad range of intellectual interests and life experiences, from at least an association with the Republican movement to philosophy to advertising to religion to art but most especially he finds interest in food and sex.

## Chapter Six (Episode IX)

Episode nine takes place at about two o'clock in the afternoon at the National Library on Kildare Street, next door to the National Museum. Although Bloom appears and becomes a brief topic of discussion, the chapter focuses on Stephen Dedalus. He gives a lecture on *Hamlet* and Shakespeare to a fairly prestigious audience of Dublin scholars and writers.

The chapter begins by presenting some members of Stephen's audience and the attitudes and circumstances he encounters and will encounter as he speaks. The narrator introduces William Lyster, the chief librarian, by identifying his religious faith, Quaker, and his temperament, urbane and calm. Lyster begins by quoting Goethe, one of his enthusiasms. After a brief remark by Stephen, John Eglinton speaks. He is an essayist and assistant librarian who graduated from Trinity College. Eglinton is a pseudonym for William Kirkpatrick Magee. He treats Stephen with thinly veiled patronizing contempt. AE, a pseudonym for George Russell, speaks next. He espouses his artistic theory of the irrelevance of a writer's life to the eternal, spiritual truths of the work. Stephen thinks of Russell and his mystical practices and theories. Richard Irvine Best, the assistant director of the library, enters and tells Russell that Haines left to purchase a copy of Douglas Hyde's *Lovesongs of Connacht*.

The discussion turns to Shakespeare by way of a Stephen MacKenna translation of a prose poem by Mallarmé, which told of a French translation of *Hamlet* subtitled *Le Distrait* (*The Distracted*). Eglinton makes a disparaging comment about the French, an indirect challenge to Stephen Dedalus, before directly challenging him by way of a condescending remark to Best about the topic of Stephen's lecture. Stephen vigorously responds by challenging Eglinton's characterization of the theory as simply making *Hamlet* a ghost story. He sets a compelling scene in which Shakespeare, playing Hamlet's father's ghost, speaks to Hamlet, declaring his form and identity. Stephen argues that it could not have escaped Shakespeare's imagination that Hamlet's name bears a striking similarity to his dead son's name, Hamnet. Russell then challenges Stephen, arguing that a writer's personal life—his debts, his habits, the gossip of the day—may be interesting but that it is irrelevant to an understanding of the poetry and ideas of a work. Stephen does not respond. Rather, he muses on a variety of subjects, including some lines of Russell's verse and the idea of debt and money. Russell, like Deasy, is from Ulster. Stephen recalls Deasy's words about money and conflates IOU with the vowels and with AE's name. Eglinton interrupts Stephen's thoughts by challenging his characterization of a Shakespeare who would indict his wife in the play as a murderer. Stephen answers by indicating that Shakespeare's relationship with an estranged wife, after the birth and death of their child, carries a significant relevance to his work. Shakespeare, Stephen argues, prompted by Best's question, may have resented his wife because she seduced him and he regretted marrying her. Russell interrupts the discussion, saying he must leave. Lyster mentions a book planned by Russell featuring the work of young Irish writers; Stephen's work will not appear. He does, however, offer some polite words to

Russell and then, prompted by a parting question by Russell, suggests that Shakespeare's wife may have been unfaithful to him.

Stephen's thoughts then turn to death and aging. He associates Shakespeare's wife with falling leaves and a corrupted text, then muses on the library as a type of graveyard. In response to challenges and questions by Eglinton and Best, Stephen explains certain aspects of his theory. Specifically, he asserts not, necessarily, that Hamlet is Shakespeare's son but rather that Hamlet is a youthful version of Shakespeare, that father and son, as Stephen uses the terms, refer more specifically to younger and more mature versions of the self. The conversation then turns toward the symbol of the daughter in Shakespeare's works as a healing figure. The female child for the male author also, according to Stephen, represents continuity but, in addition, change enough to not repel the artist with his own likeness. Stephen then turns the discussion toward the theme of the betrayed artist drawing the image of his wounded self as a ghost father that haunts and demands that the temporal version of himself, Hamlet the son, become an agent of revenge.

At the height of Stephen's rhetoric and argument, Mulligan enters and attempts to draw attention to himself, as an act of revenge against Stephen. Stephen thinks of him as a clown, the sort of jester that forces those that laugh at him to serve him. Mulligan, according to Stephen, uses comedy as a tool for power and control. After a discussion of Wilde's theory of Shakespeare's devotion to a young actor in his company, Willie Hughes, Mulligan reads from Stephen's telegram. Mulligan then proceeds to ruthlessly and threateningly mock Stephen, using language that parodies Synge's peasant dialect. An attendant interrupts, announcing Bloom's presence to Lyster. Bloom wants to see the model for Keyes's advertisement in the Kilkenny paper. Mulligan then mocks Bloom, making fun of his attention to the Greek statues' bottoms in the National Museum. Mulligan also makes reference to Bloom as knowing Stephen's father, linking the two.

The discussion then returns to Shakespeare and, more specifically, to his sexual exploits in London, far away from his wife. Stephen suggests that Shakespeare acted out of the impulse for revenge, resenting his wife's betrayal of him. Stephen cites two proofs for this. The first involves Shakespeare's failure to mention his wife in the thirty-four years of their marriage and his bequeathing her his second-best bed. Stephen then turns on Shakespeare's self-image created in his other plays, arguing that Shylock represents the tendency to exploit others' need and popular events for selfish monetary reasons. Stephen's argument thematically, in terms of the text, links Shakespeare and Bloom. Stephen then returns the conversation to Shakespeare and to father and sons, rearticulating his theory that Hamlet and his father's ghost refer to younger and older versions of the artist. Mulligan mocks Stephen's theory as absurd, but Stephen continues. At this time, he outlines his thought processes of how various figures of Shakespeare's family appear in the plays and even suggests the appearance of his uncles in a sequence without a narrator and in dramatic form. The remainder of the section covers much the same ground, adding thematic levels to Stephen's reading of Shakespeare. At one point, Eglinton makes a condescending comment about Stephen's name, which causes Stephen to think of himself not as Dedalus the artificer but as Icarus, falling to the sea. Best makes a connection between the brother themes in Shakespeare's plays and a similar thematic construction in ancient Irish literature; Patrick Dineen, an Irish-language scholar and writer, enters the narrative briefly. Stephen then discusses brothers as betrayers and the artist as self-creator, before Mulligan interrupts with boisterous articulations and exaggerated gestures.

As Mulligan pretends to write down some of Stephen's ideas, Eglinton mocks Stephen, who admits that he does not believe his own theory, at which point, Eglinton declares that Stephen should not expect to be paid and points out that he is the only contributor to *Dana*, a literary magazine, who expects payment. Stephen responds by letting Eglington know that he can publish this interview for a guinea. Mulligan again interrupts, sarcastically representing Stephen as "Aengus of the birds," the wandering Irish god of youth, beauty, and love who continually searches for a mate. At Mulligan's invitation, Stephen follows him out of the library for a drink. Mulligan makes a series of jokes and satiric rhymes, making fun of Stephen, Eglinton, Yeats, and Synge before reproaching Stephen for an unkind review of a work by Lady Gregory after she helped him obtain the position as reviewer. Mulligan then suggests that Stephen, like Yeats, could have written a false review and offers a few lines, praising the work as the Irish *Odyssey*.

The chapter comes to a close with Mulligan declaring that he will write a play for mummers. One tradition associated with the mummers involved going from door to door on Saint Stephen's feast day, singing songs and hunting the wren, the bird that supposedly betrayed Stephen to the Romans to be martyred. Mulligan relays a bawdy portion of his mummers' play as the two leave the National Library. Stephen looks for signs of birds and sees none; these were the symbols of inspiration he noticed in his younger days; Mulligan earlier flapped his arms mimicking a bird's movements. Bloom passes between them. Mulligan refers to him, derisively, as the "wandering Jew." The chapter ends, as Stephen reaches for peace and reconciliation, thinking of the lines that end Shakespeare's *Cymbaline*.

The chapter focuses attention on Stephen's new aesthetic theory; in *A Portrait of the Artist as a Young Man*, he sought to create work as an objective artist. Here, Stephen argues, half seriously, for subjective artistic creation. More important, the chapter reveals how disdainfully some in the Irish artistic and scholarly community view Stephen. Moreover, Mulligan's mockery unites Bloom and Stephen and establishes a relation between them as despised outcasts and wanderers.

### Chapter Seven (Episode X)

Episode ten begins almost exactly at 2:55 in the afternoon; one of the characters checks his watch at the beginning of the chapter. It ends at about four o'clock, the time of Boylan's appointment with Molly. The chapter contains nineteen sections or episodes that communicate the sometimes concurrent actions and occasionally the thoughts of a number of characters during this hour period.

The first section focuses on Father John Conmee, the Jesuit rector of Clongowes and prefect of studies at Belvedere while Stephen studied at both schools. Fr. Conmee's journey takes him from the Jesuit residences on Upper Gardiner Street, north of the River Liffey and quite close to Bloom's house on Eccles Street, to Artane School in the northeastern part of Dublin. Conmee checks his watch at 2:55 before setting out on his journey to Artane to oblige Martin Cunningham's request for Dignam's son. In the course of his walk, he encounters a one-legged sailor, whom he blesses but to whom he does not give money; he has only a single coin in his purse. Fr. Conmee also encounters a member of parliament's wife, with whom he exchanges a few words. Afterward, he reflects on a Jesuit preacher whom she admired before speaking to three young boys. He asks one of them to mail a letter for him. He passes along his way Denis Maginni, Mrs. M'Guinness, some boys enrolled at the Christian Brothers' school, William Gallagher, and others before taking the tram. Considering the other passengers, Conmee recognizes one of them from his church, thinks about the missions and the possibility of salvation without baptism, and other topics. Leaving the tram to finish his journey on foot, Conmee reflects on the countryside and streets before him, prays his daily prayers, and stumbles across a young man coming from a gap in the hedgerow with a young woman carrying daisies. The narrator also reflects on the priest's kindness during his time as rector at Clongowes, a time that encompassed Stephen's enrollment.

The next two sections focus on Corny Kelleher and the one-legged sailor. Kelleher chews on some hay while speaking to a policeman and lazily observing the characters and scenes around him. The one-legged sailor sings a patriotic British song while begging for money. Molly, her arm appearing out of her second-story window, throws him a coin.

The next three sections focus on the Dedalus household, Blazes Boylan, and a conversation between Stephen and Almidano Artifoni. Section four takes place at the Dedalus home on Saint Peter's terrace in Cabra, south of Glasnevin and the Royal Canal. Katey, Maggey, and Boody Dedalus discuss a range of subjects, including their lack of food, money not received for books one of them tried to sell, and, in disparaging terms, their father. The section closes with the narrator's reference to the throwaway, that Bloom earlier discarded, floating down the Liffey. Section five takes place in a florist's shop on Grafton Street, just south of Trinity College. Blazes Boylan, while flirting with the sales girl, orders a fruit basket to be sent to Molly, telling the girl that it should be delivered immediately as it is for an invalid. Section six takes place outside the main gate of Trinity College. Stephen and Artifoni discuss the possibility of Stephen making a living by singing, while they observe English tourists and British soldiers nearby.

Sections seven and eight focus on Boylan's secretary and on Ned Lambert. Section seven takes place in Boylan's advertising office, probably in central Dublin. Miss Dunne, his secretary, types the date onto a letter, arranges appointments for Boylan, and reschedules one to allow time for his meeting with Molly. Section eight occurs at the old chapterhouse of Mary's Abbey, just north of the River Liffey and east of the center of the city. Ned Lambert tours Rev. Hugh C. Love through the old council chamber pointing out its historic significance as a place marking resistance to British rule and its relation to the old Bank of Ireland building and to Dublin's first synagogue.

Section nine, which takes place in or about the center of Dublin along the Liffey from Crampton Court to the Grattan Bridge, opens with Tom Rochford demonstrating an invention for Flynn, Lenehan, and M'Coy. Lenehan and M'Coy leave after the demonstration and once outside discuss Rochford's act of heroism. He risked his life to rescue a man from the sewer. M'Coy then waits for Lenehan as he checks the odds for a horse race that afternoon. The two subsequently catch a glimpse of Bloom buying a book and discuss his cleverness at making purchases. A narrative interjection announces an advertisement for unfurnished apartments in the upper rooms of Bloom's house. Lenehan then describes Molly and an outing where he observed her physical attractiveness. He goes on to disparage

Bloom's sexual prowess but backs off after M'Coy appears unreceptive to the comments.

Section ten finds Bloom searching for a pornographic book for Molly at a stall in Merchants Arch, between the Temple Bar and the Metal Bridge on the southern banks of the Liffey. Bloom considers several titles before settling on *The Sweets of Sin*. While reading sections of it to himself, Bloom feels a sexual response. A narrative intrusion summarizes cases before the Dublin court that day and the coughing fit of the bookshop's proprietor.

Section eleven focuses on Stephen's sister, Dilly, waiting outside an auction house along Bachelor's Walk on the north side of the Liffey just to the east of the Temple Bar. Dilly listens to bids on curtains as her father approaches. He tries to correct her posture, but she stops him, asking if he has come up with some money. He responds angrily but gives her a shilling and a few pennies.

Section twelve, set in the area around the Guinness Brewery, just south of the Liffey, focuses on Tom Kernan. He recalls a recent advantageous business deal and a conversation with his client regarding the *General Slocum* disaster. Kernan suggests that corruption caused the explosion. Traveling on, he catches a glimpse of himself in the mirror and fancies that he makes a dashing and distinguished figure in his fashionable but second-hand suit. Walking on, he considers Robert Emmet and Dignam. He also considers various Irish rebels and rebellions, revealing his pro-British sympathies. He also just misses paying formal respects to the vice-regal cavalcade.

Section thirteen, set on Fleet Street and Bedford Row just east of the Temple Bar, returns the focus to Stephen. He begins the section gazing into the dusty and dark offices of a gem cutter, describing him as an "ape" with "Moses' beard." As Stephen turns the corner, he catches sight of the cockle pickers, hears the dynamos of the power plant, and gazes in shop windows before approaching a book cart. Speculating that he might find some of the books he won as prizes and sold by his sisters, he thumbs through a religious book before running across Dilly. She apologizes for having to sell some of Stephen's books after she asks his opinion of a French primer. Stephen quietly encourages her, although he privately recognizes that she, despite sharing his intellectual curiosity, will find despair because of her impoverished circumstances. Stephen finds himself overcome by guilt and sadness.

Section fourteen focuses on Simon Dedalus, who finds himself on Ormond Quay Lower between the Metal Bridge and the Grattan Bridge on the north bank of the Liffey. The section begins as he talks to a "Father" Cowley; the title is a nickname and does not designate a clergyman. Cowley, beset by debt, discusses his attempts to forestall collection while inter-jecting some anti-Semitic phrases. Ben Dollard approaches them. He promised to help Cowley by asking the Dublin sheriff to order the bill col-lectors to stay away from Cowley's house. Simon and Cowley tease Dollard about his clothes. Dollard answers them by saying that he has not paid the Jew who made them. As they walk on, Dollard announces the discovery of a loophole that will not permit the repossession of Cowley's property. Ap-parently, the landlord has a right of prior claim, and the landlord holds Dollard's property as security for the rent.

Section fifteen takes place in the vicinity of the city hall, just south of the Grattan Bridge. The section opens as Martin Cunningham discusses his proposed arrangements for Dignam's son. Cunningham mentions his letter to Fr. Conmee and discusses, with John Wyse Nolan and Power, Bloom's donation. The group spots Blazes Boylan and pauses for a conver-sation with Long John Fanning, the Dublin subsheriff. He regales them with stories of the council chamber and his frustrations at general ineffi-ciencies and at requests to have the sessions conducted in Irish. As they proceed to his office to talk about a contribution to Dignam's family, the group catches sight of the cavalcade.

In the sixteenth section, Mulligan and Haines discuss various subjects including Stephen and his lecture in the tearoom at the Dublin Bakery Company, located on Dame Street about midway between City Hall and Trinity College. They begin their conversation by talking about John Howard Parnell, who sits at another table. Mulligan quickly changes the subject to Stephen's lecture and brags about putting him off balance with disruptive comments. Haines and Mulligan then speak patronizingly of Stephen's capabilities and plans to write a book in about ten years; Joyce began *Ulysses* in 1914. Haines, however, observes that Stephen may in fact produce something. The section ends with the narrator describing Bloom's throwaway religious flier floating into Dublin Bay.

Sections seventeen and eighteen focus, respectively, on Artifoni and young Dignam. Artifoni wanders along Nassau Street as it changes its name to Leinster, Clare, and then Mount Street Lower. He observes the blind piano tuner and accuses him of not being blind. Young Dignam trav-els from the pork butchers on William Street South, just south and west of Trinity, then along Wicklow and Grafton Street to Nassau Street. Dignam, as he returns home with meat from the butcher's shop, considers the scene of mourners at his house, advertisements for boxing matches, staying away from school another day, and finally, on the arrangements for his father's fu-neral and the specifics of his father's death.

The chapter's final section follows the progress of the vice-regal's caval-cade as it passes through Dublin from the Vice-Regal Lodge and Phoenix Park across the Liffey to Sandymount. The procession passes various char-acters and situations described in the chapter, receiving tributes from some observers but mostly passing noticed but ignored by the people of Dublin.

## Chapter Eight (Episode XI)

Episode eleven begins at about 3:40 and ends at about 4:30. The chapter's action takes place in and around the bar at the Ormond Hotel, located on the north bank of the Liffey between the Grattan Bridge and the Richmond Bridge, where Bloom spends a portion of the time during Molly's scheduled meeting with Boylan. The layout of the Ormond's bar allows Bloom and Richie Goulding to eat in a room and to view an adjacent room, which is par-tially obscured by a bar that serves both rooms, while remaining unseen by the patrons in the adjacent room, who sing and talk around a piano.

The chapter's first two pages suggest a type of musical introduction to its characters and themes.[23] The words indicate characters, songs, and sounds associated with both characters and songs. The people involved in the chapter fall, roughly, into three categories: (1) the bar's employees—Miss Douce (bronze) and Miss Kennedy (gold), the barmaids, and Bald Pat, the waiter; (2) the bar's patron's—Simon Dedalus, Lenehan, Ben Dollard, the blind piano tuner, Father Cowley, Richie Goulding, George Lidwell, Tom Kernan, Bloom, and Boylan; and (3) absent women—Martha Clifford and Molly. The numerous musical allusions to almost four-dozen songs, gener-ally fall into two categories: (1) songs associated with lost love or leave-taking and (2) patriotic songs. Of the many songs to which the chap-ter refers, critics consider five the most important. The three that fall into the first category are "Goodbye, Sweetheart, Goodbye"; "All Is Lost Now"; and "When I First Saw That Form Endearing." The two that fall into the second category are "Love and War" and "The Croppy Boy."[24]

After the introductory passages, the chapter begins as Miss Douce and Miss Kennedy discuss the vice-regal's cavalcade. Douce catches sight of a gentleman in one of the trailing coaches wearing a silk hat and rushes to the window to catch a better glimpse of him. When he looks back at her, she jokes about manly eagerness. Miss Kennedy, however, considers that men have much more fun than women do, as she mopes about the bar play-ing with her hair.

The narrator subsequently focuses on Bloom and the novel, *The Sweets of Sin*, he purchased for Molly. Returning to the bar, the narrative focuses again on Douce and Kennedy as they discuss the busboy/shoe-shine boy, their personal appearance, and various men. After the narrator wonders about his location, Bloom passes the hotel, thinking of Stephen, Mulligan, and the statues, when the barmaids catch sight of him, joking about his dark, Jewish eyes, pronouncing the word "grease" as grace with their Dublin accents.[25]

Bloom, after considering some advertisements, his advertisement for Keyes, and the present he will buy for Molly with his commission, decides to have lunch. At the bar, Simon Dedalus enters, pruning his nails. He and Miss Douce flirt, discussing her recent vacation at a seaside resort in County Down, when she got a bit of a tan, which makes her self-conscious; fashionable women possessed pale skin in 1904 Dublin. As Lenehan enters the bar looking for Boylan, Bloom, approaching the bar, resolves to write to Martha Clifford. Lenehan and Dedalus then discuss Stephen, whom his father does not initially recognize, and the piano, which has recently been tuned.

The narrative focus then returns to Bloom, who stops to buy flower stationery on which to write his letter to Martha. As he buys his stationery, Bloom sees Boylan's cap and remembers his wife's meeting. Back at the Ormond bar, the patrons discover a tuning fork left by the blind piano tuner and begin singing songs while Lenehan teases Miss Kennedy about a detective novel she is reading. As Boylan enters the bar flirting with the barmaids, Richie Goulding invites Bloom to the Ormond bar for lunch. As Bloom enters the dining room, he sees Boylan across the dividing bar and wonders if he forgot his rendezvous. Boylan, however, prepares to leave but only after teasing Douce into snapping her garter.

As Ben Dollard tries to persuade Simon Dedalus to sing, Bloom and Goulding order drinks. Bloom and Douce both notice Boylan's departure. She looks after him longingly while Bloom's thoughts about his leaving trail off in incomplete fragments. As Goulding and Bloom order their food, Dedalus and Dollard, who do not notice Bloom's presence in the dining room, discuss buying secondhand clothes from Molly and Bloom, who sold them for extra cash. Dedalus then discusses Molly's physical charms at length and considers her origins as a soldier's daughter born in Gibraltar.

The narrator then describes Goulding and Bloom eating their lunches in silence and Boylan's progress toward Eccles Street. Ben Dollard sings a song about love and war, and Miss Kennedy asks some bar patrons about the cavalcade. Bloom, mixing his gravy and potatoes, hears Dollard singing and then recalls the night he wore the secondhand trousers and remembers that Molly laughed because of the extremely tight fit.

Douce then greets and exchanges words with a solicitor as Bloom eats and thinks about his surroundings and hears the piano. Bloom considers music and Molly and their relationship together, the romantic times, and Boylan's rendezvous. The group then persuades Simon Dedalus to sing. He chooses a romantic love song. The narrator updates Boylan's progress once again before shifting focus to Bloom, who thinks about Simon Dedalus's spending habits, as he sings an English folk song about Dublin in decline. Afterward, Bloom and Goulding discuss the next song, about love lost. Bloom's thoughts consider women and love, and he, resignedly, comes to the conclusion that he cannot do anything about Molly's infidelity.

As Simon Dedalus sings another love song, Bloom casually notices that the piano has been tuned. However, his thoughts and actions take on a more melancholy tone as he plays with an elastic band and thinks about Simon's voice, women, and singing. Bloom also experiences an erection because of the music's emotional tone. The song, "M'appari," reminds him of Martha Clifford, whom he resolves to seduce. Bloom's thoughts then return to Molly and their first meeting at Matt Dillon's, where they fought over the last chair in a game of musical chairs and where he turned the pages of a score as she sang. Simon's singing reaches its climax and, the narrator suggests, captures the imagination of all present, and he receives cheers as he finishes.

The narrator then updates Boylan's progress as he grows impatient at the cab horse's progress along O'Connell Street, as it retraces the path of the funeral procession. Bloom's thoughts turn toward death, the death of love, and his own death, as he anticipates being mourned then forgotten by Molly. The narrator once again updates Boylan's progress as his cab approaches Dorset Street, very near to Eccles Street.

The narrative then returns to more flirtatious subjects. Miss Douce playfully withdraws her hand and cautions George Lidwell, the solicitor, not to be so free with her. Bloom asks Bald Pat, the waiter, for a pad and pen for Martha's letter. Before he returns with them, Goulding and Bloom exchange a brief comment about music, which stimulates Bloom's thoughts about music, its mathematical arrangements, its beauty, and its misuse. Bloom does not enjoy hearing girls practicing their scales and thinks a mute keyboard would do for them. He also thinks about Milly's complete lack of musical talent. Simon Dedalus then tells Ben Dollard about hearing Italian as a boy, as sailors sang drinking songs at Queenstown (Cobh) in County Cork. Bloom writes his letter to Martha, under the cover of answering a job advertisement. The narrator then updates Boylan's progress as he passes the pork butcher's shop that Bloom visited that morning.

Bloom reflects on several of the people he met that day and their troubles and preoccupations before entertaining himself with a pun on Bald Pat as a waiting waiter. Bloom also observes Lidwell and Douce listening to a shell she brought back from her seaside vacation. Bloom reflects that Miss Douce's ear is like a shell with her braided hair circling it. Douce and Lidwell continue their conversation. Douce informs him that she walked by the shore with a gentleman. As Cowley plays the piano, Bloom thinks about music and his creative talent of enjoyment rather than composition. As the narrator relays Boylan's arrival at 7 Eccles Street, Bloom thinks of another pun involving "Chamber Music" and the sound of a chamber pot in use.

As Bloom gets up to leave, Ben Dollard sings "The Croppy Boy," which compels Bloom to stay and listen. Bloom thinks about the song; he considers its parallels with his life that day and his life in general—the Latin rituals of the Catholic church, of Molly, of Milly as his heir rather than his lost son, of writing and women's bodies, and of the lure of empathetic women. Miss Kennedy, meanwhile, considers her own reflection in the mirror. Bloom resolves to leave quickly before Dollard finishes the song. As Bloom leaves, the crowd congratulates Dollard on his singing, and Simon teases him about his weight.

As Bloom walks away from the Ormond Hotel and Bar, he experiences some intestinal discomfort and passes gas while considering difficulties of conversation and anger. Back at the bar, the company realizes that Bloom was in the dining room. Simon observes that Molly has or had a fine voice as the blind tuner arrives to claim his lost tuning fork. Bloom, walking on, thinks of attorneys and their fees, of bands and musical instruments, of Molly, and of death. Spotting a prostitute, Bloom becomes aroused, considering the comfort she might offer him. She taunts him, mentioning Molly's name. Bloom looks into a shop window, which sells musical instruments, till she passes and thinks about learning to play the melodeon. He experiences intestinal discomfort again. As the chapter comes to a close, the group at the bar toasts Ben Dollard, the blind piano tuner stands in the bar's door, and Bloom reads Emmet's promise of an epitaph when Ireland is free as he passes gas, making sure no one notices him.

### Chapter Nine (Episode XII)

Episode twelve takes place in and around Barney Kiernan's pub on Little Britain Street, around the corner from the Courthouse on Green Street and a few blocks north of the Ormond Hotel. The chapter, which begins just before five o'clock, focuses on a number of characters, including a citizen, a barfly/narrator, Martin Cunningham, and Bloom, among several others. They discuss Irish politics, horse racing, other sports, money and debt, religion and the Jews, and punishment and forgiveness. The chapter also contains several narrative voices. In addition to the usual narrator and the barfly/narrator, a journalistic narrator appears as does an epic/mock-heroic narrative voice, a legal voice, a theological voice, a children's story voice, and a scientific voice.[26]

The chapter begins with the barfly/narrator describing how, in the course of his attempt to collect a debt for Moses Herzog, he spoke with a member of the Dublin Metropolitan Police and Joe Hynes, nearly had his eye poked out by a chimney sweep, and engaged in a heated argument with the debtor, identified by a pseudolegalese narrative voice as Michael Geraghty. Hynes, subsequently, suggests that the barfly/narrator join him at Barney Kiernan's for a drink. Hynes wants to inform one of the bar's regular patrons, identified as the citizen modeled, on the Gaelic Athletic Association's founder Michael Cusack, about a meeting regarding hoof-and-mouth disease.

Subsequently, a narrative voice interjects a mock-heroic description of the area around Kiernan's pub. The passage specifically parodies fashionable translations and nineteenth-century versions of Irish saga literature. The description focuses on Saint Michan's, located just west of the pub on Church Street Lower. The passage makes reference to the church's tower, dating from the fifteenth century, and the crypt, where dry conditions preserve bodies of the dead. The mock-heroic narrator then describes the Dublin Fish, Meat, and Vegetable Market. After a brief interval featuring the barfly's imagined challenge to Geraghty, the mock-heroic voice returns, describing the market's livestock and fish. Flynn and the barfly then arrive at the pub, where the citizen argues with a dog named Garryowen. After introducing themselves, the three discuss the markets and war before deciding to order drinks. After the citizen quiets the dog by grabbing its throat, the mock-heroic narrator describes him as an Irish hero, providing a litany of names for comparison.

The barfly then observes Hynes paying for the drinks with a sovereign. At Bloom's suggestion, Hynes obtains an advance from the cashier, which he uses to pay for the drinks rather than to repay Bloom. The mock-heroic narrative voice then describes Bloom as an ancient Irish knight before the citizen reads with disgust the English names from the birth and death notices section of *The Irish Independent*, a paper founded by Parnell.

The mock-heroic narrative voice then describes the entrance of little Alf Bergan, followed by Denis Breen and his wife. He carries law books under his arm and wears slippers. After the barfly notices Bob Doran, drunk and sleeping, Alf Bergan explains that Breen spent the day walking between lawyers' offices trying to file a libel suit about the "u.p. : up" cards. The mock-heroic narrator then describes Bergan ordering, receiving, and paying for drinks with a coin with Queen Victoria's face on it. The narrator also describes the inscriptions on the coin and the expanse of her empire.

The citizen then asks about Bloom, whom he sees walking up and down the street outside the pub. Subsequently, the conversation turns to Paddy Dignam. Alf Bergan claims to have seen him five minutes previously. A parodic Hindu/spiritualist narrative voice then makes contact with Dignam's ghost. He receives buttermilk, sends greetings, and discloses the location of a lost boot; it is under the toilet. A mock-epic/Irish-language poetic narrative voice then mourns Dignam's passing. The citizen, once again, notes Bloom's passing presence as Bob Doran drunkenly curses God for taking Dignam. The citizen invites a reluctant Bloom to enter, over the growls of the dog, as Hynes reads a letter of application from an Englishman for the job of hangman/executioner in Dublin. As the group discusses English executioners, Hynes offers Bloom a drink. Bloom declines but does ask for a cigar. A biblical/spiritual narrator then celebrates the executioners.

The conversation turns to capital punishment. The barfly/narrator mocks, in anti-Semitic terms, Bloom's attempt to explain its origins and intended purposes. Alf Bergan raises the issue of a hanged man's erection. Bloom also volunteers an explanation for this and a pseudoscientific narrative voice parodies him. The barfly then, in an exasperated tone, observes that the citizen takes any opportunity to discuss politics, as Bob Doran plays with the dog. The barfly then describes a discussion between the citizen and Bloom regarding the 1798 uprising and Robert Emmet, whose girlfriend later married a British soldier. The barfly describes Molly before telling the story of how Bloom, in an attempt to purge Dante Riordan's nephew of alcohol dependency, actually exacerbated the problem. As Bloom and the citizen engage in a more heated discussion, the mock-heroic narrative voice describes it in epic terms, concluding with the glories of Bloom's execution. Subsequently, the barfly/narrator describes how the conversation turns to the Irish-language issue and how, when the dog acts up out of hunger, the citizen growls back at it in Irish. A pseudoscholarly/scientific narrative voice describes the scene, comparing the citizen's use of Irish with ancient Celtic bards and with then-current Irish writers like Hyde (Little Sweet Branch) and Synge.

Offered another drink, Bloom declines, saying he must wait for Martin Cunningham so they can negotiate with Dignam's insurance policy's mortgage holder. The barfly/narrator describes Bloom's explanation, revealing that when Bloom was caught selling illegal Hungarian lottery tickets his Masonic connections saved him from jail time. A drunk Doran interrupts, asking in an assumed formal tone to convey his condolences to Dignam's widow. Doran leaves and the barfly describes the drunken departure and tells stories about Doran's drunken exploits with two prostitutes and his marriage, which his wife's brother forced by threat. Doran married because his future wife was pregnant.

As the group receives its drinks, hoof-and-mouth disease is discussed. The narrator, once again, derisively describes Bloom's contribution, pointing out that he feels qualified to discuss the issue because he once worked at a slaughterhouse. Later, Bloom discovers that Nannetti plans to leave for London to debate in parliament the cattle issue and the restrictions on Irish games in Phoenix Park. A mock-parliamentary narrative voice then dramatizes the debate, conflating the practitioners of Irish sports with slaughtered cattle. A pseudojournalistic narrative voice describes the debate, indicating that Bloom opposes the citizen's views. The narrative description ends with a list of clergy present, satirizing a common journalistic practice of the time.

Hynes, the citizen, and Alf Bergan then discuss boxing, speculating on Blazes Boylan's betting prowess. Bloom, however, tries to change the conversation, bringing up lawn tennis. A pseudojournalistic voice interjects with a description of a boxing match, drawing the two opponents as representatives of England and Ireland. Ultimately, the group discusses Boylan and his upcoming concert tour. Bloom yields to the conversation and even praises Boylan's organizational ability. The barfly/narrator, using colorful metaphors, recognizes Boylan's true designs for Molly. A mock-heroic narrative voice injects a description of Molly as a pure and faithful maiden.

J.J. O'Molloy and Ned Lambert enter the bar; the mock-heroic narrative voice introduces them to the reader. The barfly speculates about their activities before the conversation turns to Breen and his libel suit. The group then jokes about Breen. Bloom intervenes, pleading that they stop for the sake of his wife. The group proceeds to insult Breen's manhood. The barfly/narrator then comments on Bloom's explanation and Breen's arrogance. O'Molloy argues, perhaps teasingly, that Breen might have some cause for legal action. Joe Hynes then spots the Breens outside the pub talking to Corny Kelleher. The group discusses several other court cases involving swindle and fraud. The barfly/narrator injects some anti-Semitic comments before a pseudolegalese narrative voice discusses a court case. Through metaphor, the legal language links ancient Irish law and ancient Jewish custom.

Bloom takes Hynes aside to discuss Hynes's debt under the guise of the Keyes advertisement. Bloom does not want to embarrass Hynes. The group discusses immigration, in negative terms, and adultery. The citizen, bored, changes the topic to the Irish-language question and city hall proceedings. The mock-heroic narrative voice then summarizes the news that the council had voted to recognize Irish. The group then, in vigorously negative terms, discusses England and English culture. Specifically, the citizen indicts their sailors and prostitutes for having venereal disease, indicts their literature and art as empty save for what has been stolen from the Irish, and indicts their language. J.J. O'Molloy attempts to moderate the discussion by suggesting that all are part of a European family. The citizen condemns that interpretation, arguing that he has been to Europe, with Kevin Egan in Paris, and that English is not spoken there.

The barfly and Lenehan then discuss the Gold Cup, a horse race. Apparently, the horse that Bloom unknowingly recommended won the race, whereas Boylan's horse, the favorite, lost. Bloom, the citizen, and O'Molloy discuss history and law. The citizen poetically describes the renowned products of Irish craft and textiles, praising their quality, and wonders about the Irish lost to emigration, pointing out that England ravishes Irish land, people, and resources to benefit itself. The mock-journalistic narrator follows with a lengthy description of a wedding between Nolan and a tree;[27] he had just been speaking about trees. In the description, Bloom, as Senhor Enrique Flor, plays the organ. The citizen then advocates and predicts closer trade and alliances with Europe, specifically, Spain and France. The barfly/narrator observes that the citizen speaks in an exaggerated way and, although he will buy the land of a tenant to prevent eviction, he lacks the courage to directly confront the forces of oppression and imperialism.

As the group decides on more drinks, the barfly/narrator notes that Bergan looks for sensational stories in the paper and not for news, such as the lynching of a black man in Georgia. Ned Lambert then goads the citizen into expressing his views on the British navy. The citizen brings up corporal punishment and flogging in the navy and continues his criticisms of England by attacking the nondemocratic power of the House of Lords and the economic barons of the extended empire. Bloom logically attacks the citizen, indicating that forceful overthrow of British rule is the moral equivalent of corporal punishment and oppression. The citizen responds by listing the English use of force in Ireland during the famine, characterizing it as an attempted genocide. Bloom presses his point, but the others, excited by the citizen's rhetoric, recite the glories of Irish soldiers fighting in foreign armies against the British. After brief mention of an elitist clergy playing to the British authorities, the group discusses nationality. The citizen asks Bloom about his nationality. To the shocked horror of the citizen, Bloom declares that Ireland, the place of his birth, is his country. To the citizen's further shock, Bloom also claims his Jewish heritage and notes that the Jews were and are persecuted.

Bloom brings the argument to a rapid conclusion by declaring that "life" is the opposite of war and hatred and punishment, that life is "love." The others ridicule him. The citizen declares him the new messiah, the barfly/narrator makes Bloom's love into sex and romance. The citizen then discusses missionaries and their love philosophy and the presence of the Zulu chief in London. After a few more words about missionaries, the group notices Bloom's absence. Lenehan tells them that Bloom is not going to the courthouse, as he claimed, but, rather, to collect winnings on Throwaway, the horse that won the Gold Cup. The barfly urinates, narrating the action and commenting on Bloom and his discussions. Returning, the barfly discovers that Bloom, Nolan suggests, gave Griffith the idea for *Sinn Fein*. Martin Cunningham and Jack Power arrive to meet Bloom. Cunningham enters, after a mock-heroic narrative interlude, asking for Bloom and confirming Nolan's claim. After listening to some disparaging comments about Bloom, Cunningham defends him, telling them he cut an amazing figure before his son died.

Cunningham accepts a drink and defends Bloom once again against the citizen's attacks. Bloom enters, after a narrative describing a religious procession. Bloom apologizes, saying he was waiting at the courthouse. The barfly/narrator attacks Bloom in anti-Semitic terms, and the citizen aggressively accuses him of keeping a secret. Cunningham suggests they leave, and the mock-heroic narrator describes their exit as a journey in an enchanted boat. The citizen follows them, cursing after them and taunting Bloom as a Jew. Bloom defends himself, declaring the names of great Jews, adding that Christ and his father were Jews. Cunningham cautions him against this declaration, and Bloom concedes, declaring that his uncle was a Jew instead. A narrative description paints Bloom as Elijah on his chariot and as savior of Ireland. The citizen throws a biscuit tin at Bloom, and the barfly/narrator declares that the citizen threw it with such force that if it had been aimed better, the sun inhibited his aim, it would have done damage. A pseudoscientific narrator describes Bloom's cart rattling down the street in exaggerated terms. The chapter comes to a close as the citizen orders the dog after Bloom and the narrator sends Bloom off as Elijah on his golden chariot.

### Chapter Ten (Episode XIII)

Like episode three, episode thirteen takes place on Sandymount Strand. In this chapter, which takes place from about eight o'clock to nine o'clock in the evening, Bloom does not find himself alone contemplating philosophical questions. Rather, he carries on a silent but mutual romantic/sexual liaison with Gerty MacDowell, a young woman on the beach. Two clearly defined sections comprise the chapter. In the first, Gerty MacDowell contemplates a variety of romantic subjects, including Bloom, before her section climaxes in a fireworks display. In the second section, Bloom considers a range of subjects as well, including, but not limited to, romantic/sexual issues. In addition, a service at Saint Mary's Star of the Sea Catholic Church serves as backdrop to both sections.

The first section begins as a rather heavily romantic narrative voice, mirroring Gerty MacDowell's state of mind, sets the geographic scene. The action takes place on Sandymount Strand near Saint Mary's Catholic Church. Gerty, Edy Boardman, Cissy Caffrey, twin four-year-old boys (Tommy and Jacky Caffrey), and a baby enjoy a pleasant summer evening on the shore. The twins, dressed in matching sailor suits with Royal Navy insignia, build a castle in the sand and begin to disagree about the shape of the castle. Cissy, Tommy and Jacky's older sister, notices the twins fighting and intervenes, drawing a tearful Tommy toward her. After Edy teases him about having a crush on one of the girls, Cissy suggests that Edy take Tommy out of sight so he can relieve himself without a nearby gentleman, Bloom, seeing.

The romantic narrator then focuses on Gerty, describing her as a bit frail and waifish. She has pale skin, blue eyes, and thick dark-brown hair. She is also a bit shy and heavily romantic. Apparently, she had a flirtatious relationship with a young Protestant boy, about seventeen years old, who would ride his bicycle up and down in front of her house, until his father forbade him to go out in the evenings, so he could study for a scholarship to Trinity College. She also wears some blue clothes to bring her romantic luck, and she has indulged in fantasies about a life with the boy, about joining the ascendancy class, about cooking and keeping house, and about spiting her friends who teased her about him.

As the narrator's attention returns to the activity on the beach, Tommy just finishes urinating and begins to tease Edy, who cannot control him. Cissy comes to the rescue by indulging the boy. She also reveals herself to be a willful young woman who occasionally shocks her companions. She even dressed as a man in her father's suit, wearing a black moustache fashioned from burned cork. Walking up and down a busy city street, she proudly smoked a cigarette. It becomes clear that the other girls see Cissy as a leader and that her considerable charms complement their shyness.

As a service begins at the nearby church, Gerty hears the prayers of men petitioning to the Holy Spirit and for the Virgin Mary's intercession to help them abstain from alcohol. Gerty thinks of her father and her family's relatively impoverished circumstances as a consequence of his drinking habits. She comes across as a concerned and dutiful daughter, if a bit resentful about her father's proclivities. She manages her home on a daily basis and, the narrative suggests, uses her romantic imagination to escape from and to make tolerable her circumstances.

The twins then, while playing with a ball, accidentally kick it toward Bloom. Cissy calls to him, asking that he throw the ball to her. Bloom, however, tosses it toward Gerty. While trying to kick it back to the twins, Gerty misses. Raising her skirts to give the ball a solid kick, Gerty successfully knocks it across the beach. She also catches sight of Bloom and, realizing an attraction to his sad and dignified appearance, begins to blush. Meanwhile, the church service continues as the penitents pray to the Virgin, the twins play in the background, and Edy and Cissy focus on the baby. Gerty, frustrated by their presence, wishes she were alone on the beach and notices and indulges in Bloom's now avid attentions. As she considers Bloom, she romanticizes him, fantasizing about his dark eyes and foreign appearance. She imagines giving him emotional and empathetic support and reflects, with happiness, that she wore sheer stockings that evening. Her thoughts, interrupted by the sounds from the church, consider a local Dominican priest and a long-past confession. She reveals herself as innocent, having confessed her first menstrual period. Growing frustrated by her companions' presence, Gerty grows irritated at the twins' behavior and at Cissy for running after them with immodest athleticism. All the while, the sounds of the service come from the church.

Responding to Cissy's display, Gerty takes off her hat and spreads her hair, displaying its fullness and texture. She also realizes that she has aroused Bloom sexually and encourages his attentions. Edy, noticing the action, teases Gerty, who hints that Edy and Cissy should take the twins and the baby home, as it is getting late. Cissy, who also notices Gerty's in-teraction with Bloom, walks over to him, asking the time. His watch stopped, Bloom speculates that it must be after eight. Gerty admires him the more because of his passionate attentions and his ability to control them while speaking to Cissy. As the sounds of the church service con-tinue, Gerty notices that she will have her period soon. Edy makes an in-sensitive remark about the young boy losing interest, but Gerty responds positively, even though the comment wounded her, by saying that she can have any man.

The narrator imagines a Gerty with renewed confidence briskly refusing the young, would-be Trinity scholar's attentions and, in the process, spiting Edy and Cissy. Cissy, unaware of Gerty's thoughts, cleans the toys, little shovels, and buckets from the beach while Edy prepares the baby for depar-ture. Cissy tickles the baby, who was fussing, and the baby vomits over the bib. Gerty lets out a small cough of joy at Cissy's misfortune, as the service at the church proceeds to the benediction. Gerty then thinks about litera-ture, revealing a taste for sentimental romance novels and poetry. She also considers Bloom, once again romanticizing him, thinking to heal his deep wounds and longings.

As Cissy, Edy, and the children race away to better see the fireworks from the bazaar, Gerty remains behind. As the fireworks burst in the air around her, Gerty notices Bloom's sexual attention directed at her. She begins to excite herself sexually, leaning back and gradually revealing her stockings and garter. As the fireworks reach their climax, Gerty leans back father, no-ticing a bat circling the sky. Letting her handkerchief fall as a token for Bloom, Gerty walks away. Bloom notices her limp. Gerty is lame.

The chapter shifts its focus to Bloom, who, even though he notes her limp, thinks Gerty particularly attractive. He also rightly guesses that she is about to menstruate, which prompts him to consider a variety of subjects concerning women, from menstrual habits to sexuality to female friendship and homosocial behavior. Bloom also reflects with gladness that he did not masturbate earlier over Martha's letter or at the pretty young girls in town. In a succession of vivid images, Bloom considers Gerty's appearance, par-ticularly her hair, and how she must have enjoyed his attentions, despite what he sees as his unattractive qualities, particularly his weight. He also considers Molly's hair and how they sold a portion of it to help them finan-cially years ago. Thinking, at last, of his watch, he reflects that it must have stopped when Molly and Blazes consummated their relationship. Just then, Bloom lets out a cry and smoothes his wet shirt. He then thinks about uri-nating earlier, about how it enabled him to masturbate just now. Bloom also briefly considers talking to Gerty but dismisses the idea, thinking instead about Molly and her first kiss. She was fifteen and the man was an officer stationed in Gibraltar.

Bloom then thinks about the various women in his life and their sexual games, as Gerty walks away to watch the fireworks. Bloom also thinks about the fireworks before focusing on Milly and her naturally intuitive flirtations. He also reconsiders Gerty and her stockings, comparing them with the rumpled stockings of an older woman he saw in town that day. Bloom then thinks about women aging and losing their charms, about women in childbirth, and about them gaining weight and producing milk. He stops thinking for a moment in order to readjust his penis, which, relaxing, had positioned itself uncomfortably.

As he considers women's comfort after sex, Bloom catches a whiff of Gerty's perfume; it carries the aroma of roses. Bloom then thinks about Molly's perfume and her scent before thinking if women can smell men and what smell men have. He catches the scent of the lemon soap he carries and recalls that he forgot to return to the chemists to pick up the lotion and to pay the bill. He then worries about the chemists withdrawing credit and thinks of a way for Hynes to repay his loan.

Catching sight of a passing stranger on the beach, Bloom thinks to write a story for a magazine. He also observes the sunset and the changes the setting sun and shadows create on the environment and perception. He envies the rock that Gerty sat on and the chairs at the library where pretty girls sit before remembering Molly on Howth when they first met. Bloom then observes the bat flying along the shore and his thoughts turn to advertising, religion, metempsychosis, and sadness. Shaking off his melancholy thoughts, Bloom thinks about the bat's eating habits, only to return to thoughts of death, the sea, infidelity, absence, and love.

After thinking again about Milly, Bloom reviews his day. He reflects that he perhaps went too far in speaking against the citizen. Bloom even grants that the citizen may not have meant harm to Bloom. He also considers death and widowhood, the Breens, and his advertisement for Keyes before thinking about returning to see Gerty the next day. He resolves to write a note for her in the sand, going so far as to write a few words but reconsiders, realizing that the tide would wash it away. Throwing the stick away, Bloom sees it stick itself into the sand, standing erect. Closing his eyes briefly, Bloom's thoughts wander over the scene on the shore that day. As the chapter comes to a close, a cuckoo clock chimes in the distance as Gerty MacDowell looks on the sleeping Bloom.

### Chapter Eleven (Episode XIV)

Episode fourteen takes place from about ten o'clock to eleven o'clock at night. Bloom, Stephen, Mulligan, and several other characters find themselves at the National Maternity Hospital on Holles Street, located south of the Liffey and just east of the National Library. The chapter stresses several familiar themes, including death, paternity, sexuality, conception, gestation, and birth. However, the chapter primarily focuses on language, using a variety of styles and nine sections to create a parallel between the evolution of an embryo from fetus to child and the development of languages and forms of communication.[28] Essentially, the chapter begins, after a brief invocation, with an imitation of classical Latin writers and ends with an imitation of twentieth-century prose. Don Gifford, in *Ulysses Annotated*, identifies more than thirty stylistic shifts in the chapter, and the content outline that follows utilizes these shifts as a guide.

The chapter begins with an invocation repeated three times; three has particular significance in the Roman Catholic, the pre-Christian Roman, and the Celtic religious traditions. The first word is a phonetic match for the Irish-language word "deiseal," meaning the direction of the sun or "turning to the right."[29] The second word stands for Holles Street, and the third word is Latin and means "let us go." The three together indicate that we should follow the sun and go to the maternity hospital on Holles Street. The second paragraph, again in the form of a threefold petition, appeals to the sun god and the horned god of fertility to give the speaker a child. Critics also suggest that the passage refers to Dr. Andrew Horne, a director of the hospital. The third paragraph represents the cry of a midwife at the birth of a male child.

The next three paragraphs imitate the styles of Latin writers. The first mimics classical Latin historians and argues that every citizen has the duty to procreate, thus passing on a society's culture and traditions and, moreover, ensuring their continuance. The next two paragraphs imitate the styles of medieval Latin chronicles. The passages trace the development of medicine and maternity care, first among the ancient Celts and then in contemporary Ireland, praising the skill and wisdom of Irish doctors.

The next few paragraphs, imitating the styles of Anglo-Saxon poets, initially suggest that, prior to birth, the hospital and mother provide for all a baby's needs. The passage then notes the appearance of Bloom, the condition of the hospital, and a conversation between Bloom and a nurse, who tells him about a doctor's death.

The next few stylistic sections model themselves on a variety of medieval and Middle English literary conventions. The first, an imitation of

Middle English prose, begins with a contemplation of death but soon transitions to a discussion of Mrs. Purefoy's labor. The nurse tells Bloom that the baby will soon be delivered but also that it has been the most difficult childbirth she has attended. Bloom then expresses empathy for women in general and Mrs. Purefoy in particular. Subsequently, in a passage that imitates the style of fanciful medieval travel narratives, Bloom speaks with Dixon, a medical student who recently treated a bee sting for Bloom. Dixon convinces a reluctant Bloom to come into another room to have some food and rest. The chapter's style then transitions to an imitation of Sir Thomas Malory. The passage details, after a request by the nurse for silence, a conversation between Dixon, Bloom, Lenehan, and several medical students about, if given the choice, whether it would be better to save the life of the mother or the child. Bloom joins the conversation but privately reflects on his dead son, the cries of a mother in childbirth, and on Stephen, whom Bloom considers to be wasting his promise on drink, unworthy companions, and prostitutes.

The next few stylistic variations take as models Elizabethan through early seventeenth-century prose. In the form of Elizabethan prose chronicles, the narrator describes Stephen's description of himself as artist. Beginning with a parody of the eucharistic celebration and treating the group to drinks, Stephen asserts that artists are greater creators than women in general and the Virgin Mother in particular because, among other reasons, the product of artistic creation possesses immortality and also because the Virgin was treated as a type of prostitute by the Holy Spirit. Punch Costello then begins to sing a bawdy song on the subject before the nurse, once again, asks that the group be silent. In imitation of sixteenth- and seventeenth-century Latinate prose, the narrator details Stephen's response to Dixon's questions about not becoming a priest. Stephen answers jokingly, and the group responds with teasing and bawdy jokes about Stephen and brothels. Stephen then defends his virginity, which prompts more humor. Specifically, the group jokes about Stephen, as priest, taking the virgin wives before the service. Costello then commences a song, when a thunderstorm interrupts. The storm frightens Stephen, but Bloom comforts him. Subsequently, in a passage imitating John Bunyan's prose, Stephen and the group joke about prostitutes and the diseases they carry and the means by which they avoid the consequences of their actions.

The next few passages imitate the styles of various other seventeenth-century and early eighteenth-century writers. The narrator, modeling his prose after Pepys and Evelyn, describes the city and its response to the storm, eventually discovering Mulligan and Bannon together, talking about Milly Bloom before going on to the hospital. Subsequently, in a prose style imitating Daniel Defoe, the narrator describes the group discussing possible solutions to diseases infecting Irish cattle. The narrator, in Swiftean prose, then details the group's bawdy discussion of Pope Adrian IV, Nicholas Breakspear and his Papal Bull, granting Henry II the right to invade Ireland, justified by supposed Irish moral corruption. In imitation of Addison and Steele, the narrator then describes Bannon's and Mulligan's arrival. Mulligan jokingly declares to the company that he intends to purchase an island and to establish himself as chief inseminator of all the women of Ireland. In fact, he suggests, he will not accept pay for his services. The narrator then describes, in imitation of Sterne, Crotthers interrupting Mulligan, begging for a drink. Crotthers then bends over, revealing a locket with a young girl's picture, and jokes about raingear and contraception. The narrator, in a style reminiscent of Goldsmith, describes how Nurse Callan interrupts the revelries by asking that Dixon come to the ward. Mrs. Purefoy has delivered a baby boy. Dixon then defends Callan to the group after they mock her and make sexual innuendos about her. In Burkean prose style, the narrator subsequently considers Bloom's private thoughts. He apparently does not wholly approve of the group's irreverent tone, with Mrs. Purefoy suffering so close to them, but forgives them because of their youth. He also feels relief because she delivered the baby. The narrator, in the style of R.B. Sheridan, then describes the group's reaction to Bloom's words of caution; he suggests that they not joke about Mrs. Purefoy. Crotthers responds by telling Bloom that they will soon be transformed into doctors and that laughter helps them deal with their circumstances.

In passages, in further imitation of late eighteenth- and early nineteenth-century writers, the narrator details further events at the hospital. Specifically, in a passage modeled on Junius the satirist, the narrator attacks Bloom for criticizing the group, when his sexual proclivities are questionable, and when he will not make love to his wife. Subsequently, in imitation of Gibbon, the narrator describes the group's discussion of various childbirth procedures and regulations regarding abortion, ending with Stephen's reminder to the group of the official Catholic church's teaching regarding abortion. The narrator then shifts attention to Mulligan and, in a conglomeration of styles reminiscent of Walpole, Sheridan Le Fanu, and Synge, describes Mulligan and Haines. Mulligan's story carries subtle overtones of colonialism and imperialism and far less subtle references to Bloom's father's suicide, Stephen's Shakespeare theory, and Stephen's effort to escape from Mulligan and Haines. Subsequently, as the narrator models Charles Lamb's style, Bloom finds himself taken by thoughts of his schooldays, of his early years at work, of his first sexual experience with a prostitute, and of his dead son.

Subsequent passages imitate early nineteenth-century writers. Bloom, in two paragraphs modeled on De Quincy, reflects on the history of the world. His passes through generations and lands of his ancestors to the beginning of time and beholds the first woman, his daughter, wearing a ruby. The narrative, in a style similar to that of Walter Savage Landor, portrays a melancholic Stephen, reminded by an old acquaintance of their schooldays and his promise. Stephen finds encouragement for his literary promise, broken by a sarcastic and disinterested Lenehan who, after joking about Stephen's mother's death, talks about his lost bet on the Gold Cup. One of the others interrupts, telling the story of seeing, while emerging from the bushes with his girlfriend, Fr. Conmee earlier that day. A Macauly-like narrator interrupts and offers a lengthy description of the company engaged in debate and discussion. Subsequently, in the style of Thomas Henry Huxley, the narrator describes and comments on the subjects of discussion, mentioning various characters and their thoughts. Mulligan discusses bacteria and disease. Bloom takes about sexuality and women; the narrator describes him as a type of comic interlocutor. Stephen speaks of God, much to the narrator's dismay, as an omnivorous creature, devouring all sorts of beings.

The narrator then transitions to a series of mid to late nineteenth-century narrative styles. Initially, a Dickensian voice describes Mrs. Purefoy and her thoughts about her newborn child, her eight other children, and her husband, an aging accountant at Ulster Bank. In a brief paragraph, stylistically reminiscent of Cardinal Newman, the narrator then discusses the nature of sinful thoughts before making a transition to a Pateresque description of a "stranger," Bloom, contemplating young maidens on a green, fertile field accompanied by a young boy dressed neatly in a wool suit. The narrator then transitions to a Ruskinesque voice, describing the falling off in conversation and the lull before the thunderous suggestion, in a style reminiscent of Carlyle, that the group go to Burke's pub. The group, joined by Dixon, rush to exit, while Bloom lingers awhile, asking Nurse Callan to convey his best wishes to Mrs. Purefoy. The narrator then celebrates Dublin, as the group emerges into the outside air, fresh from the recent rain. The narrator also celebrates in hyperbolic terms Mr. Purefoy, comparing him to God, as creator.

The chapter comes to a close in a conglomeration of styles that suggest twentieth-century literary experiments. In the first paragraph, the narrative voices touch on, in a mix of Latin, French, stereotypical Chinese English, in half-finished English and various other forms, several key themes of the chapter, including God, the priesthood, sex, childbirth, literary production, Ireland, the Catholic church, and cattle. The group arrives at the pub, ten minutes until its eleven o'clock closing time and orders drinks, discussing, among other topics, Molly and Milly, while Bloom has yet to arrive. As the bar closes, they discuss, yet again, the Gold Cup race and Bloom. As the group leaves the bar, Lynch and Stephen turn toward the brothels, while the rest of the group walk away. Stephen and Lynch comment on Bloom in anti-Semitic terms and once again identify him as a Freemason.

### Chapter Twelve (Episode XV)

Episode fifteen begins sometime between eleven-thirty in the evening and midnight and ends approximately one hour later. The action takes place in and around Dublin's brothel/red-light district, located north of the Liffey between Amiens Railway station to the southeast and Gloucester Street to the northwest and between Gardiner Street to the west and Buckingham Street to the east. The chapter focuses mainly on Stephen and Bloom but also includes appearances by most of the other characters in the book and touches on most of the other themes in the book, including duty, family, paternity, nationalism, sexuality, and artistic/priestly vocation. The chapter's dramatic stylistic structure varies from the rest of the novel. However, rather than an objective presentation of events, the chapter functions as an expression of the subconscious and conscious minds of not simply Stephen and Bloom but many of the other characters as well.

The chapter's opening scene presents a tableau of grotesque figures, combining human and animal forms, that eat and bargain for and offer sexual favors in "nighttown," Dublin's brothel district. Children also appear, playing easily among the figures and speaking Irish words. A construction worker hunts for sex, and an Italian man sells ice cream. In addition, Cissy Caffrey appears as a prostitute, who sings suggestive songs referencing Molly and flirts with two British soldiers, who fart through their mouths and carry swagger sticks. The soldiers wear scarlet tunics, their dress uniform, and shop for sex.

Stephen and Lynch come on the scene, and the soldiers mistake Stephen for a priest. He, taking their cue, begins to chant the Easter service in Latin. The Easter service references water as a cleansing force. Edy Boardman also comes on the scene, muttering a jealous complaint as a bawd speculates that Stephen and Lynch are Trinity medical students, who, as a consequence, are not likely to pay for the services of the girls. Stephen declares salvation to all in Latin and raises his staff, spreading light to all. A dog cowers in response but eyes him suspiciously as he declares gesture the new universal language, subsequently invoking, in French and in Latin, women as pitiless nymphs and saving goddesses, as he through gesture offers himself up to sacrifice.

After Stephen and Lynch exit, Bloom then enters the scene, searching for something to eat. He rejects fish and potatoes, marking himself as an outsider; at that time, Fridays were days of abstinence from meat for Catholics. Instead, he buys pigs' feet and sheep trotters. Catching his breath, Bloom nearly finds himself run over by boys on bicycles and by a street cleaning truck. Grabbing the shriveled potato he carries in his pocket, a charm from his mother, Bloom thinks about exercise and catches sight of a darkened figure who probably has syphilis because of the mercury on the face. Bloom addresses the figure at first in Spanish but then, after the figure calls out the street name in Irish, Bloom answers in Irish. Subsequently, the Caffrey boys run into him.

An image of Bloom's father appears, bearing the marks of poison and condemning him for spending time and wasting money, hunting Gentiles in the red-light district. Bloom speaks submissively to him in German and English and remembers his father's other chastisements. Bloom's mother also appears, muttering prayers and carrying tokens, including the potato. Subsequently, Molly's image comes before him, wearing Oriental garb and in an Eastern setting. Bloom becomes submissive and apologetic to the domineering Molly. Successive images of other women appear. Bridie Kelly, Bloom's first sexual experience, becomes a type of vampire figure. Gerty MacDowell accosts Bloom for taking advantage of her and then thanks him for doing it. Mrs. Breen teases him about reporting his presence in the brothels to Molly. Bloom, again, appears frightened and submissive, explaining that Molly likes exotic things such as brothels and minstrel shows. Black-faced minstrels appear before him. Bloom then reminisces with Mrs. Breen about their youth. He, as a consequence of her flattery, becomes a younger, more handsome version of himself, but then he becomes chatty and almost feminine before she fades away. In the background, after her image leaves the scene, the half-animal creatures speak to one another and a woman urinates in an archway.

Bloom then resumes his search for Stephen but finds himself distracted and put on trial. Taunted by prostitutes and stopped by the police, Bloom gives a correct name but identifies himself as a dental surgeon with wealthy relations. Asked for identification, Bloom drops a card reading Henry Flower and finds himself arrayed in Eastern clothes. Cautioned by the police, Bloom offers them the flower that Martha sent him. Martha herself then appears, asking Bloom to clear her name. The police ask him to accompany them, Bloom offers a Masonic gesture and then accuses Martha, who identifies herself now as Peggy Griffin, of drunken behavior. Bloom appears before a court and, pleading for sympathy, claims Molly's father as his own, praising British soldiers. Bloom then claims to be a writer, until Philip Beaufoy appears, accusing him of plagiarism. Mary Driscoll also appears, accusing Bloom of lewd and boorish conduct. Bloom defends himself by speaking in indecipherable language and in pidgen English. A series of other women appear, accusing Bloom and calling for his punishment. Bloom, excited by the prospect of public humiliation, finds himself judged by a jury composed of a faceless man and a number of men who know of his humiliation at the hands of Boylan. The faceless man accuses Bloom of orchestrating and profiting from Molly's infidelity. They sentence Bloom to death. He tries to defend himself by confessing a number of other sins and by forgiving Hynes's debt, but to no avail. Paddy Dignam also makes an appearance before the prostitutes recall Bloom to the present.

Zoe Higgins, a young English prostitute, asks Bloom if he is looking for a friend and informs Bloom that Stephen and Lynch are in Bella Cohen's. Zoe also asks if Bloom is Stephen's father. Bloom denies this as she probes his genital region. Discovering his mother's potato talisman, she politely asks for it as she takes it from him. Bloom has a vision of Eden, and Zoe sings Hebrew words into his ear. Encouraged by his attentions and praise, Bloom begins to speak about potatoes, becoming the lord mayor of Dublin. He receives tributes from Ireland and the world. Specifically, the archbishop of Armagh anoints him, as religious, civic, business, community, and even feminist leaders attend the ceremony and praise him. John Howard Parnell names Bloom the successor to his brother, and Bloom makes a series of confident and inspired speeches. Holding court, Bloom dispenses wisdom and judgment over some minor offenses and some comic characters. Bloom also becomes a great entertainer, but Lenehan and Paddy Leonard accuse him of plagiarism and of being a traitor. A mob, led by Dr. Mulligan, accuses Bloom of sexual deviance and libertine behavior. Dr. Dixon temporarily saves him, pronouncing him the new "womanly man" and declaring that he will soon deliver a baby. The crowd praises him, as the papal nuncio reads his lineage, proclaiming him "Emmanuel." However, a message from "a deadhand," an indisputable ecclesiastical source, declares him a fool, and the crowd, with the exception of the Jews, turns on him. Bloom gives himself up as a sacrifice, reciting a song summarizing his day's activities, as Bloom becomes the image of his mother's shrunken and carbonized potato.

Zoe recalls Bloom to reality, but he responds in a stage-Irish brogue and speech patterns, declaring his imminent death. She misunderstands. Thinking him about to go, she invites him into Bella Cohen's to hear some music. Inside, a drunken Stephen lectures on music, the piano, and other subjects. The group discusses the end of the world, including the revival meeting announced on the pamphlet that Bloom threw into the Liffey. Reuben J. appears carrying from a long pole his drenched son, whom he retrieved from the Liffey. A number of characters appear, including Elijah who speaks like an American tent-revival preacher, soliciting confessions from the prostitutes. The medical students appear as the babbling beatitudes, and the Irish god of the sea, Mananaan, speaks like a Hindu swami. Bloom's paternal grandfather also appears. He, in scientific language reminiscent of pseudopsychoanalysis, describes the prostitutes. After several graphic descriptions and reasoned responses from an equally analytical grandson, Bloom declares his frustration. The grandfather sings a simple ditty and flaps his wings like a moth, rushing toward a shaded lamp. Immediately afterward, Henry Flower appears, carrying a dulcimer and looking every part the romantic poet. He even has Christ's face and sings in a famous Italian tenor's voice.

The chapter's focus then shifts to Stephen, who sits at the piano, telling himself to imitate his father's playing posture and habits. Stephen's thoughts continue, touching on playing technique and his teaching at Deasy's school; however, his thoughts remain incomplete, as the crowd yells requests at him. Ultimately, two sides of his personality appear, representing his sober and his inebriated thoughts. As they push lawnmowers about the room, one of the crowd once again mistakes Stephen for a priest, prompting a prostitute to relate a story of serving a clergyman. A discussion ensues, that includes Virag, about celibates and their progeny. Ben Dollard enters, to the delight of the prostitutes, and Henry Flower sings from "M'appari," before exiting like Moore's minstrel boy. Virag unscrews his head, while the group presses Stephen again about his being a priest. Lynch jokingly declares him a cardinal's son. On cue, Simon Dedalus appears, arrayed as the cardinal, archbishop of Armagh. He sings some comic songs and then exits.

The chapter once again shifts focus to Bloom. He hears someone near the door and nervously assumes Boylan has arrived. Feeding chocolate, an aphrodisiac, to Zoe, Bloom, dressed as a magician, orders the figure outside the door to appear. Bella Cohen enters, carrying a large fan. The fan and

Bloom engage in conversation. It discerns that Bloom is both married and controlled by his wife. Bloom speaks in awkward metaphors about his age and impotence, regretting his lost potato talisman. Kneeling before Bella as she lifts a hoof to a nearby chair, Bloom knots her lace and suddenly finds himself transformed into a woman, as Bella becomes a man called Bello. The two engage in dominance games and sadomasochistic interplay. Bello declares Bloom a woman and condemns him to suffer all the ignominies of societal convention regarding women's dress and behavior. Bloom confesses that his desire to be a woman began when he dressed as one for a school play. Subsequently, the sins of Bloom's past appear, accusing him of homosexual acts, voyeurism, and sexually aggressive telephone calls. Bello urges a complete confession, as inhuman faces grunt and throng about him. Bloom, hesitant, stutters and stammers. Bello commands him to be silent and declares him one of her prostitutes. Clients appear, bidding on him. Bello declares him pathetic and mocks his impotence and taunts him about Boylan. Bloom admits his weakness and his inability to satisfy his wife. Bello turns him into a type of Rip Van Winkle. Old and bearded, Bloom mistakes an image of Milly for Molly. Bello condemns Bloom again, accusing him of creating his pathetic condition. She condemns him to death. Jewish mourners pray the Hebrew death ritual.

An image of a nymph appears before Bloom. She comes from a photo he clipped from a magazine and hung above his bed. She thanks him for his courtesy and homage. He apologizes for all she saw or heard in his bedroom. She recalls a broken commode. Bloom then finds himself transformed. Wearing the cloths of a schoolboy, he confesses to an early act of voyeurism. Roundly condemned for his proclivities, the nymph then accuses him of violating her. Bloom suddenly stands up for himself and condemns the nymph for her hypocrisy. Bella Cohen appears. Bloom also stands up to her, telling her to clean herself up and hide her weight. He also insists that Zoe return his potato talisman. She, after several objections, relinquishes it to him.

Bella's attention turns to Stephen. She asks for money and he gives over more than he should, while trying to focus on the piano. As Lynch enjoys the prostitutes, Stephen sings a song, whose subliminal meaning suggests his mother's death. Stephen, a little drunk, fumbles in his pockets, dropping money and matches. Bloom intervenes with Bella, rescuing Stephen's money and retrieving his matches. At Bloom's insistence, Stephen hands over his money for safekeeping. Stephen lights a cigarette and begins to speak to Lynch but drops the cigarette. Bloom throws it into the fire and orders Zoe to bring Stephen some food. She draws closer to Stephen, reading his palm. His hand outstretched, Stephen recalls a paddling he received at school and images of Fathers Dolan and Conmee appear. As she continues to inadequately read his fortune, Bloom, exasperated, intervenes and tells her to read his palm. She does so, accurately suggesting that his wife dominates him and that he traveled beyond the sea and married for money. He denies these things and shows her an injury received twenty-two years ago when he was sixteen. Stephen, noting that he is twenty-two years old and noting also that he fell when he was sixteen, remembers that it was his fall that precipitated Dolan's paddling. Stephen links himself and Bloom.

Blazes Boylan arrives on a carriage, accompanied by an admiring Lenehan, Mina Kennedy, and Lydia Douce. Boylan, flower in mouth and his straw boater on his head, parades past Bloom, hanging his cap on antlers that have grown on Bloom's head. Boylan informs a passive Bloom that he is welcome to watch through the keyhole and masturbate as Boylan and Molly engage in sex. Bloom eagerly watches as his wife and Blazes romp in exaggerated fashion around the room. The crowd cheers them on, as does Bloom. However, he and Stephen gaze into a mirror where a beardless Shakespeare appears, wearing cuckolded antlers through a trick in reflection. Mrs. Dignam then arrives, trailing four whining children. Martin Cunningham's face appears in the mirror and merges with Shakespeare's face; Cunningham's beard covers Shakespeare's bare chin. Cunningham's wife also appears, as a merry widow in Asian dress. Stephen then mutters a Latin phrase about the horns of the just being exalted, and Bella cautions him. Lynch reminds the group that Stephen was just in Paris, and Zoe begs him to speak French. Stephen obliges them, sprinkling French phrases in tales mixing religious images, sexuality, and vampire images. Ultimately, he calls on his father to free him. Simon Dedalus appears and conjures the wallpaper, depicting racing and foxhunting scenes, to life. The horses run a version of the Gold Cup, with the "dark horse" winning. Garret Deasy also appears, riding a horse called Cock of the North and wearing the orange, green, and gold colors.

Two British soldiers pass by the window singing, interrupting the scene. Zoe, exultant, dances around the room. Stephen searches for his ashplant. Laying it aside, he dances furiously with Zoe, then Florry, then Kitty as Maginni orchestrates his movements. Throwing Kitty into Lynch's arms, Stephen takes up his staff and whirls it around. His father appears and Stephen conducts a glorious dance involving many of the characters of the book. Ultimately, his mother appears, speaking of her youthful beauty. Mulligan's image also appears, mocking Stephen as he questions his mother. She tells him to repent as he protests and as guilt consumes him.

She presses the issue, and a green crab appears, sinking its claws into Stephen's heart. Stephen continues to struggle, ultimately declaring his freedom from the image and smashing the chandelier with his ashplant.

Bella calls for the police as Stephen flees, chased by the prostitutes. Turning to Bloom, she demands an exorbitant price for the chandelier. Bloom inspects the damage and discovers that Stephen broke only the shade. He hears reports of a fight outside and leaves, throwing down money for the damage. A hooded Bloom leaves the establishment, evading Kelleher and two of his friends, insults, gravel and other debris, hounds, and numerous other characters, hooting at him. Eventually, Bloom catches up with Stephen and two soldiers involved in a misunderstanding. Amid appearances by the king, Edward, and Lord Tennyson, Stephen and the soldiers exchange insults and taunts. Bloom, calling Stephen a professor, much to the delight of the girls in the street, tries to intervene. Kevin Egan, the Croppy Boy, and an aged woman, a symbol of Ireland, also appear, as Stephen and the soldier gradually become more and more aggressive. Molly's father, Major Tweedy, and the Citizen also appear, cheering on the violence as Stephen and the soldier get dangerously close to hurting one another. Bloom pleads with Cissy Caffrey to say something. A voice calls for the police, but a fire ensues that conjures the dead, including many Irish heroes. As a battle begins, a priest says mass, society ladies pulls their dresses over their heads to shield themselves from the sights of battle, and even Mrs. Purefoy makes an appearance. An Anglican clergyman named Haines holds an umbrella over the priest's head as he invokes the black mass. The soldier ultimately strikes Stephen, pushing him to the crowd. The crowd of onlookers shouts cheers and taunts. The police come, and the soldier pleads his view to them. The officer of the watch, inclined to press charges against Stephen, ultimately withdraws at Bloom's and Corny Kelleher's urging. Finally, Bloom remains to help Stephen home.

The chapter, a series of confrontations and violent resolutions, comes to a close as Bloom stands above Stephen. He lies moaning on the ground as Bloom observes him, thinking how much Stephen resembles his mother, May. Bloom's son, Rudy, then appears, carrying a small staff with a paschal lamb in his pocket. Bloom, unheard, calls to him.

## PART III

### Chapter One (Episode XVI)

Episode sixteen takes place from about one o'clock to two o'clock in the morning. The action occurs in and around the cabman's shelter under the

Loop Line Bridge, adjacent to the Custom's House and just west of Beresford Place. The chapter touches not only on themes of loyalty and compatibility but also falsehood, misunderstanding, concealment, and disguise, particularly in terms of the written and spoken word. Other than Stephen and Bloom, W.B. Murphy and Skin-the-Goat Fitzharris feature prominently in the episode. Murphy, a sailor from the *Rosevean*, and Fitzharris, a decoy driver associated with the Phoenix-Park murders, weave fantastic stories and romantic pasts, which may or may not be true.

The chapter begins as Bloom helps Stephen get himself together after his activities in the brothel district. Bloom, responding to Stephen's request for something to drink, suggests they proceed to the cabman's shelter. On their way, Bloom offers Stephen some paternal advice about squandering his money and time on prostitutes and on drink as Stephen catches sight of and tries to avoid one of his father's friends. Stephen does, however, stop for conversation with an acquaintance, John Corley, while Bloom gives them some privacy by moving away but keeps close enough to keep watch for any danger. Corley tells Stephen that he has no job and nowhere to stay that evening. Stephen informs him that there will be a position open at Deasy's school and gives him some money. Corley, thanking Stephen, asks him to see if Bloom could talk to Blazes Boylan about a job; Corley had seen Bloom and Boylan together. Bloom, after Stephen volunteers that he gave Corley money so he could find a place to sleep, asks Stephen where he will sleep that night and suggests he return to his father's house. Bloom also pays Simon Dedalus some compliments. Stephen, privately thinking about his family's desperate poverty and hopelessness, does not respond. Bloom discourages Stephen from returning to Mulligan and Haines. Their immediate conversation comes to a close as they approach the cabman's shelter and hear men engaged in animate conversation, speaking Italian.

Entering the shelter, the proprietor, Skin-the-Goat Fitzharris, and the other patrons, especially W.B. Murphy, take note of Bloom and Stephen. After suggesting that Stephen eat something, Bloom remarks on the beauty of the Italian language. Stephen reveals to Bloom that the men outside were arguing about money. Bloom confesses to loving the sound without knowing the substance. Stephen observes that sounds are deceptive, as Bloom discreetly nudges coffee and a bun in Stephen's direction. Murphy interrupts their conversation, asking for Stephen's name. When he tells the sailor "Dedalus," Murphy proceeds to tell Stephen that his father was a sharpshooter and an Irish rebel. Interestingly, the sailor also reveals that he, like Simon Dedalus, is from County Cork. Murphy explains that he has not been home for years, that he has been sailing around the world, and that he also expects his wife to welcome his return.

Bloom, questioning the truthfulness of the sailor's stories, contemplates traveling to London and relishes the adventure of the journey. He also considers laying the groundwork for a concert tour to England before thinking about tourism in general. He regrets and finds frustrating the lack of ferry service from Rosslare in County Wexford to Fishgaurd on the southern Welsh coast. He also contemplates the beauty of Wicklow, relatively close to Dublin, and of County Donegal, thinking that they are also ideal retreats from the urban world of Dublin.

The sailor continues with his tales, relating exotic stories about Chinese cooking and toys. He also discusses knives and assignations, focusing on an Italian man who skillfully used a knife. Murphy also argues that foreigners, like Italians, have a natural ability for killing with knives and suggests that, because of this, rumors spread that Italians committed the Phoenix-Park murders. As Bloom and Stephen glance at Skin-the-Goat Fitzharris for any reaction, Bloom reflects on the park incident, noting that he was fifteen at the time. Bloom then asks if the sailor traveled to Gibraltar, hoping for some common memory, but Murphy avoids answering. Bloom then quietly contemplates the sea and the romance, the dangers, and the adventures associated with it, before the sailor interrupts with another story. He discusses life on land and his family. Murphy reveals that he has a son, also a sailor and, subsequently, displays his tattoos. They tell the story of parts of Murphy's life and of his friends, acquaintances, and adventures. Specifically, he displays a tattoo that, when manipulated, details the story of a young sailor named Antonio, laughing at stories and defying authority. Murphy then explains that sharks killed Antonio and, subsequently, offers a short comic rhyme about his lost friend.

Bloom then notices a prostitute lurking outside the shelter. Recognizing her as someone whom he saw that afternoon and who asked for his washing, Bloom distracts himself by reviewing an advertisement printed on pink paper and by thinking about washing and soiled undergarments. After she leaves, Bloom drops some comments to Stephen about her and prostitutes in general, arguing that they should be licensed and inspected for disease. Bloom, subsequently, asks Stephen's opinion about them and the soul and the mind. Stephen responds to Bloom's practical logic with a detailed theological statement. Bloom, although he does not quite understand Stephen's reasoning, presses pragmatic evidence in favor of philosophical abstraction and also presses Stephen to eat something.

As Stephen begins to eat the roll, Bloom gently urges Stephen to eat more and questions the sailor's veracity. Bloom also considers that Murphy may not be a sailor at all but, rather, a prisoner, who was jailed for murder, perhaps even the murder of Antonio. Bloom then allows that, although Murphy may be a sailor who exaggerates the truth, he can be forgiven, considering the public's thirst for exotic tales. Bloom then discerns some truth in the essence, if not the details, of the sailor's stories, mentioning to Stephen that Latin blood does indicate passion enough to kill. Bloom even observes that his wife, born technically in Spain, possesses a very passionate nature. Stephen indicates that Dante and Leonardo were very passionate and romantic themselves. Bloom excitedly begins talking about the statues he observed in the museum, about how the representation of Latin women far exceeds the actual beauty of Irish women. However, the group, bored with this topic, speaks instead about shipwrecks and disasters at sea.

Murphy excuses himself from the conversation, going outside to urinate. Bloom watches him surreptitiously take a drink of whisky, look across the bridge, and, despite the presence of a public urinal, relieve himself noisily in the street. The sounds of the sailor's urine hitting the ground disturbs a horse standing nearby. The horse's movements shake the coal in the watchman's fire, which in turn disturbs the watchman, who quickly returns to sleep. The narrator explains the watchman's position in life, his fall from comfort and a modest inheritance, and his current drunken state of desperation. Gumley, the watchman, is an old friend of Stephen's father, who shares a similar personal history. Murphy, returning to the shelter, sings an irreverent song as Fitzharris extols the virtues of Ireland, its soil, its cattle, and its men. Enthusiastically, he proclaims that the Irish soldier maintains the British Empire, before catching himself on and declaring that no Irishman should serve the empire. Bloom reflects quietly on Fitzharris's declarations, giving the English more credit than Fitzharris does and noting the hypocrisy of Irish soldiers serving in the British military, going so far as to compare them with prostitutes. Bloom then engages Stephen in direct conversation, telling him about his encounter with the citizen earlier that day, mentioning the errors of anti-Semitism, and extolling the virtue of tolerance as opposed to hatred disguised as patriotism.

Bloom then suggests to Stephen that he should work, any type of work, but, especially, literary work, if even for a newspaper. Stephen does not receive Bloom's observations favorably yet Bloom persists, suggesting he has a value to the country. Stephen responds unfavorably to the very mention of the word country. They agree to change the subject. Subsequently, Bloom searches for another topic as his mind rambles from Stephen's physi-

cal similarity to his father and sister to youthful promise unfulfilled to public morality. Ultimately, Bloom thinks about the money he expended on
Stephen. Bloom dismisses his concerns, justifying the expenditures as an
investment. Stephen's intellectual observations stimulate Bloom and may,
perhaps, serve to inspire him to write a short story about their experiences,
which will allow him to recoup his financial loss.

Bloom's thoughts then wander to the daily newspaper. He scans several
of the day's stories, including coverage of the disaster in New York, Deasy's
letter, and the Gold Cup results, comparing Throwaway's victory to an earlier "dark horse" winner. Bloom's attention settles on coverage of the
Dignam funeral. He reads the article out loud, noting several errors, including the reported presence of M'Coy, Stephen, and a man named M'Intosh.
The story also misspells Bloom's name as Boom. As Bloom focuses on the
coverage of the horse race, a cabman declares that the newspaper will one
day report Parnell's return. The cabman then discusses Parnell at length,
including reported sightings and speculating on his political mistakes.
Bloom privately reflects on the unlikelihood of Parnell's return and, even if
he lived, the advisability of it. Bloom then reflects on the funeral and remembers that the ship that brought Parnell home to Ireland was the *Bella*.
Bloom also reflects on what he considers the tragedy of the public disclo-
sure of Parnell's affair with Katherine O'Shea, of their moving love letters,
and the scandal and sadness of their public display.

Bloom then reflects that she, like Molly, had Spanish blood. He proceeds to show Stephen a photograph of Molly taken in 1896. The photo
displays Molly's sensual charms, and Bloom regrets that it does not represent her artistically. Certainly, he reflects, photography cannot capture the
artistry of the human form the way sculptures can. Bloom, becoming increasingly nervous about suggesting to Stephen that he stay at Eccles
Street, wishes that Molly's charms could be on personal display for the
young man. Bloom also gives a passing thought to his son before thinking of
Stephen. Bloom considers Stephen intelligent and distinguished, especially because he admired Molly's picture. Thinking again about Molly's
picture, Bloom considers popular taste and public innuendo in connection
with women and marriage. His thoughts turn toward Parnell, whose hat he
had retrieved some years earlier, and his public scandal. Blooms dislikes the
way people joke and speak about that situation. He considers infidelity and
romantic liaisons between men and women a private affair.

Bloom refocuses his attention on Stephen, worrying about his association with prostitutes and their diseases. Bloom also worries about Stephen's
eating habits. Apparently, he has not had anything to eat since the previ-

ous day, which causes Bloom to reflect on the habits and views of his youth, when he had political aspirations. After thinking about the best way to propose that Stephen stay in Eccles Street and after worrying about Molly's reaction, Bloom declares to Stephen that they should leave the bar and go home to Eccles Street. As Bloom asks for the bill, his mind wanders over various possible benefits of Stephen's company, including education and a concert tour.

As Bloom and Stephen prepare to leave, the sailor begins reading some more stories out of the paper, disclosing that he is very fond of reading and can read in the dark. Stephen and Bloom then leave the shelter. Exhausted, Stephen wonders why the chairs are put upside down on the tables in restaurants. Bloom, practical-minded as always, tells Stephen that it makes sweeping the floors easier. Stephen, at Bloom's suggestion, then leans on him for support as they travel home, discussing music and dodging a horse with its absentminded driver. As the conversation returns to music, Bloom again introduces the topic of Molly, suggesting that she and Stephen would get along very well. Bloom also considers how much Stephen resembles his mother and, more practically, the potential profits of a concert tour featuring Stephen and Molly. As the chapter comes to a close, the narrative perspective shifts to the driver of the horse-drawn street cleaner as his horse defecates. The driver takes note of Bloom and Stephen walking off together continuing their conversation.

### Chapter Two (Episode XVII)

Episode seventeen takes place sometime after two o'clock on Friday morning, June 17. Most of the chapter, with the exception of the opening passages, is set in Bloom's home, 7 Eccles Street. Although many characters and events haunt Stephen and Bloom's thoughts, only they appear in the chapter, which details their first completely private interaction. Bloom makes repeated gestures of affection and offers of shelter, which Stephen initially appears to accept but in the end rejects. Bloom for his part, remains optimistic and maintains the relative self-assurance he found after episode fifteen. Episode seventeen has a unique narrative style composed of a series of questions and answers. The style, like Bloom, tends to be practical and straightforward but also follows the pattern of Catholic catechisms, and critics suggest that the style reflects the combined mental processes of both Stephen and Bloom.[30]

The chapter opens as the two travel from the cabman's shelter to Bloom's home. As they walk, they discuss a wide range of subjects, including women, friendship, travel, music, Ireland, and literature. They also discover that they share much in common. Specifically, they both distrust political and religious extremism. They both enjoy music, and they both, they assure one another, are heterosexual. They also discover they disagree on matters of diet and exercise and on the value of literature in affirming the human spirit. Bloom values the former while Stephen values the latter. Bloom also reflects on the decreasing frequency of meaningful conversation in his life, as he grows older. He recalls speaking about substantive subjects quite often in his youth but really has not engaged in such quality conversation since his late twenties.

Arriving at 7 Eccles Street, Bloom discovers he forgot his key. Initially frustrated, he decides not to disturb his wife but rather climbs down below the stairs leading to his front door and forces open an area door that leads to the scullery. Walking through to the kitchen, Bloom lights the gas lamps and a candle for himself and then proceeds to invite Stephen into the kitchen. As Bloom lights the coal fire, Stephen recalls his father, sister, mother, and various Jesuits lighting similar fires. Bloom then prepares the kettle and, washing up, invites Stephen to do the same. Declining, Stephen recalls that it has been months since he washed himself; more specifically, Stephen has not bathed since shortly after his mother's death. Bloom decides not to advise the young man about hygiene or anything else at that moment. Privately, Bloom reflects on Stephen's resilience and seeming confidence. As the water comes to a boil, Bloom moves to the cabinet to prepare tea and considers the day, focusing on the results of the Gold Cup and his apparent premonition. Bloom serves the tea to his silent guest and takes care not to disturb him. Bloom, thinking Stephen contemplates some creative endeavor, considers his own efforts at writing poetry. He sent a verse in to a magazine as part of a contest and wrote a poem for Molly. He also thinks about his failure to write some songs for a musical.

Bloom then thinks about his connections and previous meetings with Stephen, remembering that they had met when Stephen was five, then later when he was ten. Bloom had also received an open invitation to dinner from Simon Dedalus but never accepted it. They both also had known and lived in the proximity of Dante Riordan. Reminiscing about his past, Bloom thinks of ways to regain some youthful energy. The narrative then considers their divergent educational experiences, the family histories, and their racial differences. Bloom thinks about his practical experiences and creative advertising ideas, before focusing on how he must carefully explain things to Molly. Bloom seems a bit frustrated at his wife's lack of intellectual ability and discipline. Bloom and Stephen then discuss the Hebrew and the Irish languages, comparing their sounds and histories. Each man begins to see commonality in the other despite superficial differences.

However, Stephen sours the convivial atmosphere by singing an anti-Semitic song. The song tells the story of a little boy who, while playing, put a ball first into the garden of a Jew and then through his windows. Retrieving the ball, the Jew's daughter, dressed in green, charms the little boy into the house and then kills him. Bloom receives the song with private discomfort, thinking of his daughter. He concentrates on his memories of her birth, infancy, and girlhood. He thinks of her pretty hair and of the positive attention strangers gave her good looks when she was a child and of the more recent attentions of young men. He also thinks about teaching her when she was younger and of the gifts she has given him. Bloom then proposes that Stephen spend the night in his house, offering him the privacy of his own room. Bloom would welcome the opportunity to introduce his wife and daughter to Stephen, hoping for a possible romantic connection between Stephen and Milly. However, Stephen politely declines.

Bloom then returns the money he has been holding for Stephen, and the two discuss arrangements for vocal instruction and language lessons. Before Stephen takes up his hat and walking stick, Bloom thinks about two events in his life. In the first, a clown teasingly declared to a circus audience that Bloom was his father. In the second, Bloom had marked a coin, thinking that he would know it if it ever made its way back to him. Bloom considers that the coin never returned and that the clown is not his son. Bloom escorts Stephen, by candlelight, into the garden at the rear of the house. Bloom then points out the star formations to Stephen, speculates about astronomy and astrology, and the connection between women and the moon before pointing to a light coming from Molly's window. Bloom and Stephen by mutual consent then urinate simultaneously, allowing their individual flows to converge. As they urinate, Stephen thinks about ecclesiastical feasts while Bloom considers the penis in various circumstances. The narrator points out that both, however, observed the same star. The narrator then describes Bloom using a key to open a door in very sexual terms.

Bloom and Stephen shake hands as they take leave of one another. In the distance, the bells of Saint George's Church sound the time. Each man applies different words to the music of the bells. Bloom then thinks about the night sky, the cold vastness of the heavens, and of dead friends and companions. Bloom thinks of remaining outside to watch the changes in the evening sky but decides instead to return to the house. Entering the front room, Bloom bumps into some furniture. That day, while he was away, someone rearranged the room, making him feel a bit disoriented in his own house.

Left by himself, Bloom takes some time to think about his life and sur-roundings. He begins by lighting some incense; he uses the Agendath Netaim prospectus to fire the incense cone. Bloom, looking in the mirror, observes an old clock and a stuffed owl, both marriage gifts. He also consid-ers himself alone but not unhappy and looks at various books on a shelf in another part of the room, whose inverted titles he reviews. He also consid-ers the order and discipline of learning, and gives some disparaging thoughts to what he considers women's taste in literature and the inade-quacy of using a book as a hiding place. The books also remind him of places and people he has known, specifically, his wife's father. Relaxing, Bloom unbuttons his collar, suit, and trousers. He then makes out a budget of the day's earnings and expenses before allowing himself the fantasy of a home with gardens and beehives, an ideal of middle-class comfort. He then thinks about several money-making ventures and schemes that could gen-erate the money necessary to build or purchase his dream home.

Bloom then reveals his vulnerability. However, through introspection, he ultimately discovers his resilience. At first, he acknowledges to himself the impossibility of his money-making ventures but indulges in them to help him sleep. Subsequently, he discloses that his nighttime fears include thoughts that he might, in weakness, commit suicide like his father. The narrator then focuses on the contents of Bloom's private drawers. In one, he keeps various items, including his daughter's old copybook, one of her drawings of him, some old foreign coins, Christmas cards, romantic tokens and letters, and some pornographic postcards, among other items. Before considering the contents of the second drawer, the narrator relays Bloom's personal thoughts about the positive attention he received that day from various women. In the second drawer, Bloom keeps official documents, in-cluding birth certificates, insurance policies, and savings certificates. Bloom also keeps mementoes of his father in this drawer, notably the sui-cide note. Bloom thinks also of his son, Rudy, before going to sleep. The narrator then focuses on the potential and possibility of Bloom leaving his home to wander across Ireland and, perhaps, the world.

Deciding not to wander off because of the darkness and his tiredness, Bloom decides instead to go to sleep. He first, however, reviews his day, from cooking breakfast to bathing to attending the funeral to the hospital and the brothel district. He also takes note of what he considers to be his failures, including not getting an advertisement renewed, not discovering some intimate details of female statues, and missing a theatrical performance. Thinking of Molly's father and noticing her personal items, Bloom takes off his cloths and climbs into bed next to his wife. Before going to sleep, he takes note of the impression in the bed of another man's form and of the presence of some potted meat crumbs also left in the bed. He then considers several of Molly's possible lovers, including Simon Dedalus, before focusing on Boylan's vigor and arrogance. Plagued by a series of negative emotions, Bloom eventually deals with his wife's infidelity with equanimity. He briefly considers killing Boylan or divorcing Molly but dismisses both contingencies. Kissing Molly's bottom and laying his head by her legs, Bloom goes to sleep.

However, the narrative continues, focusing on the things omitted from Bloom's review of his day. Further, the narrator explores in detail Molly's and Bloom's sexual relations, noting the conception and birth of both Milly and Rudy, and also noting that Bloom and Molly have not had sex since Rudy died. The chapter concludes with a detailed scientific description of Bloom and Molly's sleeping positions and Bloom's weary, restful sleep. The narrator also takes care to mention Bloom's wanderings, playing with sounds and puns associated with literary travelers.

### Chapter Three (Episode XVIII)

Episode eighteen takes place in the bedroom at Bloom's home. While Bloom sleeps, his wife, Molly, shares her thoughts on Bloom, on her day's activities, and on her life. She touches on numerous themes, including sexuality, womanhood, men, love, duty, and numerous other topics. Her extended soliloquy gives voice to numerous stereotypes, but she also articulates within these conventional representations various and individual perspectives that belie the stereotypes. The narrative style of the chapter follows the pattern of a stream-of-consciousness interior monologue. The chapter contains only two periods and eight paragraph divisions, and Molly's flow of thought can sometimes be confusing.[31]

Molly begins her reflections by commenting on an apparent request by Bloom to have his breakfast served in bed. She considers that he has not made such a request since they lived in the City Arms Hotel. Thinking of the City Arms, Molly's thoughts turn toward Dante Riordan, whom Molly considers a cheap and selfish woman whose life focus involved excessive piety and a contemplation of the end of the world. Molly prefers to enjoy life and comments that Mrs. Riordan's piety and prudishness stemmed from her undesirability as a woman. Molly, however, does allow that Mrs. Riordan was well educated but found her talk boring and monotonous.

Molly then considers her husband. She likes his kindness but complains about his propensity, like all men in her view, to make the slightest sickness or ailment into a search for pity and female empathy. She also correctly observes that he has reached sexual fulfillment but mistakenly thinks he was with a prostitute. She considers that he could have been with the woman he engages in secret correspondence with and thinks about his other lustful adventures, particularly with a former maid. Molly then fantasizes about seducing younger men and priests before considering Boylan. She does not appreciate the casual familiarity of his patting her on the behind before he left that afternoon. She also considers his sexual prowess. Apparently, he reached climax several times that afternoon. Molly, however, did not enjoy the experience as thoroughly as he did, and she reflects on men's sexual selfishness and what she considers women's physiological disadvantages. Molly then reflects on men's weakness when it comes to women's attentions. She focuses particularly on Bloom, whom she can control and manipulate, and reflects on their courtship, thinking, specifically, about when he asked her to marry him. She also thinks about a woman who was a rival for Bloom's affections. The woman, Mrs. Breen, Molly comments, made an unfortunate match. Molly also thinks about how aggravating men can be and about a woman, Mrs. Maybrick, who killed her husband. After initially considering the act desperate and wrong, Molly develops sympathy for Mrs. Maybrick, speculating that she was motivated by love for another man or driven to desperate measures by her husband.

Molly begins the second section by speaking about Boylan. Her feet attract him, and he noticed them when Molly and Bloom were having tea one day. Molly noticed Boylan as well and returned to the same place two days afterward on the chance of seeing him. Molly's thoughts then wander to Bartell d'Arcy, whom she kissed after choir. She thinks about taking Bloom to the place were it happened and surprising him with the tale. Molly also considers Bloom's proclivities for undergarments, remembering their courtship and his odd requests for tokens and also remembering the women's bottoms he admired in the park. Bloom also courted Molly secretly and exerted himself sexually all too quickly for her tastes. Molly also brings to mind her activities with Boylan. She likes the idea that he agreed to come back on Monday at four o'clock, even though she was initially put off by the fruit basket he sent her. Molly also considers the upcoming concert tour and when she will have the opportunity to be in Belfast with Boylan while her husband is in County Clare. She contemplates making love with Boylan on the train before thinking about other singing engagements canceled because the current political climate resents that her father

was a soldier and considers that Bloom is not Irish enough. Bloom's association with the Freemasons, Molly reflects, also cost her some church jobs,
particularly with the Jesuits' church. Thinking about her father, Molly remembers a brief fling with a British soldier before he left for the Boer War
and remembers, with great fondness, watching Spanish and British Imperial troops on parade in Gibraltar. She then thinks again of Boylan, considers leaving her wedding ring behind while on the tour, and considers his
love-making habits and physical characteristics. Considering her physical
characteristics, Molly worries about her weight and thinks about her undergarments, remembering the Spanish girls in Gibraltar who went without them. She then wonders if Bloom remembered to buy her skin lotion
and worries about her aging; she reveals that she is thirty-two, the same age
as the number of counties in Ireland and the same number of feet a body
falls per second. She then thinks about Bloom's business sense, his unmas-
culine habits and odor, and his unfortunate taste in women's clothes.

The chapter's third section begins with Molly's comment on Boylan
sucking her nipples. She proceeds to contemplate her body in detail, comparing what she sees as the beauty of women's bodies to men's bodies.
Thinking about statues and erotic pictures and postcards, Molly remembers Bloom asking her if she would be willing to pose for one, at a time when
he lost his job. Molly, thinking about other men and Bloom, then considers
his explanations for complicated subjects. Finding them inadequate and
even humorous, she also remembers that he burned his breakfast that
morning. Returning to her body, Molly remembers nursing Milly and the
times Bloom had to relieve her pain by suckling her. Seeing him as an en-
larged baby who wanted to farm her out for extra money as a wet nurse,
Molly thinks again of Boylan. He, apparently, gave her a great deal of sexual
satisfaction that afternoon, and she anticipates his return on Monday.

Molly begins the fourth section of her soliloquy by commenting on the
power of trains, with their strength and abundance of water. She then remembers the heat of the afternoon, comparing it with the heat of Gibraltar.
Remembering Gibraltar, she recalls the rock's size and strength and, again,
the heat of the days and nights there. She also remembers various friends
and activities she experienced in Spain. Specifically, she recalls the bull-
fights, remembering the pain of the dying animals. She also thinks of an
early lover. She recalls her excitement and enthusiasm for life that she had
there, the adventures of watching the soldiers and dignitaries passing
through, and also remembers her father talking about heroic deeds and acts
of glory. She compares her contemporary surroundings and acquaintances
unfavorably with her youthful memories of Gibraltar and acknowledges

the death of almost all the people that she knew in Spain, recalling only the odd card or note. Molly also longs for romance, for someone to write her a love letter, and regrets her lost youth and fears getting older.

Molly begins the fifth section of her narrative thinking about a woman named Mrs. Rubio, a pious servant from Gibraltar, who disapproved of Molly's lack of religious piety and reserve. Mrs. Rubio also was less than pleased about English control. Molly remembers Rubio because she served Molly the morning of her first kiss to a British sailor named Mulvey. She kissed him under the Moorish wall with such enthusiasm he managed to crush the flowers he bought for her. Molly, to tease him, told him she was engaged to a Spanish nobleman. The relationship grew more physically intense, despite Mulvey's imminent departure. She allowed him to touch her breasts but not to penetrate her one day. Remembering this, Molly also recalls her curiosity about sex, admitting she once thought to, but never did, insert a banana into her vagina. Returning to thoughts of Mulvey, Molly recalls bringing him to sexual climax with a handkerchief and promising herself to him on his return. She never heard from or saw him again and speculates on his fate, thinking to make his current wife jealous. Molly then thinks about her marriage and considers her name and her other possible married names. She then recalls other men in Gibraltar and the landscapes and views of Southern Spain and Northern Africa. She also remembers one of her young paramours who died in action in South Africa. A passing train interrupts her thoughts, and Molly contemplates singing and performing so well as to spite those individuals who would deprive her of opportunities because of politics and misguided cultural nationalism. She thinks of her singing rival's relative inexperience in life and recalls some of her exploits, thinks of Boylan's sexual prowess and Bloom's annoying presence. She reveals that she would like him to sleep somewhere else so she could at least fart in peace.

Molly begins the sixth section expressing relief that she passed wind; she used the sound of the passing train to cover up that sound. Molly recalls her childhood, dancing wildly at night in her shift or stripped to the waist. She also speculates that a neighbor watched her from the cover of darkness. Her thoughts returning to Bloom, Molly hopes that he does not make a habit out of returning late at night, thinking he might try to recover his youth by hanging around with young men. Molly wonders at his breakfast order, thinking him a bit full of himself, but still she notes his polite manners. She then considers the cat and its habits. She sarcastically speculates about the food she will serve him and thinks to plan a picnic where couples could experiment with other partners. She also remembers Bloom bragging about his rowing ability on one particular outing and nearly drowning the people in the boat because of near incompetence. She then wonders about the book Bloom brought her, before thinking again of the sea, her ruined clothes after Bloom's exploits, and how the sea excites her sexually. She also recalls Bloom's various business ideas, thinking he would probably fail like his father did. She also thinks of all his dreams and romantic plans that never come to fruition and thinks also of his cowardice; he cowered noisily down the stairs one evening to investigate suspicious sounds coming from the kitchen. Molly then thinks about her daughter, concentrating on her maturing physical form, her girlish mannerisms, her interactions with her father, and on her flirtatious adventures with boys. Molly also thinks about her rivalries and disagreements with Milly. Molly then considers the difficulty of finding good servants and what she considers Bloom's ridiculous behavior that evening, jumping over railings and entertaining Stephen Dedalus in the kitchen. She expresses relief that her underwear was not hanging in the yard for the young man to see. Molly feels her period coming and wonders if it will pass in time for Boylan's Monday visit. Molly then recalls a particularly vigorous menstrual bleeding that came on when she was at the theater, during a play about adultery. She expresses relief that Boylan did not make her pregnant and recalls the sound of the bed jingling with their movements. She recalls their foreplay and reminds herself to obliterate the signs of sexual contact that might still be around the apartment before wondering what it would be like to be a man during sex.

The seventh section begins as Molly expresses concern over the frequency of her cycles. Her last period was only three weeks prior to her current cycle. She also considers consulting a doctor and remembers the clinical nature of his language and manner. She then thinks of Bloom and of their early days together, when he had political ambitions. She recalls his tricks to catch sight of her privately. As she stoops above the chamber pot, she thinks disparagingly of her husband's habits, including his sleeping in an inverted position, his pretensions, and his smell. She considered what she considers their relative poverty and his failed business schemes and his variety of unsuccessful jobs. She considers the pretensions of his associates, comparing their assembly at Dignam's funeral unfavorably with the military funerals she witnessed as a young girl. Molly acknowledges too that she knows the men mock Bloom behind his back. She also expresses empathy for Dignam's family. However, her thoughts turn negative again when she considers the good voices but poor performances of Ben Dollard and Simon Dedalus. She then thinks of Stephen and Bloom's proposals for tutoring and collaboration. She recalls Stephen as a young boy, innocent and childishly cute, riding with his parents. She also wonders if Bloom wants to arrange an affair between herself and Stephen. She begins to consider an affair with Stephen, romanticizing his poetic tendencies, imagining herself his muse, and thinking of him sexually. Hoping he keeps himself clean, she imagines him sexually innocent and hopes to teach him sexual things as he teaches her intellectual things. Molly goes so far as to imagine herself his famous romantic partner, before remembering Bloom.

Molly begins her final section thinking disparagingly of Boylan and his presumptive manners and of his unrefined habits. She thinks also of sexuality, again wondering what it would be like to be a man and to have a penis. She speaks enviously of men's relative power in sexual games and politics, regrets that Bloom does not embrace her or satisfy her sexually, and fantasizes about anonymous sexual contact with a sailor or a stranger. She then considers men's rude behavior and drunken habits and thinks the world would be a better place if women were in charge. She also thinks piteously of Stephen, seeing him as a motherless boy in need of love and regrets that he did not stay the night. She considers Stephen once more as a companion, longing for his intelligent company. She thinks of serving him breakfast in bed or of Bloom serving both herself and Stephen. She also wants to impress him by teaching him Spanish while he teaches her Italian. Subsequently, a now-angry Molly turns her thoughts to Bloom, revealing that at least a partial motivation for her affair with Boylan was to make Bloom jealous and to punish him. She also reveals guilt and self-blame in her angry thoughts. As she tries to fall asleep, she contemplates cleaning the piano and the house, ordering flowers, and wearing nice clothes in case Stephen returns. Molly then thinks of the freedom of flowers and the open countryside before reflecting with great enthusiasm of her early days with Bloom on Howth, when she passed seed cake to him from her mouth. She thinks of their passionate embrace afterward and of his warm kiss. As the chapter comes to a close, Molly recalls her days in Gibraltar, imagining an Eastern paradise with sun and flowers and romance and passion, ending her soliloquy as she began it, with affirmation.

## NOTES

1. Richard P. Davis, *Arthur Griffith and Non-Violent Sinn Fein* (Dublin: Anvil Books, 1974).

2. Joseph E. Duncan, "The Modality of the Audible in Joyce's *Ulysses*," *PMLA* 72 (March 1957): 288–290.

3. R.J. Schork, *Latin and Roman Culture in Joyce* (Gainesville: University of Florida Press, 1997), p. 125.

4. Duncan, "Modality of the Audible," p. 287.

5. Ibid., p. 288.

6. Ibid. Also see *A Greek-English Lexicon* (Oxford: Oxford University Press, 1996). It provides definitions for both diaphane and adiaphane, as the ancient Greeks understood them.

7. Declan Kiberd glosses "sconce" as "head" ("Notes," *Ulysses*, James Joyce [London: Penguin Books, 1992], p. 959). Don Gifford references Samuel Johnson's refutation of Berkeley's theory regarding the nonexistence of matter (*Ulysses Annotated* [Berkeley: University of California Press, 1989], p. 45).

8. Duncan, "Modality of the Audible," p. 287.

9. The allusion is to Dante's *Inferno* 4:131.

10. Duncan, "Modality of the Audible," p. 290.

11. Ibid., p. 288. See also Kiberd, "Notes," p. 959.

12. Ibid., p. 288.

13. Declan Kiberd glosses "made not begotten" as "a reversal of the usual formulaic reference to Jesus in the Apostle's Creed" ("Notes," 960). Kiberd's deduction is correct, but the prayer is the Nicene Creed.

14. Stephen's predicament closely matches Coleridge's distinction in the closing sections of chapter thirteen of the *Biographia Literaria*, between the "primary imagination," the "secondary imagination," and the "fancy." J. Shawcross glosses Coleridge's terms as follows: "The primary imagination is the organ of common perception, the faculty by which we have experience of an actual world of phenomena. The secondary imagination is the same power in a heightened degree, which enables its possessor to see the world of our common experience in its real significance. And the creations of art are the embodiments of this vision" ("Notes to Vol. I," *Biographia Literaria*, S.T. Coleridge [Oxford: Oxford University Press, 1907], p. 272). Stephen goes on, in subsequent chapters, to adopt Coleridge's methods of literary criticism in his analysis of biographical data to support a theory regarding Shakespeare and Hamlet.

15. Kiberd, "Notes," p. 960.

16. Gifford, *Ulysses Annotated*, p. 60.

17. Ibid., p. 66.

18. Ibid., p. 88.

19. Ibid., p. 109.

20. Mrs. Sinico is a character in Joyce's story, "A Painful Case."

21. Zack Bowen, *"Ulysses." A Companion to Joyce Studies*, ed. Zack Bowen and James F. Carens (Westport, Conn.: Greenwood Press, 1984), p. 462.

22. Tom Corfe, *The Phoenix Park Murders: Conflict, Compromise, and Tragedy in Ireland 1879–1882* (London: Hodder and Stoughton, 1968).

23. Zack Bowen, "The Bronzegold Sirensong," in *Bloom's Old Sweet Song*, ed. Zack Bowen (Gainesville: University of Florida Press, 1995), pp. 26–27.

24. Zack Bowen, *Musical Allusions in the Works of James Joyce: Early Poetry through Ulysses* (Albany: SUNY Press, 1974).

25. Kiberd, "Notes," p. 1047.

26. Bowen, "*Ulysses*," pp. 497–498.

27. The reference creates an interesting parallel between Nolan and "Mad Sweeney" of Irish legend, who, driven mad by battle and a curse, wanders in the wilderness and lives in the trees.

28. Stuart Gilbert, *James Joyce's Ulysses: A Study* (New York: Vintage Books, 1955), pp. 294–312.

29. Brendan O Herir, *A Gaelic Lexicon for* Finnegans Wake *and Glossary for Joyce's Other Works* (Berkeley: University of California Press, 1967), p. 348.

30. Bowen, "*Ulysses*," pp. 539–540.

31. Shari Benstock, in *Who's He When He's at Home: A James Joyce Directory* (Urbana: University of Illinois Press, 1980), traces the antecedents of Molly's pronouns.

# 3   Texts

Between the time Joyce first conceived *Ulysses*, as the subject of a short story he might include in *Dubliners*, and the final publication of the novel, the framework of the story and its themes and techniques underwent considerable revision. Indeed, the text has never stopped seeing itself revised and altered since its initial publication date, on Joyce's fortieth birthday in 1922. Joyce himself constantly reworked and revised sections of episodes, altering their form and reworking their thematic motifs, up to the last possible moment prior to publication. After its initial printing, Joyce devoted time and energy revising the text and correcting errors in its initial and early printings. Joyce never did see a nonflawed version of the text published in his lifetime, and the general public and academics alike are still waiting for a definitive text, despite the efforts of numerous scholars and editors.

The story of Odysseus and his journeys occupied Joyce's thoughts and excited his imagination since he was a schoolboy. Long before he considered writing about Leopold Bloom, he found himself preoccupied with the adventures of Odysseus, as told by Charles Lamb in his *Adventures of Ulysses*.[1] Lamb's version of the text attracted Joyce's attention because of its depiction of the ancient Greek heroes as human figures involved in superhuman events and incidents. Lamb fashioned his retelling of the *Odyssey* with the intention of making the ancient Greek hero more accessible to a wider audience. Likewise, Joyce wanted to model a contemporary hero on the ancient Greek hero, initially thinking to write a short story for *Dubliners* on the theme.[2] Joyce's choice for his modern-day wanderer was a Dublin Jew named Hunter, and "Mr. Hunter's Holiday" is the earliest title for *Ulysses*. In 1906, Joyce disclosed the title and his intention to write the story to his brother Stanislaus. Joyce's intention seems to have been to take Lamb's design of the ancient legend a step further. If Lamb wrote the story of Odysseus so as to make its themes accessible to contemporary readers, then Joyce wanted to demonstrate those themes in contemporary life, choosing an unlikely hero to embody the ancient themes; Mr. Hunter was an outsider whose wife reportedly cheated on him.

A year after writing Stanislaus regarding the subject of Mr. Hunter, Joyce chose to focus instead on his first novel. He apparently decided that a short story would not allow him to explore the potential broad range of themes and issues that a modern *Odyssey* offered. However, Joyce's first novel moved away from Odyssean themes in favor of the life and evolution of a young writer. Nonetheless, even as he completed *A Portrait of the Artist as a Young Man*, Joyce considered that *Ulysses* would be a fitting sequel. Between the official beginnings of the novel in 1914 and his early conception of the story, Joyce read and reread Homer and various academic commentators on Homeric epics. He was preparing himself for his later work.

In 1914, he laid down a rough outline of the text, patterned on the *Odyssey*, and began writing some of the episodes. Interestingly, Joyce worked on the later chapters first.[3] Apparently, he wanted to anchor the initial chapters with a view toward the novel's ultimate conclusion. His composition process also allowed him to discover possible interrelations between episodes and allowed for variation and improvisation within an overall pattern or structure. However, Joyce did fashion near-final versions of the first three episodes by the end of the First World War. By this time, the chapters began to appear in serial form in magazines in the United States and in England. By 1920, Joyce had completed more than half of the final eighteen episodes when he decided to dramatically revise and expand them. During the previous two years, he decided to make the themes and the structure of the novel far more complex. Even as the page proofs came back to him from the publisher in 1921, Joyce revised and expanded the text so drastically that his publisher had to send as many as five versions of each episode.[4] Although his creative process may have annoyed his editors, Joyce sought to weave into each episode subtleties of theme, character, and narrative form that would create an organic whole of his entire text. Each episode then had to be revised as other episodes changed in order to keep the intricacies of theme, plot, and structure unified. Joyce's revisions reshaped his narrative, producing an entire text that reflects the unified vision of the latter stages of composition. Essentially, Joyce's basic plan for the text as a modern-day *Odyssey* remained constant. However, his artistic rendering of that initial design grew and changed with the process of composition, and Joyce's artistic integrity demanded that every facet of his text manifest his mature creative vision for the novel. He refused to compromise his epistemological designs in favor of expediency or convenience.

Joyce organized his expanding vision by using note sheets.[5] Each episode would find its basic design and its intended expansion outlined on large single sheets of paper. The notes reveal that even passing or seemingly incidental detail from the text reinforces an intricate and subtle plan. The sheets also reveal the extent to which Homer's characters and designs influenced even the late revisions. Joyce apparently chose to weave his own unique reading of Homer's text into his *Ulysses* at every stage of composition. Joyce not only anchored his text in Homer's epic but also in realistic details. He explored maps of Dublin and Gibraltar, wrote friends and family for accurate details of Dublin scenes and views, and scoured newspapers and magazines in order to enhance the realistic flavor of his novel. Joyce calculated the exact time it would take each of his characters to journey from place to place within each episode. He asked for the height of railings and doors, the layout of gardens, and the exact sightlines of churches and beaches.[6] Joyce also drew on many of his early notebooks, collecting details he jotted down as a young man wandering the streets of Dublin. *Ulysses'* design seeks to root the workings of an epic, with its ephemeral and sublime themes, to the realistic and ordinary lives of ordinary people.

From these anchors in the epic and in realistic detail, Joyce then expanded the designs of each chapter. He accumulated associative details of color and movement endemic to themes and characters. He built these associative details around his anchors, accumulating more and more layers of related detail with each subsequent revision. He, subsequently, added related details to earlier episodes and chapters in order to produce a texture of interconnected relationships and meanings.[7] Moreover, Joyce never sacrificed the quality of his language. He labored not only over detail but also over the sound of his words, ensuring that on the aural and visual levels his written work reinforced his overall thematic structure. Significantly, in his process of revision, Joyce seems to have nearly always added material and rarely to have edited out sections of his text, a process suggesting that his initial design and structure remained fairly constant despite his numerous and extensive revisions. A. Walton Litz, in *The Art of James Joyce*, likens *Ulysses'* form and method of composition to an artist working in mosaic form. The early stages of composition laid out a broad pattern. From there, the overall outlines of images emerged. Subsequently, motifs of color and texture and subtleties of form took shape. Finally, nuances of color and shape emerged in all parts of the text simultaneously. Joyce then layered his designs and motifs to create not only an integral artistic work but also a deeply textured manifestation of numerous related themes and patterns. *Ulysses* takes the artistic aesthetic of Joyce's earlier works to its logical and extreme conclusion. In *Dubliners* and *Portrait*, realistic details lead to epiphanies, sudden insights into the sublime or transcendent. *Ulysses* plants the seeds for epiphanies in associative detail that layer a character's and a reader's experience in the text and with the text. When an epiphany emerges, it comes as a sudden insight but its origins and growth can, subsequently, be traced through the text's layers of detail, narrative design, and symbol.

The first published forms of *Ulysses* appeared in *The Little Review*, an American periodical, and *The Egoist*, a London periodical. In 1917, with the help of Ezra Pound and Harriet Shaw Weaver, Joyce began the serial publication of individual chapters. *The Egoist* produced only the first three-and-a-half episodes; no printer could be persuaded to typeset the rest. However, *The Little Review* published fourteen episodes, starting in March 1918 and continuing through December 1920. Margaret Anderson and Ezra Pound quietly edited some passages from some of the episodes in order to avoid legal trouble over their explicit sexual references and their graphic descriptions of bodily processes. Despite the efforts of Anderson and Pound to avoid legal trouble, the United States postal authorities confiscated and burned four issues of *The Little Review* precisely because of their "obscene" content. More troubling still, the July-August 1920 issue of the magazine was accidentally sent to the daughter of a prominent New York attorney, who promptly informed the district attorney's office. The July-August number contained part of the "Nausicaa" episode. The district attorney's office passed the episode on to the New York Society for the Suppression of Vice; they filed suit against *The Little Review*. John Quinn, a prominent lawyer in his own right, led the defense, arguing that *Ulysses*, despite its content, would not encourage deviant behavior but would rather deter it, in the tradition of the explicit literature of Swift or Rabelais. The prosecuting attorney grew frustrated with Quinn's arguments, and the judges appeared ready to side with the defense. They actually found the supposedly offensive passages from the text incomprehensible. However, the court delivered a ruling against Joyce and *The Little Review*, effectively preventing

*Ulysses*' publication in the United States. In order to see his book in print, Joyce would have to go to extraordinary means.

*Ulysses* found publication in book form under the imprint of the Shakespeare and Company bookshop in Paris. Sylvia Beach, the bookshop's owner, sympathized with Joyce's efforts to find a publisher, made more difficult because of the negative United States court ruling. Ultimately, she decided to arrange for its publication. A limited edition of 1,000 signed copies appeared on Joyce's birthday, February 2, 1922. The cover of the edition carries with it a symbolic meaning. The title and Joyce's name appear in white on top of blue covers. The white represents the rock of Ithaca rising from the blue covers, the color of the sea. The blue itself stands for not only the sea but also for the color blue in the Greek flag. In order to match the color of the flag exactly, the dye had to be specially mixed.[8] London's Egoist Press also issued the Shakespeare and Company edition in two limited editions. Five hundred of the 2,000 first Egoist Press copies were burned by New York postal authorities, and customs authorities in Folkestone confiscated 499 of the 500 second Egoist Press copies. Shakespeare and Company issued several more editions of the text in the next few years; however, they also had to issues pages of corrections at the end of the volume. The French typesetters who set the first edition made numerous errors in transcribing Joyce's corrections and text.[9] Ultimately, for Shakespeare and Company's eighth printing, in May 1926, the text was completely reset; the final Shakespeare and Company edition, its eleventh, came out in May 1930. Without exception, the various editions of the Shakespeare and Company version offer an attractive but very fragile text. The covers were thin cardboard, and the pages of the copies that survive are very brittle.

The Odyssey Press then published *Ulysses* in Germany in 1932. Stuart Gilbert, under the direction of Joyce himself, supervised and submitted corrections for the Odyssey Press edition,[10] which saw four reprintings; the last edition appeared in April 1939, just months before the outbreak of the Second World War. The edition divides the text into two small paperback volumes, with brief introductions by Gilbert, Ernst Robert Curtius, and Edmond Jaloux. The volumes also contain blurbs by Curtius, Middleton Murry, and Valéry Larbaud. A number of influential critics argue that the Odyssey Press edition remains the most authoritative and accurate edition of *Ulysses* yet printed.[11] Unfortunately, it is not widely available.

Indeed, difficulties surround the mass market editions of Random House in the United States and the Bodley Head in London. A favorable and influential court ruling enabled *Ulysses* to be published in the United States. Throughout the 1920s, Americans had smuggled copies of *Ulysses* into the country under various disguises. However, in 1933, Bennett Cerf of Random House decided to force the issue. He openly imported a copy and managed to challenge the ban in court. On December 6, 1933, Judge John Woolsey ruled that the book did not violate any law and, therefore, could be printed and distributed in America. Random House issued the first American edition in 1934. Unfortunately, Random House set the text not from the Odyssey Press edition or even from the Shakespeare and Company edition but rather from a pirated edition that appeared illegally in 1929.[12] Samuel Roth, in defiance of the legal ban on the book and in utter disregard for Joyce's rights as author, began to serialize the text in his (Roth's) New York–based journal *Two Worlds Monthly*; in 1929, he issued *Ulysses* in a single volume. Joyce, joined by writers and intellectuals ranging from Einstein and Eliot to Hemingway and Mann, vigorously protested the edition. Random House, in setting its legal and authorized version of the text from the pirated edition, incorporated thousands of Roth's misprintings into the text. Fortunately, the British publisher Bodley Head used an Odyssey Press edition to set their version of *Ulysses*, which appeared in 1936; a limited edition with drawings by Matisse that was published in New York in 1935 also used the Odyssey Press version as its source. In 1960, the Bodley Head issued a corrected text, which was used to print subsequent Penguin, Modern Library, and Random House editions. Declan Kiberd also used the Bodley Head text for his "Student's Edition" of *Ulysses* published in the early 1990s. Kiberd provides extensive annotations to the text, offering translations of Latin, Irish, and other material as well as explications and detailed explanations of Joyce's various sources and references. However, many critics still dispute the authority of the original and reset Bodley Head editions, citing thousands of errors and variations from Joyce's manuscripts.

Garland Publishing, making primary source materials more widely available, published the *Ulysses* manuscripts, typescripts, notes, and proof sheets between 1977 and 1979; *The James Joyce Archive*, arranged by Michael Groden, also published extensive notes, typescripts, manuscripts and proofs for Joyce's other works. Students and critics can now examine Joyce's methods of revision and composition more thoroughly than before. Using *The James Joyce Archive* as a source, Hans Walter Gabler issued what he believed to be an authoritative edition of *Ulysses*.

Gabler, working with a staff in Munich, also used computers as editing tools. They transcribed and collated different versions of each episode, enabling the team to lay side by side different versions of the text. Gabler's work methods combined German genetic research with traditional Anglo-

American editing techniques.[13] Briefly, an Anglo-American editor would use a base text, most likely the last authorized published edition, and then consider revisions and emendations to the authorized edition. German editorial practice focuses on the author's process of revision, establishing the stages of composition. In 1979, Gabler presented an episode to the James Joyce Symposium in Zurich and received permission from the James Joyce estate to proceed with a full edition.

Gabler then proceeded with his work, choosing a number of what would later prove controversial editorial practices. He created what has come to be known as a "continuous manuscript text" that privileges extant Joyce notes and manuscript materials over printed and published versions of the book. Critics point out that not all of Joyce's manuscript material survives, raising issues of comprehensiveness and extant manuscript authority over published texts.[14] When Gabler published his critical version of the text through Garland publishing in 1984, he included his new text and the continuous manuscript text, laying them side by side. The advisory board, overseeing the project, objected to Gabler's editorial techniques, almost at the same time as his text was being submitted to the publishers. Gabler objected to their concerns, raised so late in the editorial process, and declined to rework the book based on their objections. His advisory board resigned but withdrew their resignations only after agreeing to publish *Ulysses: A Review of Three Texts*, pointing out their concerns over Gabler's editorial practices and their reservations about the finished volume. Nonetheless, the volume, published to great acclaim, received high praise, at least initially. The publisher declared the subsequent reader's edition title as *Ulysses: The Corrected Text*. Gabler objected to the title, preferring to see his work as a variant and counterpart to the 1922 edition.[15]

The Joyce community also praised the volume; many had been part of his editorial team or had served on his advisory board. Moreover, many had little or no training in textual editing. However, the seeds for what would become known as the "Joyce Wars" were planted in 1985 at the meeting of The Society for Textual Scholarship. John Kidd, participating on a panel with Hans Walter Gabler, organized a public relations coup against Gabler. Kidd appealed to the media, particularly *The Washington Post*, and presented himself and his position as the innocent defenders of Joyce's text against the heavy-handed editing procedures of Gabler, the new Teutonic menace. Gabler's response seemed heavy-handed. Consequently, many flocked to Kidd's defense.[16] During the 1988 Joyce Symposium in Venice, Fritz Senn set up a panel to discuss the controversy. Gabler attended but did not participate in the discussion. Kidd declined to attend but published, while the conference was in session, an attack on the Gabler text in *The New York Review of Books*; copies of Kidd's article were distributed to the conference participants. Kidd accused Gabler of misreading the manuscripts, of spelling errors, of relying too heavily on facsimile copies of manuscripts, and of departing from the published text far too often. The popular press took up the story, and Gabler and Kidd became types of celebrities. Time and time again, Kidd managed to score media victories against Gabler, who could not manage to effectively counter the charges publicly.[17]

In February 1989, the Joyce Wars came to Miami for the annual Miami J'yce Birthday conference. Gabler and Kidd faced each other, as did teams of supporters for each side. Despite the rather contentious atmosphere of the sessions, Gabler agreed that some changes to his edition were necessary. Kidd, at the conference and later in an article in the *Papers of the Bibliographical Society of America*, outlined his charges against Gabler, seemingly unwilling to compromise. Critics defending Gabler's position point out that he used sound editorial practices because Joyce never fully revised any published version of *Ulysses*, Gilbert's corrections to the Odyssey Press edition aside. Therefore, the use of a manuscript text seems appropriate, especially considering various printer's errors in the production of the 1922 text. Ultimately, Kidd petitioned Random House to cease publication of the Gabler text and return to its old edition. Random House responded by publishing both editions. Many scholars and teachers use the Gabler text, and with great success, although many see the need for a new, corrected Gabler edition.

The next major edition of *Ulysses*, and one that promised to establish a definitive text, came out in June 1997. Danis Rose and Picador Press published in Dublin what they claimed to be the "Reader's Text" of *Ulysses*. The edition became a best seller in Ireland, the United Kingdom, and Canada. It was not released in the United States. Rose estimates that he made 8,000 to 10,000 changes to the text, including "correcting" misspellings; changing punctuation and even adding apostrophes to Molly's final soliloquy; breaking up compound words; and changing the order of words so that they flow more logically. Rose, perhaps anticipating scholarly objection to his editorial practices, declares that his text is not for the scholars but for the people, the average reader.[18] Picador, in its press releases, declares the edition the best available because combining "the better features of current theories of text-editing, previously assumed to be incompatible," Rose has "removed a plethora of small, yet not insignificant, obstructions between writer and reader that have hitherto marred the enjoyment of this most human and extraordinary of novels." Publicity information also contains a statement attributed to Danis Rose, asserting that his edition "is designed pre-eminently for the lover of literature, and the aesthetic qualities—the sense, the sound and flow of words—have been subjected to a refinement which only a craftsman, not a scholar alone, could hope to bring to bear." Presumably, Rose considers Joyce's craftsmanship to have been obscured by printers' errors, and, therefore, does not feel that Joyce needs the assistance of a craftsman of language. In fairness to Rose, he assembled an "isotext"[19] to produce his version of *Ulysses*, meaning that he assembled all possible variations to each chapter and passage and then chose the version he felt best reflected Joyce's creative desires, later obscured by printing errors or by errors in transcription.

Critical reaction has been predictably strong. Some defended the edition. The *New York Times*, of June 23, 1997, quotes Seamus Deane as saying that Rose's text is "one of the most important editions of 'Ulysses.' "[20] Robert McCrum, writing for the *Guardian* also praised the edition as "a fine and loyal act of restoration."[21] However, others attacked the edition. The Joyce estate, led by Stephen Joyce, argues that the text does not represent Joyce's work at all, that it is, essentially, an entirely new book.[22] Lawrence Rainey, in the *London Review of Books*, writes that Rose's edition is a "self-aggrandizing fantasy." Many more early supporters of Rose's text withdrew their support after the extent of his revisions became clear. John Kidd sarcastically suggests that Rose next publish "a *Reader's Digest* condensed version of *Finnegans Wake*."[23] The Rose edition did bring *Ulysses* back into the popular consciousness and did tap into widely held prejudices against the academy but, in truth, does go too far in changing and altering the text. It is as if Joyce was in desperate need of Danis Rose's cleverness to make his work accessible to contemporary readers. Rose obscures, by clarification, many words or phrases Joyce wanted to remain obscure, argue many critics. His use of compound words and lack of punctuation point toward Joyce's dissatisfaction with the written word and toward Joyce's efforts to create a new way of using the written word to communicate.

John Kidd plans to publish his own version of *Ulysses* through W.W. Norton and Company. The projected edition, held up by copyright disputes, promises to correct about 2,500 errors present in other editions. Kidd also promises that his edition will restore the original pagination and lineation of the 1922 text. Kidd is especially enthusiastic about the planned big, bold headlines in episode seven, printing them just as Joyce intended them to be printed. However, scholars, many of whom fell victim to Kidd's various attacks, suggest that the copyright laws are a convenient excuse. Indeed, unless Kidd's version is perfect, many Joyce scholars will be all too happy to discredit it. Many relish the chance to do to Kidd what he has done to Rose and Gabler. The truth is far more complicated. As early as 1992, Norton had page proofs for the Kidd edition in hand. However, they lost them, wasting hundreds of hours of work. Moreover, the 1994 "General Agreement on Tariffs and Trade" does protect *Ulysses*. However, Norton has opened discussions with the Joyce estate, and there is at least the possibility that Kidd's edition will be published soon.[24]

John Kidd is also engaged in producing a CD-ROM version of *Ulysses* with himself acting as a tour guide through the text, which will also include more than 2,000 photographs and 15,000 annotations. Michael Groden, of the University of Western Ontario, is also currently working on a "hyper-media" version of *Ulysses*.[25] Groden's project not only includes a text of *Ulysses* with annotations and explications but also an archive of major critical articles; copies of source books, including the *Odyssey* and *Hamlet*; period maps and photographs of Dublin and of people from the text; recordings of songs and a list of musical allusions; an audio version of the text; and a search and index feature. Groden's version will also lay side by side various editions of *Ulysses*, including the 1922 text, the Odyssey Press text, the Random House editions of 1924 and 1961, the Bodley Head editions of 1936 and 1960, and the Gabler text. Hypermedia editions of Joyce's works promise to open up *Ulysses* to an even wider variety of readers, viewers, and listeners. Finally, even as Joyce's masterpiece enters the computer age with all its high-tech promises and possibilities, the Orchises Press, a Canadian publisher, has made available an edition of *Ulysses* that re-creates the 1922 Shakespeare and Company edition. Printed on acid-free paper and under hard cover and cloth boards, the edition promises to give readers the "experience" of "what it would have been like to hold, handle, and leisurely read one of the first 1,000 copies of *Ulysses*." The edition reproduces all the front matter, cover lettering, broken type, and cover color of the original edition.

## NOTES

1. Richard Ellmann, *James Joyce* (New York: Oxford University Press, 1982), p. 46. Ellmann tells the story of Joyce, as a young student at Belvedere College, writing an essay on Ulysses as his favorite hero. Joyce also recommends that Mrs. William Murray read Lamb's book to better understand *Ulysses*. (See James Joyce, *Letters of James Joyce*, vol. 1, ed. Stuart Gilbert with revisions by Richard Ellmann. [New York: Viking Press, 1966], pp. 193, 198.)

2. Zack Bowen, "Ulysses," in *A Companion to Joyce Studies*, ed. Zack Bowen and James F. Carens (Westport, Conn.: Greenwood Press, 1984), p. 421.

3. A. Walter Litz, *The Art of James Joyce* (London: Oxford University Press, 1961), pp. 2–4.

4. Ibid., pp. 5–8.

5. Ibid., pp. 5–13.

6. Joyce, *Letters*, pp. 135–136. These letters offer a representative sample of Joyce's requests for information.

7. Litz, *The Art of James Joyce*, pp. 5–13.

8. Edward L. Bishop, "Re: Covering *Ulysses*," *Joyce Studies Annual* 5 (summer 1994): 24.

9. Ellmann, *James Joyce*, pp. 504–508.

10. Ibid., p. 653.

11. Michael Groden, "A Textual and Publishing History," in *A Companion to Joyce Studies*, ed. Zack Bowen and James F. Carens (Westport, Conn.: Greenwood Press, 1984), p. 107.

12. Ibid., p. 108.

13. Geert Lernout, "Anglo-American Textual Criticism and the Case of Hans Walter Gabler's Edition of *Ulysses*," *Genesis* 9 (1996): p. 62–64.

14. Michael Groden, "Perplex in the Pen—and in the Pixels: Reflections on the James Joyce Archive, Hans Walter Gabler's *Ulysses*, and James Joyce's *Ulysses* in Hypermedia," *Journal of Modern Literature* 22.2 (1999): 233–35.

15. Ibid., pp. 231–233.

16. Ibid., p. 234.

17. Ibid., p. 235.

18. Danis Rose, "The Rationale of the Reader's Edition," *Ulysses*, James Joyce, ed. Danis Rose (Dublin: Picador, 1997), pp. xi-xxvii.

19. Danis Rose, "A Technical Appendix," *Ulysses*, James Joyce, ed. Danis Rose (Dublin: Picador, 1997), p. lxxxv.

20. Sarah Lyall, "'*Ulysses*,' in *Deep Trouble Again*," *New York Times*, June 23, 1997, p. B4.

21. Robert McCrum, "McCrum on *Ulysses*," *The Guardian*, June 15, 1997 (on-line: September 14, 2000).

22. Lyall, "Deep Trouble," p. B1.

23. Mary McGlynn, "Bloomsgate," *Metanews 21st* C (2.4) (on-line: September 14, 2000).

24. Warren St. John, "James Joyce and the Nutty Professor," *Joycewars*, (on-line: September 14, 2000).

25. Groden, "Perplex," p. 241.

# 4    Contexts

Many of the cultural, historical, and political trends of the late nineteenth and early twentieth centuries find expression in *Ulysses*. Indeed, Joyce's text embodies much that comprises turn-of-the-century artistic and cultural identity. However, *Ulysses* is by no means the only literary work to give voice to the turbulent years of the late 1800s and early 1900s. George Bernard Shaw's *Heartbreak House* also embodies many of the cultural and political preoccupations that pervaded late Victorian and early modern life. As the play opens, the house, itself a metaphor for Victorian society, finds its owner, a retired British naval officer, playing host to his daughters and their suitors, including barons of industry. Essentially, Shaw's play functions as a microcosm of Victorian society, containing representatives of all the sources of turn-of-the century British pride and self-confidence. The retired naval officer, who makes his living experimenting with explosives, represents the British military, which extended British culture and commerce throughout the world. The capitalist mogul stands for the strength of British industry, and the captain's daughters represent Victorian morality and the flower of Victorian womanhood. When the play ends with the house's explosive destruction, Shaw's meaning is clear. The captain, like the British Empire, sustains himself through technological advances that will destroy not only him but also all he holds dear.

*Ulysses* also provides insights into the experiences of being Irish at the close of the nineteenth century and the first few decades of the twentieth century. Similarly, Shaw's position in Victorian society as an Irishman enabled him to perceive the hypocrisy that sustained many of the empire's institutions and to detect their underlying weaknesses. He, like many other writers and artists of the late nineteenth and early twentieth century, foresaw the consequences of political and cultural expansion through a matrix of dominance and exploitation, and anticipated that the technological and scientific advances that powered the engines of empire could be turned onto their creators. In Shaw's play, contemporary readers can see the anxiety associated with technology and cultural hegemony, and can detect a foreshadowing of the First World War and the Modernist movement in art and literature. Moreover, just as Shaw's position as an Irishman writing from the heart of the British empire enabled him to more readily accept and expose its weaknesses,[1] Joyce's *Ulysses* sets itself in the heart of Victorian Dublin, revealing many of the weaknesses of late nineteenth- and early twentieth-century society but simultaneously revealing the human strength and potential that lies dormant underneath the colonial/imperial surface.

## THE MODERN CONTEXT

In *The Time Machine*, H.G. Wells captures the Victorian faith in technology, in man's ability to survey and control other lands and territories, and the Victorian curiosity for travel. However, Wells also portrays the anxiety associated with the rapid advance of science, the insecurities that come with the encounter of other lands and people,[2] and the sense of lack and absence inherent in the Victorian worldview. Wells's traveler masters the supposed scientific limitations on time. He becomes a type of transcendent being, leaving all the temporal restraints behind him as he travels. In this sense, he epitomizes the Victorian scientist, traveler, and explorer. His pride, curiosity, and enthusiasm carry him forward. However, once he leaves the comfort of his Victorian home and his time, he encounters war, the degeneration of the species, and the eventual end of time. Books decay before his sight. The ruling and leisure class become food for the working class. The buildings and structures in which the Victorians invested so many of their resources fade and decay. Technology not only enables the traveler to view all the agents of destruction but, in many ways, it also functions to destroy the Victorian ideal. In a sense, the mechanisms of scientific advancement serve as the agents of destruction. Moreover, beyond science, Wells's traveler's survey of time is reminiscent of the Victorian explorer who leaves the comforts of home to extend the gaze of British society to distant lands. However, in extending the gaze, the explorer or missionary or military expedition encounters disturbing sights.[3] That Wells's traveler stays in England, covering only the territory of time, leaves the Englishman without his usual defense against foreign cultures and communities. Whereas the Victorian traveler could inoculate himself against the presence of the strange or the seemingly savage by distinguishing himself from the objects of his gaze, Wells's traveler must confront the reality that all he surveys is English and, therefore, a direct reflection of and challenge to his identity as superior. *The Time Machine*, therefore, embodies the typical Victorian's faith in both his abilities and his simultaneous doubts and insecurities that accompany his advances and explorations.

More specifically, technology for the Victorian represented the manifestation and self-evident proof of his superior mind. Technological advance represented a sense of invulnerability, a sense of dominance over nature, and even a sense of independence from God and religion. After all, to the Victorian mind, technological advances expanded commerce throughout the globe, enhancing wealth at home in England. Although the leaders of industry profited the most, wealth increased for all members of society. The general standard of living was continually rising. The steam engine, steel, and other technological advances created jobs at home and facilitated commerce and exploration abroad, enabling England to expand her wealth and influence across the globe. Moreover, technological advances seemed to prove man's superiority over the heavens. Percival Lowell declared, in *Mars as the Abode of Life* (1896), that he had discovered, by use of a superior telescope, the existence of life on Mars. Popular magazines predicted that man would shortly harness the power of the sun to satisfy his fuel needs, that science could also harness more earthly manifestations such as water, and that science would conquer the caprices of the environment to ensure a balanced growing season with abundant crops. In addition, technological discovery promised a further end to all of society's problems. Scientific exploration into the human gene could reveal the motivations and causes for crime and deviant behavior. Science, by understanding these genetic faults, could then conquer them. Education, utilizing the revelations of scientific discovery, could maximize human potential.

Sherlock Holmes, one of the clearest manifestations of Victorian self-confidence, embodies many of the Victorian ideals. His use of the scientific method to solve crime, his self-discipline and self-regulation, and his attention to detail, coupled with his use of laboratory equipment to assist him in his endeavors, reveal a Victorian faith in the abilities of the scientist to impact everyday life, to positively change the experience of every individual. Sherlock Holmes promised to make crime and deviance obsolete in the new society. The new face of society even promised a literal manifestation. Many Victorian intellectuals argued, without self-consciousness, that inferiorities that they considered endemic to race could be bred out of the human species. A myth of technology came into being that promised a future free from concerns associated with everyday Victorian life.

However, simultaneous with the increased optimism associated with technological advance and scientific discovery, the Victorian mind encountered a sense of insecurity. Technological advance may distance man from sources of strength and inspiration. Industry and science might destroy man's connection with the natural world, with God, and with one another. Specifically, as society advanced, it seemed to use up more and more of the earth's natural resources. Even as Percival Lowell declared the certainty of life on Mars, he warned that life there was almost certainly disappearing as a consequence of its dwindling resources, notably water. The implication was clear. Life on earth may suffer the same fate. Many, in response, thought that technology cast too much light on problems with mankind and longed for a slower advance. Robert Louis Stevenson, in "A Plea for Gas Lamps," even advocated a literal return to darkness, favoring gas lamps on the street rather than electricity. He wrote that electric light would reveal too much of the seedy undercurrent of Victorian society. Many, seeing scientific discovery illuminate not simply the more seedy members of society but all societal faults in general, saw a general collapse as unavoidable. Jack London, in *The Iron Heel*, drew a picture of a world in which markets collapsed and labor dried up, destroying the economic manifestations of scientific progress and the structures of potential recovery and advance. Similarly, many people felt that they had an ever-increasing lack of control and power over their lives. The social reformer Frances Power Cobbe even published an essay in which she gives voice to a nightmare that one day the sun would not rise. She gives a dramatic account of people standing astonished and horrified, staring at the blank horizon. Science, it seems, has mastered nature, in her vision, but cannot control the powers it has created. Indeed, many felt that with the advance in technology, humanity was becoming increasingly less powerful and increasingly more insignificant. As the vast array of scientific and industrial advances revealed the true size and complexity of the world and the universe, man's role seemed to rapidly diminish. It was as if the Copernican revelations of a heliocentric universe were being felt all over again. Specifically, in addition to the vastness of time and space, discovery suggested the presence of more advanced civilizations in the wider heavens. Victorian sensibility trusted in its superiority over other races and peoples on the earth and saw its military power as the manifest proof of its superiority. If distant worlds were more advanced, then they could do to England what England had done to large portions of the globe with the consequent implications regarding manifest superiority. Moreover, technological advance, partly because of its ability to unsettle the individual and societal certainty, was often associated with the devil or witchcraft. Robert Louis Stevenson demonstrated how technology could reveal and unleash the devil, or Mr. Hyde, that lies within the upstanding Dr. Jekyll. William Morris gave voice to another fear of the Victorian mind associated with industrial advance. In *News from Nowhere*, he at first casts light on a Victorian society in which the individual has no connection with the products of his labor and then reveals a nontechnological society that emerges after labor unrest and war, which reconnects the individual with his environment and with the objects of his creation. George Gissing's *The Netherworld* also reveals the potential dehumanizing effects of industry on the individual conscious and conscience, as people destroy and harm each other living within a nightmare of poverty, labor, and fatigue. In Joyce's *Ulysses*, the sound of the machines in the newspaper office takes over the lives of many individuals associated with its production, melding their voices into the sound of the machines. Significantly, Bloom, the epitome of the feeling individual, remains outside the machine's control but not beyond its ability to harm. He must labor to feed its need for advertising money, and his failure to secure an ad prevents him from realizing his full happiness.

The historical context of the modern era reveals a similar pattern of pride and uncertainty. As commerce opens the globe to British interests and control, expansion feeds military and imperial ambitions. However, as the British come to terms with other people and cultures, the forces of empire and conquest encounter disturbing reminders of their limitations and powers. On the face of it, however, a Victorian could survey a map of the world and discover that British military might had placed one-quarter of the globe and one-quarter of the world's population into British hands. Moreover, British power extended even to the fall of the sun and the change of the seasons. At some point in the British territory, the sun was always rising and it was always spring. Moreover, the empire extended its dominion over the world's oceans, as the Royal Navy sailed the world's seas without a significant military rival. The consolidation of British power and global influence had risen with the rise of technology. During the nineteenth century, Britain acquired territory in every region of the globe and consolidated its control over key shipping lanes in the Mediterranean, South Africa, and the Far East. Britain had most significantly solidified control over the Indian subcontinent, with its vast territories, population, and natural resources. The expanse of the empire satisfied the British need for self-government, self-support, and self-defense. Moreover, expansion fueled the belief that British sovereignty and military superiority meant the superiority of the British system of government and the British mind. Journals of the age boasted that British justice had reached the ends of the globe, replacing "uncivilized" and "savage" customs and traditions. Indeed, anthropological texts placed the British Empire and system of government and religion at the height of an evolution of societal progress that ranged from savagery to barbarism to science. The ideals of social Darwinism were prevalent, even informing James Frazer's ethnographic text *The Golden Bough*. Perhaps the most influential text for modernist writers and artists, Frazer's study surveyed the globe categorizing and detailing worldwide customs and belief. However, the ethos that underlay his analysis stressed the inherent proof of British superiority and supremacy.[4]

Nowhere was the British sense of themselves as superior more manifest than in their education system. The boy's public (private) school functioned as the training grounds for empire. Curriculum of the day placed equal emphasis on the development of the mind, body, and the soul. However, the development of the mind and soul based itself wholly on British principles of superiority and the sovereignty of empire. The development of the body found its clearest manifestation on the playing field. Boys were expected to demonstrate there the same principles that would later govern their behavior as servants of the empire. Deasy's school, featured in *Ulysses'* second episode with its emphasis on rote learning and games, reveals the shallowness that underlay the British education system and, by extension, the empire. Indeed, Deasy's distortions of history and arrogance mirror the British attitude during its period of highest global influence.

However, even as the empire reached its height, a sense of insecurity pervaded the British consciousness in association with its global holdings. There was the concern the empire might be too expansive, that it may be too difficult to defend from outside attack, that it might be too susceptible to internal rebellion that could spread across British territory. Indeed, rebellion or external threat might then find home on English soil. There was the constant fear of contamination, and not only of ideas but of people. Immigrants brought with them, the Victorian imagination suggested, secret societies, strange habits and religions, anarchy, and degenerate racial characteristics. All had the potential, in the hegemonic British mind to destroy and degenerate the British way of life. Wilkie Collins's *The Woman in White* reveals the mind-set of vulnerability, as a secret society and foreign conspiracy grips an aristocratic family, robbing it of its identity and revealing its susceptibility to attack. In the end, Collins fashions the triumph of British spirit and fair play over contamination from foreign sources, but the book reveals the general fear of contagion spreading its influences into English society. Moreover, Collins's book also reveals the inherent weaknesses that lay hidden behind the British cloak of superiority. In a similar way, Victorian melodrama might boost a general confidence in British values and a certainty of invulnerability as the hero triumphs, but the plays reveal, as does Collins's book, the pervasive fear of constant siege and vulnerability.

The British Victorian society also revealed a sense of inferiority to foreign cultures and influences. Indeed, even as technology threatened to make God obsolete and to prove man's dominance over nature, there existed in the Victorian mind a sense of longing for a more direct connection with nature and a sense of envy of more spiritual societies. At about the same time Friedrich Nietzsche declared, in *The Genealogy of Morality*, that atheism was the inevitable and logical next intellectual evolutionary step for Western man, George Gissing, in *By the Ionian Sea*, observed with longing a society seemingly in harmony with time and spirituality. He traveled the southeastern coast of the Italian mainland seeking not only the architectural relics of the classical world but also its living legacy in the peoples of the region. He discovered what seemed to him to be a natural and unself-conscious belief in God, oneness with nature, and a sense of community with the wider world. James Frazer, even as he wrote of British racial and religious superiority, expressed a desire for some of the spiritual connections that existed in the cultures he examined. In Britain, spiritualism was rampant. Joyce reveals some of these tendencies in *Ulysses* in the spiritual practices of George Russell. One of Russell's spiritual mentors, Madame Blavatsky, seduced the late Victorian intellectual and artistic elite with her seeming ability to communicate with the dead and with guiding spirits. Many even sought to establish spiritualism as a science, using technology to seemingly prove what lies beyond technical understanding. Photos showed the apparent presence of spirits or of fairies. Alfred Russel Wallace, in an 1875 essay titled "On Miracles and Modern Spiritualism," even made the case for psychical research as the newest branch of scientific enquiry. The Victorian preoccupation with the supernatural did not limit itself to conjuring dead spirits. The Victorians also conjured the objects of imperial conquest, the subjugated peoples and cultures of Ireland, Africa,

Asia, India, and the Levant into living mediums for direct contact with a more spiritual world. Through a process Edward Said identifies as "Orientalism," the people of colonial culture "invented" the Orient as the dwelling place of the "exotic."[5] More specifically, Said defines Orientalism as

> a way of coming to terms with the Orient that is based on the Orient's special place in European Western experience. The Orient is not only adjacent to Europe, . . . it is also the place of Europe's greatest and richest and oldest colonies, the source of its civilizations and languages, . . . and one of its deepest and most recurring images of "the Other."[6]

The Orient, within the matrix of Orientalism, becomes the feminine, the emotional, the spiritual alternative to the West, the repository of all that technology and science has taken from the Western industrialized view of itself and of its means of understanding the world and the universe. The process of Orientalism, which finds a common motivation and practice in the Celticism of the late nineteenth century, attempts to translate, through research and scientific enquiry, the spiritual substance of "the other" into contemporary Western forms. Individuals would literally translate ancient Irish tales or Arab stories into English but impose on them restrictions associated with Victorian morality. In Ireland, Lady Gregory has the ancient Irish hero Cuchulain cooling off from battle receiving the bare breasts of women; whereas, in the ancient tale, he makes love with them. The act of translation sanitizes the ancient while still, the translator hopes, transferring some of the spiritual substance to the Victorian reader. The process of translation not only includes the literal transcription of a story into English but also the representation of other cultures and practices into familiar Western forms.

H.G. Wells's time machine then becomes much more than a science fiction fantasy. It stands as an allegory for the late nineteenth- and early twentieth-century Western mind-set and predicament. Science and technology had advanced Western civilization to the point of its most complete dominance over the globe. The British Empire, through the technological innovations of the industrial revolution, dominated the world. Advances in scientific discovery seemingly ensured man's place as master of the world's natural forces and even, perhaps, of the divine. Wealth and commerce prospered. Art flourished. However, the same forces that drove the Victorians to preeminence among the powers of the earth created a sense of uncertainty and a sense of vulnerability. If other races and cultures were inferior to the English, then what would exposure to them and possible inter-marriage do to the superior English culture and people? Moreover, what would the inevitable cross-culturation to do English society? Furthermore, if the "other" was indeed inferior, then why did he enjoy a seemingly more happy life, in harmony with time, nature, and the divine? All these questions undermined the Victorian sense of hegemony and gave rise to methods of coming to terms with the other, such as Orientalism or scientific spiritualism, that attempted both to answer these questions and to inoculate the Victorian from possible contagion.

## THE GREAT WAR (WORLD WAR I)

The First World War, or the Great War as it was called, is the pivotal political and historical event of the early twentieth century. Casualties from the war came from every British town. Today, most have monuments or memorials to the dead of that war. In Ireland, still at that time a part of the empire, most towns were similarly affected, particularly in the North of Ireland, where the Ulster Presbyterians fought in great numbers for the British cause. Stories tell of English or Anglo-Indian officers commanding the Ulster regiments, rallying them with patriotic cries that summoned not heroic deeds of the current war but of the anti-Catholic campaigns in Ulster. Thousands went to their death wearing orange sashes. Frank McGuinness, in *Observe the Sons of Ulster Marching Towards the Somme*, gives voice to the circumstances surrounding the Ulster regiment's service and to many of the circumstances and fears surrounding the war. In one particularly moving scene, a boisterous and previously confident Belfast soldier hears the sound of the giant lambeg drums, a symbol of Ulster defiance. Rather than be rallied by the sound, he shrinks in fear, likening the banging of the drums to the sound the liner *Titanic* made as she fell into the Lagan, released from her dry-dock moorings. He tells his friends, linking the loss of the ship to the loss of life in the war, that they will die, that they will be sacrificed. In his words, the pride associated with technological advancement and the despair consequent of the destruction and loss of life, that seemed at the time to follow technological progress, come together. The Great War itself saw the utilization of frightening machines of destruction: submarines, tanks, airplanes, and, most especially, gas. The scientific advances of the previous century seemed to culminate in inhuman and faceless means for destruction and misery. Two decades earlier, Émile Zola wrote of the human cost of war in *The Débâcle*. He, in one particularly horrific scene, describes the capture and literal slaughter of a Prussian soldier by French citizens. As the

French tie the Prussian down and bleed him, the way they would a pig, he cries for his mother. A French woman, taking part in the slaughter, recoils in horror at the loss of her humanity. Indeed, the war managed to give form to many of the dehumanizing terrors and fears of the late nineteenth century. Not only technology came under harsh scrutiny but also many of the pillars of Victorian society. Wilfred Owen, himself a casualty of the war, described the horrors of a gas attack in "Dulce et Decorum Est." The poem not only vividly and horrifically reflects the death of a soldier during a mustard-gas strike, it recalls, as the title suggests, the lines of a classical Roman poem and a schoolmaster teaching the poem to his pupils, a poem that declares that it is "right and fitting [appropriate and mannerly] to die for one's country." Owen, in indicting the war, indicts the British public school and its function as a "training ground for empire."

Other writers and artists depicted the horrors of war. Yeats, in "Lapis Lazuli," writes of the images of bombing zeppelins destroying art and civilization. Yeats's poem, written after the war, takes the tone of a visionary prophecy, fearing further societal destruction at the hands of science and technology gone awry. Antonia White, in "The House of Clouds," hears the cries of the war dead as she descends into madness, linking her personal insanity to the societal madness of the First World War. James Joyce, writing *Ulysses* in a Europe devastated by war and haunted by memories of the conflict, casts his hero as a prophet of peace. Leopold Bloom, the wandering Dublin Jew, advocates the pacifist gospel of Jesus to Dublin patriots yearning for the glories of war. Indeed, Bloom stands as a voice of hope and a human response to provocations and potential conflict. He, despite the pain associated with his wife's betrayal, rejects violence as an alternative in favor of equanimity.

## MODERNISM

Informed by the anxieties associated with the late nineteenth-century's scientific and technological progress and haunted by the specter and then outbreak of open warfare, many artists and writers turned toward aspects of modernism to reflect and to cope with the tensions and internal conflicts of the early twentieth century. Of the many modernist theories and practices, a common pattern, or motif, can be recognized. Many works of art reflect one or more stages of a three-part process of coming to terms with life in the early twentieth century. The first stage involves a sense of absence and a need for contact and longing on an individual or a societal level. The second stage involves an attempted contact with another individual or society. However, something about the means of attempted contact prevents full integration with the other. The flawed means, in some artistic representations, traces its causes back to personal issues associated with the trauma of life in the early twentieth century. In other representations, the intellectual method of interaction, through processes akin to Orientalism, interferes with full contact and integration with the other. The third stage involves recognition of failed contact. Some writers and artists, understanding that the contact has failed, cannot discern the cause, and despair and depression find voice in their works. Other writers and artists construct a mask of self and of integration as compensation for lack of full communion with individuals, societies, or the natural world. The mask substitutes for full integration but, simultaneously, repeats the second stage of the process. The full process finds representation in some works but parts of the process find representation in most of what critics call modernist art.

The Anglo-Irish novelist, Henry De Vere Stacpoole, who created the now popular bucolic paradise of the "blue lagoon" in his fiction, represents two young children coming of age on an island isolated from civilization. They, because they were raised apart from the technologically advanced world, approach prelapsarian bliss. Stacpoole's work reveals a sense of dissatisfaction with Victorian culture and society. He represents an industrial world in his fiction whose inhabitants lack the basic connections with the world and with one another to survive in a meaningful way. His representations of Victorian and industrialized society find a resonance in many literary and artistic productions of his day. Kipling looks to the jungles of the Indian subcontinent for a magical antidote to the despair consequent of Western industrialism. Yeats, while living in London, considers an imaginary home on a deserted island on a lake in the Irish West. Max Beckman, in his painting *The Dream*, depicts laborers, artists, musicians, and fishermen crowded together in the corner of a house unable to escape the suffocating proximity of their fellows. The American naturalist writers Drieser and Norris depicted a Western world where the animal in human form destroys the humanity in others. Salvador Dali, in the *Persistence of Memory*, depicts a bleak and arid landscape filled with a dead tree and melting clocks, the symbols of technological advance. The natural world, in Dali's representation, retreats from the devastation of technology and science; distant mountains hold the promise of something beyond the industrial desert. For many modernist artists and writers, the empty spaces of technology, civilization, and scientific advancement haunted their imagination to the point where they had to imagine an escape. Even Joyce's hero, Leopold Bloom constructs a Levantine paradise of beautiful women, agrarian diversions, and exotic landscapes while traveling through Victorian Dublin. He even places his wife in Oriental dress and under palm trees as an alternative to her form in his Dublin apartment.

The method of coming to terms with this alternative often accomplished itself through a flawed means, through a method that conjured interaction not with the reality of an alternative to Western industrialism but with an imagined visionary alternative to the West. Fueled by the belief that non-Western culture could regenerate the Western imagination, that "Oriental culture and religion could defeat the materialism and mechanism of Occidental culture,"[7] many writers and artists re-created the East to service their needs for a sense of communion with the wider world. This Western creation then serves as a "visionary alternative" to the industrialized world. Specifically, the created East becomes "gorgeous color, in contrast to . . . greyish tonality" and "exciting spectacle instead of hum-drum routine, [and] the perennially mysterious in place of the all too familiar."[8] Henri Rousseau's *The Dream* depicts a Western woman, pale and reclining nude on a velvet couch, in harmony with a jungle world of exotic plants, birds, and even predatory animals, all living peacefully together in a type of Eden. Essentially, the process of colonialism and industrialization that created the sense of absence and disconnectedness in the Western artistic consciousness also creates a means of coming to terms with the non-Western world that belies full communication. Many writers and artists looked to the East as an alternative to Western culture, seeking to find there a sense of communion with the natural world, with spirituality, and with humanity that eludes them in the West. However, the Eastern world they saw and created was so informed by their Western consciousness that they were unable to achieve communion and integration with anything but a fanciful recreation of the East. Leopold Bloom, unlike many artists and writers of the early twentieth century, acknowledges the illusory nature of his Eastern dream. He admits to himself that the East is probably not like he imagines it and not at all like the travel advertisements and the popular writers of the day depict it. He comes to see his dream of the Orient as simply a diversion.

However, unlike Bloom, many modernist writers and artists blocked from their consciousness any awareness that their created alternative did not represent reality. In response to their ability to contact only a dream alternative to the West, many found frustration and assumed that, because they could not achieve communion with a culture and a world beyond Western civilization, no culture or world exists beyond the West. Therefore, the world existed as an empty and nonfulfilling place. T.S. Eliot, in

"The Wasteland," taking the name of his poem from the term colonial administrators used to define what they thought to be useless tracks of land controlled by the British empire, depicts a Western society spiritually bankrupt and devoid of substantive humanity, waiting for rain and redemption. Eliot uses Hindu phrases to describe thunder but, in the end of his work, the land remains parched and arid. Evelyn Waugh, in *Brideshead Revisited*, represents the flower of English aristocratic youth, withering in an Oriental hell, wasting his promise as war devastates his homeland. Emile Nolde's *The Last Supper* depicts a Levantine Christ gathered with his apostles. Their faces appear as painted, inhuman masks gathered around their supposed savior. Pablo Picasso, in "Les Demoiselles d'Avignon," portrays prostitutes in malformed and masklike bodies offering themselves to the viewer. It is as if Picasso blames the women for his inability to achieve a sense of communion with anything beyond their physical form when he sought them out for sexual satisfaction only. Indeed, much of modernist painting depicts a devastated and lost society with a sense of vengeance and betrayal attributing to the society as a whole the inability of the artist to achieve full communion. Similarly, Haines's character in *Ulysses* seeks interaction with Irish society. He, as a research student, comes to Ireland seeking the imagined Irish alternative to English civilization. He discovers his reality of Ireland only in books. However, he cannot communicate with the Irish. He treats Stephen and the milk woman with contempt and pompous disdain. He is also haunted by nightmares of a black panther, an image of Oriental danger. He never does find true fulfillment, and the model for his character, whom Joyce had met in Dublin, committed suicide. Indeed, many modernist paintings and writings reflect a cultural-wide depression and death dream. Like Stephen Dedalus, they cannot seem to find fulfillment in the world around them and reject the notion that it may be their matrix of interaction that causes their sense of despair. In the end, Stephen rejects Bloom's hospitality with an anti-Semitic song.

The flavor of *Ulysses'* modernism differs greatly from other modernist representations. Joyce, apparently, acknowledged, as did other Irish writers of his time, the misguided impulse of seeking a cure for Western cultural decay in an imagined other. Indeed, George Bernard Shaw and Oscar Wilde both represented the hypocrisy of late-Victorian society, revealing through comedy and horror the reliance on cultural masks for fulfillment.[9] Wilde's *Picture of Dorian Gray* presents the ideal Victorian gentleman, accepted and embraced for his appearance alone, while his portrait decays as a consequence of his internal corruption. Wilde's image of artistic representations dying in the face of societal hypocrisy and misguided notions of fulfillment anticipates the representations in modernist works of a society consumed by a spirit of desolation, attempting fulfillment in an imagined life and in deceiving oneself to the point of annihilation in the belief that imagined life represents substantive reality. Wilde, exiled from society because of his Irishness and his open homosexuality, represented anathema to the English who saw in him the qualities of the feminized other they so readily suppressed in themselves, qualities of emotion, vulnerability, and imagination. Indeed, exploring Wilde's career without examining his Irish heritage and the effect of it on the English society's judgment on him avoids the complexities that his life and work suggest. Likewise, *Ulysses* is as much an Irish novel as it is a work of modernist literature.

## THE IRISH CONTEXT

Certainly, *Ulysses* can also be read within the context of Irish history, an Irish literary tradition, and Irish politics. In addition to referencing historical events and specific Irish writers, *Ulysses* values a means of coming to terms with the past and with various influences in the novel's present that has a resonance with Celtic traditions and Irish literary forms. Specifically, Bloom embodies many strains of Irish history. Like the Christians, the Vikings, the Norman invaders, the Northern planters, and others, Bloom's family came to Ireland. Moreover, he assimilates to his current culture while maintaining a connection to his personal and familial past. He remembers Hebrew prayers, even though he has been baptized first as a Protestant and then as a Catholic. He cherishes his own identity while respecting and accepting the identities and cultural identifiers of those around him. Unlike many people he meets in the novel and unlike many other of the novel's characters, Bloom operates within an ethos of love and acceptance rather than of exclusion and prejudice. His own particular Irish identity values assimilation with the dominant cultural influences while contributing his own personal cultural past to the whole.

During the time Joyce spent writing *Ulysses*, Ireland underwent revolution with Britain and an internal civil war. The factors that informed the violence included a struggle to define Irish boundaries, both geographic and imaginative. In addition, cultural and literary movements at the turn of the last century attempted to come to terms with what being Irish meant. Many, like several characters in *Ulysses*, sought a pure Irish identity apart from the influences of various cultures and peoples that had immigrated to Ireland over the centuries. To the individuals that devoted themselves to the type of cultural nationalism that sought a pure expression of an Irish identity in the Irish language, in writing, and in art, immigrant influences, whether they be Jewish, British, Scottish, or other meant a movement away from a pure Irish identity. For the cultural nationalists, a purging or a catharsis needed to be achieved in order to come to terms with an authentic Irish identity. *Ulysses*, on the contrary, tends to value a multifarious Irish identity that includes Celtic influences alongside the symbols of the colonizer and the immigrant. In drawing a picture of Irish culture and life that includes a variety of cultures, religious and personal practices, and individual backgrounds, Joyce's text actually comes closer to the ancient Celtic and Irish culture than many of the movements associated with cultural nationalism that sought a direct connection with ancient Irish forms. Moreover, the cultural nationalists, in their exclusionary epistemology, more accurately approximate the most destructive tendencies of Ireland's invaders.

Ancient Celtic culture valued free will and individualism and discouraged totalitarian or exclusionary tendencies. When the Celts went to war, and they often fought, they did not seek territorial conquest but rather individual honor and glory. Their philosophy of combat and life wreaked havoc on the classical Greek and Roman world because they could not understand and because they feared the Celts. A Celtic army sacked the Roman capital in 390 B.C. and left the senate and Roman people in dismay. However, after the Celts pillaged the capital city, they left and left Rome free to govern itself. A hundred years later, a Celtic army threatened Delphi, mocking the Greeks' representation of their gods in human form; the Celts viewed the representations as limiting and unimaginative. The Greeks beat the Celts back, as they began to fight among themselves, with individual villages, tribes, and leaders vying against each other for the most advantageous positions on the battlefield. Indeed, it would be the Celts' lack of centralized authority that would actually make them vulnerable to conquest. In 58 B.C., Julius Caesar's army defeated the Celts and solidified Roman power in Gaul. Caesar had the Celtic leader ritually strangled in Rome. However, Roman authority could not wholly conquer the Celts, and they retained many of their individual traditions and customs despite Roman rule. However, during Claudius's reign in A.D. 43, the Romans invaded Britain and attempted to annihilate the Celtic way of life. Their brutal war of conquest took advantage of the Celtic tribal system and defeated the Celts village by village. However, Roman brutality had a price. When legionnaires raped a local leader's daughters, their mother Boadicea lashed out against the Romans. By force of personality, she united the Celts and drove the Romans back to London. She and her armies burned the city, killing more than 70,000 Romans. The Romans fought back, however, and conquered her army; she committed ritual suicide rather than submit to their authority. The Romans herded the people into cities in an effort to disrupt village life, to obliterate Celtic culture, and to Romanize it. However, the Celtic culture, with villages, settlements, and trade networks stretching from Ireland to Spain to Turkey, proved far more resilient than the Romans imagined. The Celtic people adapted to their conditions and, although their armies never again threatened Rome, their culture endured, assimilating many Roman customs and practices into Celtic traditions. Indeed, the values familiar to readers of Joyce's work of individualism and assimilation, rather than obliteration and conquest, permeated many aspects of Celtic society.

Specifically, Celtic art tends to be open-ended and individualistic, stressing not so much the adherence to established forms but rather to interpretive impressions of realistic forms. Indeed Celtic art tends to regularize reality, to pattern and organize it but also to develop new representations of reality. Created figures might simultaneously have elongated limbs and heads but also intricate, decorative patterns and designs that offer balance to the figure. In addition, other patterns are open-ended and decorative. For example, the peacock designs on a contemporary Irish coin pattern and order the peacock, balancing the figure throughout the space of the coin. Simultaneously, the bird leaves its natural proportions and plumage in favor of a highly decorative and elaborate representation. Moreover, Celtic weaponry and armour expressed individual creativity. The Celts were masters at metal craft, fashioning chain-mail armor, shields, and swords from strong materials before the Romans and Greeks could master the craft. In terms of literary tradition, the druids and filidh worked within an oral rather than written matrix. The druids, in their capacity as priests, doctors, lawyers, poets, prophets, and teachers, mediated between gods and men, drawing the supernatural into everyday Celtic life. Their associates, the filidh, enjoyed extraordinary prestige in Celtic society in matters of politics, learning, and literature. The filidh worked within established literary traditions, offering their own individual interpretation to the conventional forms. Specifically, the established forms included the praise poem to a lord or patron and satire of a former lord or patron, and historical forms, including genealogies, royal lists, origin legends, mythologies, heroic tales, and topographical lore. The *Tain* represents satirists as clever and feared members of any battle entourage. Moreover, it and other extant ancient texts reveal the filidh's practices of representation, which parallel Celtic artistic practices. Specifically, even while they worked within the established framework of the story and developed their heroes and villains along traditional lines, the figures in these stories reach beyond ordinary human limitations, functioning as superhuman forms empowered to escape their created physical nature and to perform beyond normal physical limitations in terms of battle, sexuality, and honor. The filidh survived the druids, eventually assimilating their traditions and representations into Christian practices. Indeed, much of written Celtic literature survives as a consequence of the cooperation between early Christian monks and the filidh.

The pattern of assimilation and eventual cooperation with a variety of invaders permeates Irish culture from the time of Roman withdraw from Celtic lands, in about A.D. 410, up to the era of Tudor administration and the Elizabethan Planters. The first of the post-Roman invasions of Ireland occurred in about A.D. 432, the traditional date given for Saint Patrick's mission to Ireland. Patrick found what he saw to be many similarities in Celtic religious practice and Catholicism. In fact, the Celtic cross represents Patrick's vision for unity between the two faiths. The Celtic sun surrounds the Christian symbol of the cross. Moreover, many holy wells and pilgrim paths in Ireland are actually Christianized versions of Celtic traditions and places. In addition, scholars see in the Celtic church a model not only for cultural inclusiveness and cooperation between Christian and non-Christian forms and peoples but also a matrix for a more democratic church, one that supports individual and community involvement in the administration of religious affairs. Celtic Catholicism recognizes a communal spirituality that respects the presence of God, the Christian God, in the landscape, and the connectedness between the land and the people and the people with one another and with the divine. The Christian faith in Ireland flourished, despite numerous invasions and despite numerous conquerors. The Vikings came to Ireland in search of wealth and power, taking their ships up through the Shannon and the Bann into Lough Ree and Lough Neagh and taking control of the strategic kingdoms of Ulster, Connacht, and Meath. Viking control lasted until the Battle of Clontarf in A.D. 1014, the battle in which Brian Boru lost his life. The Anglo-Normans invaded Ireland next, aligning themselves in a series of invasions with local authorities, essentially using the old Roman formula of conquest of one village and territory at a time. Eventually, Henry II aligned himself with Roman Catholic forces in Ireland, receiving a Papal Bull from Adrian IV, the only English pope, that authorized the English invasion of Ireland in order to reform the morals of the country and further authorizing continued English possession of the island. The Irish church and much of Irish artistic representation became anglicized as a result.

In terms of artistic and literary forms, the series of invaders contributed much to the Irish cultural tradition, assimilating and combining their practices with indigenous Irish forms. In terms of early lyric verse, dating from about the seventh century, the poet sees himself as a type of Catholic priest or monk living in and interacting with nature. Obviously, the poet combines many druidic customs with Christian clerical functions. The verse reflects a concern with the world of nature, a sense of connectedness with living things. The poetry values a simplicity of expression, focusing less on description than on a reaction to or impression of the environment in a succession of vivid images, demonstrating the Celtic propensity for individual interpretation and at the same time a tendency to communicate the Christian message. In fact, many of the poets describe the coming to terms with their poetic vocation, by choice or by fate, in Christian terms. Reciprocally, Christian monks, often former lyric poets or filidh, codified much of Celtic oral literature, infusing some Christian elements into the texts. The record of various narrative cycles also combines prose and poetic forms and carries forward former druidic lore. The mythological cycles relay the stories of ancient Celtic gods and goddesses. The King cycles reinforce the local chieftain's role as the center of the social system and the embodiment of the social order. They also traced the origin of tribes and place names, recorded the history of battles, and honored heroic and honorable deeds by certain noteworthy kings. The Ulster cycle gives modern readers a unique glimpse into ancient Celtic culture through the *Tain*. The Finn cycle tends to remove the boundaries between the temporal and the divine and between the natural and supernatural worlds, also revealing the process of Christian and Celtic assimilation; in fact, the Arthurian legends derive from the Finn cycle, with their reverence for watery places and the quest for the grail. The codification of Celtic legends and the values of cultural assimilation over cultural obliteration prove to be the most beneficial product of Irish Celtic and Irish Christian interaction. However, once the texts were written down, their evolution in oral form, a necessary component of Celtic individualized interpretation, ended. Moreover, although the monasteries created a synthesis of the two traditions, they tended to promote different aesthetic values, particularly regarding the preservation and reverence of textual over interpretive ideology. In addition, beginning with Patrick's *Confessions*, Latin began to contend with Irish as the official language of record in the country. Some monks went so far as to record Latin grammars and alphabets to guarantee the integrity of the language in the face of the pervasive use of Irish by the populace. Therefore, although the monks and the Christian tradition ensured the survival of Celtic forms and practices, they survive through a filter of Latin and Christian conventions.

The Anglo-Normans also managed to assimilate to Irish culture rather than to obliterate it, despite the intentions of the early invaders. By the middle of the thirteenth century, the Normans had penetrated most of the island. Shortly thereafter, they began to speak Irish, almost to the exclusion of French or English. They began to intermarry with the local population. The English kings, so alarmed by the failing colonization of Ireland, passed the Statutes of Kilkenny in 1366, attempting to control and to govern almost every aspect of day-to-day life in Ireland, from the language the people could speak to the sports they could play. The statutes were largely ignored. In terms of literary production, the most significant writings combined old Celtic topics of topographical lore or kingly tribute with an expression in a stylized and literary French. Anglo-Norman influence in Ireland and the spirit of cooperation largely died out with the Tudor and Elizabethan reconquests of the island.

The Irish phrase "briseadh na tseangháthaimh" literally means "breaking of the old ways" and generally describes the loss of the patronage system after the Flight of the Earls in 1601; under the patronage system, wealthy families sponsored poets and writers. However, it can also usefully be applied as a description of the general state of England's period of colonial dominance over Ireland, particularly from the mid to late sixteenth century to the reforms, however meager, of the late eighteenth and early nineteenth century. In this period, the English crown, through local colonial authorities, systematically attempted to destroy Irish culture, language, religious practices, and resistance to English rule. Ireland could and was to be made into a second England, according to the new program of colonization and imperial control. The Anglo-Norman settlers, according to the new colonists, had degraded themselves by assimilating to the local culture. In 1485, Henry VII imposed English land use laws on Ireland, destroying much of local agricultural practice and laying the groundwork for the devastating famines of later centuries. Henry VIII imposed, or attempted to impose, the Anglican Protestant religion in Ireland, confiscating local church holdings and conducting religious services in English. During the Elizabethan period, the English authorities began an effort to abolish the Irish clan and village structures. In 1609, the Articles of Plantation opened vast tracts of land to Scottish settlers by seizing them from the native Irish. A class system began to emerge in which the upper class were English, the middle class, Scottish, and the lower class, Irish. During the English Civil

War, the Irish began to reestablish some of their own practices and to regain some freedom, even staging an attack on Scottish settlers. However, Oliver Cromwell invaded Ireland and put an end to the rebellion by killing tens of thousands of Catholics. When he left the country, Protestants controlled three-quarters of the land, and political and religious ascendancy for the English was assured. In the late seventeenth and early eighteenth centuries, the English passed and imposed a series of Penal Laws on the Irish that excluded all Catholics from public life, prohibited any form of Catholic education or religious practice, and outlawed the purchase or inheritance of land by Catholics. The Test Act of 1704 went even further, making it illegal for Catholics to send their children abroad for an education or from acting as guardians over their own children. Catholics did practice their religion in secret and educated their children in "hedgerow schools" but poverty grew, and Catholic family traditions suffered. By the time some tolerance and legal relief reached Ireland in the late eighteenth century, much of Irish culture had been destroyed or irrevocably altered. In terms of literary tradition, English oppression created two separate and distinct literary traditions. The dominant tradition was an English-language tradition, while the Catholic culture practiced an Irish-language tradition.[10]

The first and one of the foremost English-language practitioners was Edmund Spenser (1552–1599), author of *The Faerie Queene*, who served in Ireland as part of the colonial administration and formulated a program for the systematic colonization of the Irish people. His plan marked the end of the tradition of assimilation and ultimate cooperation between Ireland and her invaders. Spenser, despite his considerable talents as a writer and despite a genuine and profound interest in Ireland, viewed the Irish as inferior to the English. Therefore, English economic, social, religious, and political domination over the Irish became not only necessary but right. In his *A View of the Present State of Ireland*, Spenser represented the indigenous Irish culture in negative terms.[11] He also described what he saw as the degraded state of the Hiberno-Norman population, whom he saw as having fallen from their one-time civilized condition in their act of assimilation to the Irish culture and Irish life.[12] Spenser also justified the use of force in Ireland, for both the indigenous population and those former colonizer communities who had assimilated into the Irish culture. Spenser thought force the only means by which a barbarous people could be civilized, as barbarity necessarily implied an inability to reason. Spenser's program for colonization sought to eliminate an Irish historical, artistic, and cultural heritage that flourished separate from an English tradition. Moreover, the Irish language, Catholicism, and Irish farming practices needed to become models of English practices. Spenser's colonial program for separation and dominance over the Irish served as a model for British colonial administration and imperial domination of subject peoples and cultures.

Spenser's immediate colonial successors continued Spenser's program of nonassimilation and colonization. Richard Beacon, who served in Ireland from 1586–1591, believed that the only way a truly corrupt society could be civilized was through military force. Moreover, he was one of the first colonial authorities to look to classical Rome as a model of nonassimilation and dominance. Other writers, such as Fynes Moryson and Sir John Davies, justified the continued military domination of Ireland and forceful nonassimilation policy outlined by Spenser. Their efforts not only legitimized English policy in Ireland but also gave the English imperial effort a sense of moral force and mission. Moreover, their work gave the English colony in Ireland a clear sense of community and identity within "The Pale" (the English-controlled area of Ireland), which remained distinct from its Irish neighbors.

The other major English-language literary figure of the period was Jonathan Swift. Swift, although born in Ireland, considered England his homeland and saw Ireland as a place of exile. However, he was deeply influenced by Ireland. Much of his work is about Ireland. His tone, methods, and the mood of his work are unlike his English contemporaries. His work includes a sense of dislocation, distortion of perspective, and fantasy. Moreover, he lacks the English contemporary faiths in reason, decorum, and good sense. The actual features of the physical surroundings of his life and the mental features of his aesthetic, ideological, and political landscape are Irish. Essentially, Swift assimilates to Irish culture, empathizing with the predicament of the Irish populace and viewing the English colonial administration sceptically and even negatively.[13]

The Irish-language poets, deprived of their bardic schools, adapted to the changing circumstances. Some went to Europe to pursue an ecclesiastical career but continued to write in Irish. Some worked for the Counter-Reformation. Others worked to preserve the Irish language by writing grammars, compiling dictionaries, and teaching the language. Still others continued their career in Ireland. They created the aisling form, which combined traditional Celtic themes, love poetry, and political anticolonial, themes. One writer, Geoffrey Keating, wrote *Foras Feara ar Éirinn* (*A Basis of Knowledge about Ireland*), distributing and making copies by hand rather than the printing press. The volume preserved the Irish language and the Irish version of history through the period of the most strict

English dominance. Other influential Irish-language writers include Aogán Ó Rathaille, who recorded the disruption consequent of colonial rule. His work reveals the scale of the colonial administration and sees its force as unopposable. His early work, written in the aisling tradition, hopes for political rescue, but his later poetry contains a sense of helplessness and despair. However, he does hold out a sense of individual honor and integrity as an effective weapon against intolerance. Leopold Bloom's individual sense of peace and honor in the face of anger and prejudice carries a distant echo of Ó Rathaille's work. Indeed, *Ulysses* contains many echoes of the disruptions consequent of colonial rule and distrust in traditional written forms of communication.

Joyce's immediate political and literary inheritance involved failed but glorious rebellions, nationwide catastrophe, the emergence of a Catholic middle class, and the rise of an English-language literary tradition within the Catholic middle class. A series of Relief Acts, beginning in 1772 and culminating in the Catholic Emancipation Act in 1829, gradually granted Catholics many of the voting and land-owning rights taken from them in previous centuries. Also in the late eighteenth century, a voice of independence arose in the Irish parliament, led by Henry Grattan. In 1782, the parliament established a form of independence from Britain, and in the early 1790s, under the leadership of Wolfe Tone, the Society for United Irishmen came into being with the aim of full independence for Ireland achieved with the cooperation of both Catholics and Protestants. The United Irishmen originally wanted a peaceful parliamentary revolution. However, in the mid-1790s, they sought a political and military alliance with the French, who made several abortive attempts at landing troops in Ireland. In 1798, the United Ireland movement reached its height with a rebellion that ended in failure, largely because a network of British spies and informers had infiltrated the United Irishmen. The rebellion's failure resulted in its leaders fleeing to France to escape imprisonment and death and also resulted in the Act of Union, which ended even nominal Irish independence and repealed the Irish parliament, limiting Irish political representation and rule to a minority membership in the British Parliament in Westminster. Another failed rebellion followed in 1803, led by Robert Emmet, who became a symbol for the young Irish martyr; he was twenty-five when the British killed him. A few years later, Daniel O'Connell rose to prominence. In order to force British reforms, O'Connell used many of the strategies of parliamentary reform and civil disobedience later utilized by leaders such as Ghandi in India. Indeed, O'Connell's strategies did succeed. The Westminster Parliament accelerated legislative reform and, in Ireland, a Catholic middle class began to emerge. In response, some religious and literary leaders in the Protestant community created the concept of the Protestant Ascendancy, an invented superiority that legitimized minority Protestant rule.[14] However, despite the many reforms and the increasing wealth of the Catholic community, centuries of oppression, particularly agrarian abuses by the ruling Protestant class, resulted in the catastrophe of the Great Famine, "An Gorta Mor" in Irish. The famine devastated the country, initiated a decline in population from about eight million in 1841 to less than five million by the turn of the century. The potato blight began in 1845 and continued for several years. The response of the British and the ruling class was hopelessly inadequate. Many Catholics were evicted from their homes and faced not only hunger but incomprehensible poverty. Many in the British ruling class saw the famine as an opportunity to eliminate rebellious factions within Ireland and welcomed the death of many Catholics. The famine also contributed to the decline of the Irish language and contributed, in the years after it ended, to increased emigration and to a growing puritanical movement within the Irish Catholic church. However, despite the best efforts of the British, another political movement did arise immediately after the famine. The Young Ireland movement gave a political and a literary voice to Irish independence and gave rise to the Home Rule movement of the late nineteenth century led by Charles Stewart Parnell.

Moreover, in the North of Ireland, a radical constituency among the Ulster Presbyterians began to emerge in the 1790s and continued through the late nineteenth century and into the twentieth century, a more and more radical extreme found voice within Ulster protestantism. The movement is represented in *Ulysses* by Deasy and his immoderate views regarding Catholics and Jews and in his mistaken notions about the history of Ireland. In the 1790s, the Presbyterian community in the North founded the Orange Lodges and a violent minority within the movement undertook independent and repressive measures against the Catholic community. However,

until the emergence of Home Rule as a live issue in the 1880s, Protestant voters in the north had been divided into supporters of the two main British political parties, Conservative and Liberal, while a section of extreme loyalists identified with Orangeism. . . . The more dramatic result of the Home Rule crisis in the north of Ireland was the emergence of a strong, coherent Unionist party, drawing support among all classes from a revived Orange Order. From 1905, a new coordinating body, the Ulster Unionist Council, did much "to foster a partitionist mentality," representing as it did only northern Union-ism. The Ulster Unionists, led by the Dublin lawyer Edward Carson, made clear their determination to use force rather than submit to "Rome Rule."[15]

A clear consequence of Carson's movement is a mythology of historical continuity designed to unite the entire Presbyterian community in resistance to a united Ireland.

> Presbyterians have one historical requirement—to uphold the settlement of 1689 and to try to ensure that the principle of Protestant hegemony is recognised and supported. The Siege of Derry in 1689 is their original and most powerful myth. They seem to see themselves in that, and since then, as an embattled and an enduring people. Their historical self vision is of endless repetition of repelled assaults, without hope of absolute finality or fundamental change in their relationship to their surrounding and surrounded neighbours.[16]

In addition to their effort to establish a new community based on new versions of old histories that perpetuate the notion of intrinsic protestant superiority, there exists

> a primal sense of siege infused with millennialism (the assaults may be endless but faith must recurrently be placed in the powers of some eschatologically prescient prophet); disabled by an imaginative exclusiveness which many find repellent; an emotional narrowness in a basic self-vision that has led to the literary trope of the "Black North" with its sense of restriction, bleakness, and atrophied possibility.[17]

As a consequence of these rewritings of identity, Ireland becomes a land of separation and rivalry rather than cooperation and assimilation.

Samuel Ferguson emerged as the literary voice of radical Presbyteranism and, indeed, the Protestant Ascendancy. Further, his work laid the foundations for the Celtic Revival of the late nineteenth century. Ferguson possessed a hatred and contempt for living Catholics but simultaneously an admiration for an idealized past of native Irish traditions and legends. His writings seek to merge myth and heroic legend with Victorian morality, with an aim toward "liberating" traditional stories and tales from the Catholic tradition and from the Irish language. His poems and translations reveal themes of Catholic and native Irish moral and political inadequacy. Therefore, his work argues, the Protestant community must save the Irish from themselves. Within the Catholic tradition, James Clarence Mangan emerged as the leading voice of an alternative literary tradition. Joyce admired Mangan's work and wrote an essay exploring Mangan's themes and ideas. Mangan believed that, through literature, Ireland could discover an ancient cultural identity that differentiates her from England. He felt that the English language was a necessity, not a hindrance. After all, in Mangan's view, it was the language of periodicals and the emerging Roman Catholic middle class. Mangan's work serves as an ideal counterpart to Ferguson's negative representations of the Irish Catholics and also serves as a voice against English literary representations of the Irish.

The nineteenth century marked the clear development of English representations of Ireland and the Irish as culturally inferior. As revolutions and rebellions and famines in Ireland forced themselves onto English sensibility, the continued racialization of the Irish as inferior to the English took on increasing virulence. Specifically, the character of the stage Irishman mocked both the indigenous population and those members of the colonial community who had assimilated into the Irish culture. Specifically, "[t]here were two types of stage Irishman. One, the uneducated servant whose mistakes, verbal and logical alike, provide the basis of popularity[.] . . . He is presented with a broad accent, spelt phonetically, and a tendency to contradict himself foolishly."[18] For the first type of stage Irishman, language becomes the marker for inferiority.

> Paddy the Irishman is above all the archetype of mistranslation. By concealing the labour of translation, the difficulties that many Irish people faced in learning English as a foreign language, coupled with mother tongue interference and with apparent idiosyncrasies of accent and idiom, were presented as the undistinguished hallmarks of stupidity. Depending on the state of relations between Ireland and England, the dullness was cast as sinister or endearing.[19]

The second version of the stage Irishman "was more socially elevated. He was a landowner, a man of means, with military experience. . . . [He] was ignorant by English standards and used the language ineffectively and at times ridiculously, with Gaelicisms sprinkled throughout his speech."[20] Extending itself into popular culture, these Spenserian markers of inferiority enabled the justification of oppression and violence in Ireland. Moreover, many Irish internalized these prejudices and adopted the biased representation of the Irish as their own markers of cultural identity. *Ulysses* represents many of these internalized prejudices in the voice of the Citizen and the views of Bloom's companions regarding drinking and fighting.

The late nineteenth century saw the emergence of political and literary movements that would change the face of Ireland. Parnell united the Irish members of Parliament in Westminster and used his voting block to hold the balance of power in the English Parliament. He used his power to negotiate further reforms in Ireland and was on the verge of achieving Irish Home Rule when he was devastated by political scandal in the early 1890s. A decade earlier, an abortive attempt had been made to implicate him in politically motivated killings in Dublin's Phoenix Park; Joyce refers to the murders in *Ulysses*. The murder charges against Parnell proved ineffective. However, in December 1889, a Captain O'Shea filed for divorce from his wife, naming Parnell as her lover. Parnell did not contest the charges. Indeed, he made no effort to hide their relationship. However, the Catholic church and many of his allies denounced his immorality and abandoned his cause. He died a year later. Many of the nationalists, frustrated by politics, moved their quest for Irish independence into the literary realm, giving further strength to the emerging Irish Literary Revival. Other major historical and political factors of the late nineteenth and early twentieth century include Irish reaction to the Boer War. Many in Ireland openly sympathized with and backed the Boer independence movement, seeing an echo of the Irish struggle in South Africa. Just before the First World War, the British Parliament promised home rule for Ireland but delayed action. However, distrustful of British promises and disillusioned by British exploitation of Irish troops in battle, an active political and military rebellion occurred in Ireland in 1916. The British moved so harshly against the rebels, executing many of the leadership, that Irish public opinion rallied to the cause for independence. In 1921–1922, following a protracted conflict, the British gave the Irish their independence, with the notable exception of the six northernmost counties, which remain under British control. Nineteen twenty-two also marked the publication of *Ulysses*.

The Irish Literary Revival, the Celtic Revival, emerged from a literary and cultural need for an alternative to Western industrialism, with its absolute faith in technology and commerce. The traditions and customs of nonindustrialized Ireland offered a fresh and bucolic alternative to technology, industry, and increasing urbanization. However, the writings of the revival also employed a trope of exploitation, creating a fanciful and distorted image of the Irish that bore little relation to reality. However, the idealized representations did capture the popular imagination not only among the literary Anglo-Irish elite but among many in the Catholic community. De Valera's ideal of a rural Ireland redeeming and saving the country was born in the revival's idealized versions of the Irish peasant. The Irish Literary Revival advanced the concept of cultural nationalism, which held that the essential life of a nation or people exists in its cultural inheritance. The revival sought to supply the Ireland of the late nineteenth and early twentieth centuries a sense of its own distinctive identity, hoping that a cultural awareness would lead to political revolution. Indeed the revival's writings were the source of enthusiastic energy and genuine patriotic fervor. Moreover, the revival gave Ireland some of its most notable writers and most influential literary works.

William Butler Yeats began his career by inventing an Ireland that fulfilled his imaginative and his personal spiritual needs. Ultimately though, his aesthetic grew to appreciate the complexity and reality of the Irish people. However, at the beginning of his career, his unwillingness to consider the realities of Irish life lent an imaginative substance to his collection of created myths and symbols in the sense that reality, for the young Yeats, involved the miracles of technology, urbanization, and industrialization. Yeats inherited an Irish Ascendancy tradition of idealism that he then associated with the folk tradition in Ireland and claimed that both refuted science by their apprehension of the internal spirituality of individuals. In Yeats's view then, the peasant and aristocrat stand united in the battle against science. However, to achieve the marriage between the rural peasant and the intellectual aristocrat, Yeats had to discredit the middle classes, and he earnestly discredited their financial concerns in his poetry, notably "September 1913." Moreover, he distrusted political and labor movements, as they also relied on urbanization, the middle class, and industrialization for their power and support. However, toward the middle of his career, Yeats's aesthetic began to appreciate the reality of the Irish middle class and of Irish political movements. "Easter 1916" celebrates their achievements almost, in Yeats's view, despite themselves. His poetry goes on to portray creative and dramatic tension between the ideals, including the ideal representation of the Irish peasant, and the real. In his later career, the transformative effect that the real and the ideal have on one another functions as a prefiguration of the ultimate redemption and transformation of humanity. Joyce's aesthetic and forms of representation share little with Yeats's evolutionary idealism. However, *Ulysses* does reveal the isolated and simplistic notions of the revival and offers a realistic alternative to the, in Joyce's view, misguided idealization of the Irish peasant.

Another major revival figure, John Millington Synge, actually met Joyce in France. The two disagreed about the revival's representation of

Irish rural life. Synge saw in the Western peasant and in the raw beauty of the Irish landscape the source for redemption of an industrialized world. His revivalism accepted an invented Ireland but also re-created some aspects of the reality of life in the Irish West. Critics consider his dialect to be fairly true to the Irish language spoken in the West.[21] However, most critics also agree that he imposed on the realistic representations of the peasant an ideology of transformation, of spiritual alternative to an imaginatively bankrupt, in Synge's view, English tradition. Essentially, Synge's works seek not simply to convey the passing life of an emotionally inviting world but also to posit, from that world, a model of redemption and revitalization.

Not all Irish writers endorsed the revival's image of Ireland. Certainly, Joyce's *Ulysses* condemns the revival's fanciful and distorted representations and offers an alternative to its exclusive views. Moreover, George Bernard Shaw's play *John Bull's Other Island* was written in 1904,[22] which was also the year in which veteran land league radical Michael Davitt published *The Fall of Feudalism in Ireland* and the year in which Joyce set *Ulysses*. By then, Wyndham's Land Act of the previous year had helped Irish farmers buy out more land from the aristocracy, but a sceptical Shaw attempts to show how the peoples of two islands spend most of their time acting an approved part for each other. The parts, however, fail to become a means for true self-expression. In the play, stereotypes are exploded.

In other words, just as *Ulysses* advocates a pluralistic, nonexclusive view of Irish history and culture, Shaw's play suggests that, at root, the English and Irish are rather similar peoples, who have nonetheless decided to perform versions of Englishness and Irishness to one another. Each group projects onto the other many attributes that it has denied itself. *Ulysses'* and Shaw's representation of Irish history and culture find a resonance in Joyce's other works. In *Stephen Hero*, the protagonist wandering through Dublin has an epiphany—"by epiphany he meant a sudden spiritual manifestation"[23]—and a desire to record it and other experiences like them. Specifically, "he longed for the season to lift and for spring—the misty Irish spring—to be over and gone. He was passing through Eccles Street one evening, one misty evening, when a trivial incident set him composing some ardent verses. . . . A young lady was standing on the steps of one of those brown brick houses which seem the very incarnation of Irish paralysis."[24] This juxtaposition between a "misty Irish spring" and "brick houses" is clearly reminiscent of the juxtaposition in "The Dead" between a Western Celtic dew and Dublin Victorian culture. Both stories very clearly indict both scenes as images of "Irish paralysis." The epiphany at the end of "The Dead" grants Gabriel the same revelation that Stephen Hero discovered on Eccles Street one evening. Both Dublin culture and Western reviv-alism stand for an *Irish* paralysis, not simply a Dublin or urban paralysis alone. Further, the

> closing sections of A *Portrait [of the Artist as a Young Man]* raise sharp, difficult questions about the meaning of a Gaelic culture which had been "lost," a loss which can be established by the revivalists only in terms of a valued English scheme of things. What the revivalists sought to rediscover was merely a projection of imperial fantasy, eventually embodied in the person of Haines in *Ulysses*.[25]

Throughout Joyce's work, he represents patterns of mistaken notions of an Irish past, both imperial and "native," suggesting that both the colonizer and the colonized reject the integrated reality of Irish cultural history in fa-vor of exclusive versions of an idealized past and implies that the communi-ties of both the colonizer and the colonized become "dual" forms of one another. To return to an image from "The Dead," both Usher's Island and Nun's Island can stand, in this sense, for Ireland herself, for two alternative created likenesses within the larger island, for both the imperial and reviv-alist traditions unite in a surprising symbolic union like the dance between Gabriel and Miss Ivors. "He avoided her eyes for he had seen a sour expres-sion on her face. But when they met in the long chain he was surprised to feel his hand firmly pressed. She looked at him from under her brows for a moment quizzically until he smiled."[26] They find themselves caught, im-prisoned by one another, by convention. They find themselves together dancing in unison, each mirroring the other's movements. Joyce's writings suggest that in order to move forward in any meaningful way, a society must make the repressed nonsectarian inheritance manifest—in order to under-stand its past, in order to understand its potential, in order to understand it-self.

In Gabriel's dance with Miss Ivors, there lies another metaphor. The dance represents how individuals deluded by imagined dreams of alterna-tives to Western culture align themselves with individuals who place a faith in the institutions and mechanisms of supposed societal progress. Joyce posits in *Ulysses* an alternative to the delusions of the modern world and of modernist literature. He represents in his novel the horrors conse-quent of war and hatred, both on the personal and on the political level. He also represents in his novel the destructive potential inherent in techno-logical expansion and empire when military power and scientific might ad-vance themselves void of any human components. However, Joyce ends

*Ulysses* not with the explosion of society that occurs in Shaw's *Heartbreak House* but with a human voice, speaking her heart and mind in a unique way and with the words, at least, of affirmation and acceptance.

## NOTES

1. Declan Kiberd, *Inventing Ireland* (London: Jonathan Cape, 1995), pp. 51–63.

2. James Clifford, "Traveling Cultures," in *Cultural Studies*, ed. Lawrence Grossbery, Cary Nelson, and Paula Treichler (New York: Routledge, 1992), pp. 96–116.

3. Michael Cotsell, "Introduction," in *Creditable Warriors*, ed. Michael Cotsell (London: The Ashfield Press, 1990), p. 15.

4. Bernard McKenna, "Isolation and the Sense of Assumed Superiority in Sir James Frazer's Golden Bough," *Nineteenth Century Prose* 19(2) (Summer 1992): 49–59.

5. Edward Said, *Orientalism* (New York: Vintage, 1979), p. 1.

6. Ibid., pp. 1–2.

7. Ibid., p. 115.

8. Ibid., p. 185.

9. Kiberd, *Inventing Ireland*, pp. 33–63.

10. Thomas Kinsella, *The Dual Tradition: An Essay on Poetry and Politics in Ireland* (Manchester: Carcanet, 1995).

11. Bruce Avery, "Mapping the Irish Other: Spenser's 'A View of the Present State of Ireland,'" *ELH* 57 (Summer 1990): 263–279.

12. Nicholas Canny, "Edmund Spenser and the Development of an Anglo-Irish Identity," *Yearbook in English Studies* 13 (1983): 1–19.

13. Oliver Ferguson, *Jonathan Swift and Ireland* (Urbana: University of Illinois Press, 1962).

14. W.J. McCormack, *Ascendancy and Tradition in Anglo-Irish Literary History from 1789–1939* (Oxford: Oxford University Press, 1985).

15. Eamonn Phoenix, *Northern Nationalism* (Belfast: Ulster Historical Foundation, 1994), pp. xii–xiv.

16. Terrance Brown, *The Whole Protestant Community: The Making of an Historic Myth* (Derry: Field Day Theatre Company, 1991), pp. 8–9.

17. Ibid., p. 9.

18. Christopher Murray, "Drama 1690–1800," *The Field Day Anthology of Irish Writing* (Derry: Field Day Theatre Company, 1991), pp. 504–505.

19. Michael Cronin, *Translating Ireland* (Cork: Cork University Press, 1996), p. 144.

20. Murray, "Drama," p. 504.

21. Declan Kiberd, *Synge and the Irish Language* (London: Macmillan, 1979).

22. Kiberd, *Inventing Ireland*, pp. 51–63.

23. James Joyce, *Stephen Hero*, ed. Theodore Spencer (New York: New Directions, 1944), p. 211.

24. Ibid., pp. 210–211.

25. Kiberd, *Inventing Ireland*, p. 335.

26. James Joyce, *Dubliners*, ed. Robert Scholes and Walter Litz (New York: Penguin, 1976), p. 190.

# 5   Ideas

Ulysses explores a broad range of themes and issues.[1] Perhaps the most significant include parallels with the Odyssey, political themes, ecclesiastical themes, issues of parent/child relations, and comic themes. In connection with the Odyssey, as his title indicates, Joyce consciously chose to parallel Homer's epic. In the process of creating a contemporary epic, Joyce focuses on the human elements common to Homer's ancient text and to the lives of Joyce's contemporaries living in Ireland at the turn of the twentieth century. In doing so, his text suggests that humans, throughout all time, share a commonality, a potential to become heroic, if they embrace their humanity. In Ulysses, the Odyssean parallels help to reveal that Bloom and Molly become types of heroic figures through self-examination and understanding, whereas Stephen, as a consequence of his cynicism and malaise, fails as a heroic model, becoming instead a model of inaction. In the development of political themes, Joyce uses 1904 Dublin as a microcosm of early twentieth-century life, highlighting the destructive impulses of colonialism, war, and violence. Within this context, Ulysses posits Bloom as a type of hero, a man who can come to terms with his environment and personally overcome the forces that could lead to his destruction. Conversely, Stephen Dedalus, once again, becomes a model of failed resistance. He succumbs to the debilitating pressures of his society. Stephen also fails to embrace the possibilities inherent in parent/child relations and in ecclesiastical metaphors, consistently rejecting paternal figures and also rejecting the transcendent potential of spirituality, whereas Bloom comes to terms with a sense of loss regarding his father's and his son's deaths, ultimately embracing a community larger than himself that has the potential to transcend time. Significantly, the comedic themes present in *Ulysses* offer a counterreading of Stephen's role. Through comedy, he joins Bloom as a heroic figure, as both men undermine the pretensions and debilitating forces in their society. *Ulysses'* subtleties only reveal themselves through an integrated reading of these and other themes. A single strain or idea reveals some specific information, even some valuable insights into the text; however, unless those details connect themselves with the novel as a whole, no matter how insightful and valuable they are, they can distort the general focus of the work.

## THE ODYSSEAN THEME

James Joyce, in working drafts, in correspondence, and in discussions about his novel, made explicit parallels between Homer's *Odyssey* and *Ulysses*.[2] Joyce even used chapter titles to make the connections between the two texts more explicit.[3] He, however, after careful thought and deliberation, omitted the titles from the published version.[4] After many early readers failed to discern the parallels between the two texts, Joyce authorized Stuart Gilbert to write a guide that explored some of the correspondences between the *Odyssey* and *Ulysses*.[5] Nearly all the editions of Joyce's book, before and after Gilbert's published explication, omit chapter titles. Nevertheless, attentive readers can discern clear parallels between Homer's epic and Joyce's novel. In choosing to place his work in the context of ancient myth, Joyce makes a gesture at timelessness, to say that something about his characters, living in 1904 Dublin, connects them to all people throughout time. However, Joyce clearly does not indicate that his characters are Odyssean-type heroes. The Dubliners in *Ulysses* are ordinary people, with ordinary foibles, with ordinary problems, dreams, aspirations, and concerns. *Ulysses* suggests that coming to terms with these ordinary circumstances can make an individual heroic if he or she comes to terms with circumstances by embracing his or her humanity, by exploring his or her individuality, by growing and learning from life's conditions. Such a struggle is indeed, as *Ulysses* suggests, heroic, and the humanity revealed in the struggle is timeless.

Joyce's text reveals the humanity behind the lives of 1904 Dubliners that ties their struggle to the figures from the *Odyssey* and, through these ancient metaphors, to individuals throughout time. Specifically, in drawing an extended metaphor between the ancient and the contemporary (early twentieth-century Dublin), Joyce does not diminish or devalue the ancient. Rather, he simply reduces the grandiose figures and actions of the ancient text to human level, creating a mock-heroic tale that mocks grandiose pretensions and violent consequences so often linked to grandiose pretensions. *Ulysses* mocks their presence not in the ancient text but in the effort of so many of his contemporary modernists, Yeats included, to translate the external trappings of the heroic to their times. Instead, Joyce values the humanity present in those ancient texts, elevating the human, the moral, to heroic status. The hero then becomes a type of everyman, who struggles to retain his humanity in spite of his troubling circumstances. Thus, the Odysseus of the early twentieth century may not battle monsters and seductresses but does struggle with violent urges, with lust, hatred, desire, self-discovery, loneliness, vulnerability, and intimacy.

Episode one of Joyce's text, called "Telemachus" in the drafts, consciously echoes the beginning of the *Odyssey*. Both focus on the figure of the son. For Homer, Telemachus, son of Odysseus, struggles with the long absence of his father. In *Ulysses*, the son is Stephen Dedalus. In the *Odyssey*, Telemachus decides to leave his home to search for his father. In *Ulysses*, Stephen leaves the tower, not consciously searching for anyone or anything; he simply wants to escape Mulligan and Haines. In fact, Stephen's desire to avoid direct confrontation brings up the clearest difference between himself and Telemachus. He wants direct confrontation between his father and his mother's suitors. Paralleling the ancient text, Mulligan and Haines become types of suitors, mocking Stephen and his beliefs in the same way Penelope's suitors mock the unfavorable omens of the gods. Essentially, both Stephen and Telemachus struggle to find a way to escape the ambitions and ill intentions of men. Telemachus chooses to seek conflict. Stephen tries to avoid it. However, both Stephen and Telemachus leave their home and become wanderers. The ancient figure leaves with certainty and confidence, if not about the result of his quest at least about the righteousness of his cause. Stephen, the modern figure, also dispossessed, leaves only with uncertainty and doubt.

*Ulysses'* second episode, titled "Nestor," focuses on figures supposedly representative of wisdom and age. In the *Odyssey*, Telemachus seeks advice from a respected warrior named Nestor. In *Ulysses*, Stephen receives unsolicited advice from Garrett Deasy. However, both Homer's and Joyce's text represent these ancient figures not as venerable sources of wisdom but as pompous, self-important figures who provide little useful information. Nestor tells Telemachus the story of the Trojan War. Deasy relates to Stephen the histories of several wars and conflicts, often misrepresenting the facts. Moreover, in Deasy's tales, he blames women for war and the downfall of great men, specifically mentioning Helen of Troy and Kitty O'Shea, Parnell's mistress. Essentially, Deasy attributes war to women and not to the impulse that drives men to want to dominate women or to use women as trophies. His superficial understanding of history parallels Nestor's superficial information. However, in other ways, Deasy comes across as a weak shadow of his ancient counterpart. Nestor raises horses for war. Deasy simply keeps horse-racing mementoes and souvenirs. Nestor commands soldiers on the battlefield. Deasy commands boys in school and on the athletic field; Deasy, in this context, also serves to parody the beliefs of English colonialists who felt that the schoolyard was the proper training ground for the rulers and warriors of the empire. Essentially, the juxtaposition between Deasy and Nestor deflates war to a boy's games, reduces warriors to children, and reduces the trophies of war to simple souvenirs and mementoes.

"Proteus," the working title of Joyce's third episode, explores the human response to seemingly overwhelming events and circumstances. In Homer's text, Proteus, the ever-changing Egyptian god of the sea, becomes a source of information about Odysseus. Menelaus takes hold of the god, while he assumes human form on the shore at midday, and discovers Odysseus's circumstances. In *Ulysses*, the complexities of Stephen's intellectualizations parallel Proteus's ever-changing form. However, Stephen's mind, mired as it is in complexities and abstractions that change with the flow of his consciousness, never takes hold of a focused idea but rather mesmerizes him with the constant flux of ideas. On the shore at midday, Stephen cannot even choose to visit his mother's family. Instead, he remains paralyzed, imagining his father's ridicule. Conversely, Telemachus confidently seeks out Menelaus for information about Odysseus. Telemachus, by taking action, breaks through chaos and discovers information and receives direction and motivation. Stephen, by allowing his maze of thought and indecision to stay him, does not receive direction and continues to wander aimlessly. Stephen's circumstances suggest that in the early twentieth-century world, heroic gestures are not possible. Events and circumstances overwhelm the individual, who receives no clear sense of direction.

"Calypso," *Ulysses'* fourth episode, explores themes of lust and desire. In Homer, a beautiful nymph holds Odysseus on her island against his will. Similarly, in *Ulysses*, several beautiful women and images of beautiful women captivate Bloom. Most significantly, his wife appears to control and to be the focus of his every action. He fetches her breakfast. He attempts to make it exactly right. He responds to her desires. Not coincidentally, Molly's girlhood home on Gibraltar, supposedly served as a model for Calypso's island. Ultimately, Odysseus, with the help of Zeus and Athena, escapes the island. Conversely, Bloom leaves his home willingly and returns willingly, seemingly unaware of his captivity. Indeed, to the extent that women and their various qualities enchant Bloom throughout the day, but particularly in this episode, he never really leaves his lust behind. Similarly, while Odysseus longs for his home, Bloom never seems to be aware, at least not in "Calypso," that his lust robs him of his self-control, an allegorical home. Essentially, Odysseus possesses self-control, whereas Bloom has none, yielding to sexual temptations and food throughout the episode. Odysseus constantly struggles against self-indulgence in an effort to leave the island. Bloom yields to it. Higher forces intervene to help Odysseus in his struggles. Bloom receives the assistance of no transcendent powers. He has only his desires, his human frailties.

In the "Lotus Eaters," Ulysses' fifth episode, themes of escape abound. In the Odyssey, Odysseus and his men come to a land of people generous to outsiders. Conversely, the Dubliners in Ulysses appear polite and generous on the surface; however, their kindness carries with it a desire for some advantage or return favor. M'Coy would like Bloom to record his name at the funeral. Lyons wants a tip for the Gold Cup. Moreover, in the Odyssey, the men receive sustenance, which induces lethargy and forgetfulness. In Ulysses, Bloom occasionally yields to forgetfulness. The letter from Martha helps him forget Molly's infidelity for a time. Views and conversations with women distract him. Anticipating his bath enables him to put aside some of his concerns. Bloom also indulges in fantasies of the East, of prelapsarian gardens, of exotic locations, and of legendary places. Carrying forward the contrast between Homer and Joyce, Odysseus tries to persuade his men to leave; whereas Bloom does not try to disabuse his fellow citizens of their delusions, and, in fact, he both knowingly and unknowingly encourages their distractions and fantasies. He agrees to record M'Coy's name at the funeral and, unwittingly, gives Lyons a tip on the horse race. Bloom does, however, recognize the distractive power of religion and the Communion wafers but remains unaware of the most basic rituals and symbols of his adopted faith. For Dubliners in Ulysses, escape enables them to avoid the pain of everyday life. Unlike the sailors of the Odyssey, no heroic journey, great responsibility, or glorious homecoming awaits the people of Dublin. More pain, however, does await. The distractions put aside the pain for a few moments.

Ulysses' sixth episode, "Hades," concentrates on themes of life and death. In the Odyssey, Odysseus once again receives advice, this time from

Circe, to go to the underworld and seek the counsel of Tiresias on the best way to return to Ithaca. Like Odysseus, Bloom also journeys to the underworld not seeking wisdom and not prompted by the advice of a powerful observer but as a gesture of courtesy and politeness. In the underworld, he receives no consul from the dead but simply a reminder of death. The monuments to O'Connell and Robert Emmett stand mute before him. Indeed, Emmett refuses to write an epitaph as his words to the living. Odysseus receives consolation from the familiar dead, whereas the characters in *Ulysses* have only their grief at a loved one's absence, felt more acutely in the proximity of their bodies. In addition, Odysseus, a true outsider in the land of the dead, finds courtesy and welcome, although Ajax does snub him, whereas Bloom receives discourtesy or polite deference. He becomes the outsider in his traveling party. However, Odysseus receives tokens of the dead's advice. Bloom embraces life in his land of the dead, embracing it even in its unpleasant forms. He observes the remnants of lovemaking, considers the sexual life of the cemetery's caretaker, and contemplates a rat, grown fat on the meat of corpses. Both Odysseus and Bloom take lessons from their respective journeys to the underworld. Odysseus carries with him what is available to only a privileged few. Bloom takes with him information available to all but considered only by a few.

*Ulysses'* seventh episode, with the Odyssean title "Aeolus," considers the topic of fruitless labor. In the *Odyssey*, Odysseus receives unfavorable winds in a bag as a gift from Aeolus, to help speed the journey home. In *Ulysses*, Bloom receives no gifts and no one singles him out for special consideration. In the *Odyssey*, Odysseus's men open the bag of winds, which blow the ship off course. Similarly, ill winds blow Bloom off course. Bloom runs afoul of arrogant, self-important people, cliquish groups of people that treat him with polite deference: Keyes who snubs his ad, the machinery of the office, and the sounds of a mechanized Dublin. Stephen too finds himself distracted, set off course. He succumbs to the praise and camaraderie of the boys in the office, who distract him from his necessary quests and vocation. Stephen, like Odysseus, essentially falls asleep. Both men's inattentiveness contributes to their falling off course. Conversely, Bloom remains attentive. He is industrious, but his labors come to nothing. Bloom becomes a modern counterpart to the Odyssean hero. Unlike Odysseus, Bloom is not favored or singled out for special consideration. He labors unnoticed and unappreciated. Even for Stephen, who receives praise, there is no Odyssean moral for the falling off course, for the frustration. In *Ulysses*, there is no cause for fruitless labor. It simply happens.

"Lestrygonians," the Odyssean title of *Ulysses'* eighth episode, explores issues of cruelty and violation. In the *Odyssey*, giants devour Odysseus's men. Similarly, Bloom encounters many in Dublin who prey on their weak and vulnerable fellow citizens. Mr. Breen falls victim to a cruel joke. Bloom falls victim to Boylan's sexual appetite. Bloom recalls Protestants who gave soup to starving Catholics in exchange for conversion. However, the *Odyssey* offers an example of escape, whereas Bloom's Dublin offers no such possibility. Bloom can choose to leave an environment that particularly disgusts him, but the voracious appetite for exploitation surrounds him. He must learn ways to cope with his condition. Internal forces devour Bloom. He offers sustenance to ungrateful gulls, but he receives no token of generosity. Like the birds that devour the remains of Odysseus's men, forces eat away mercilessly at Bloom. Essentially, Bloom finds cruelty in the world outside him, answered by a literal hunger and by an emotional longing within himself. Unlike Odysseus, Bloom cannot sail away from the cruelty and violence he discovers. Rather, he must find a way to negotiate it.

"Scylla and Charybdis," episode nine, takes its title from a scene in the *Odyssey* in which Odysseus must choose to take a path that, on the one side, leads him to a whirlpool, Charybdis or, on the other side, leads him past a six-headed monster, Scylla. On the advice of Athena, Odysseus chooses to pass close to Scylla. Athena explains to Odysseus that the whirlpool offers certain death. The monster, however, will devour a man with each head, but the ship and remaining crew members will pass safely. In Joyce's twentieth-century counterpart, Stephen and Bloom, once again, receive no advice on the best way to negotiate their hazards. In fact, Stephen finds himself snubbed by higher powers. Stephen, relying on his ingenuity, does avoid the hungry mouths of the literary establishment but falls prey to Mulligan's ridicule that takes bites not so much out of Stephen's ideas as much as it attempts to devour Stephen's personal identity. Mulligan also mocks Bloom. In the *Odyssey*, sacrifice yielded benefit. In *Ulysses*, no such benefit comes from suffering. Moreover, in another Odyssean counterparallel, Odysseus must pass by Scylla. He does not want to take the journey. Bloom, however, wants to draw close to Stephen, even though it will later mean that Bloom will himself fall victim to Stephen's snipping wit. In addition, Bloom, unlike Odysseus, does not know what dangers lie ahead. Bloom cannot always see the enemy in the way that Odysseus and his men see Scylla and, even as they try to fight the monster, observe the whirlpool. Similarly, Odysseus and his men fight their enemy with the conviction of self-preservation. Stephen fights to present his ideas, admitting he does not wholly believe in them. Stephen and Bloom do not see the benefits of sacrifice and survival that Odysseus and his men perceive. For Bloom and Stephen, no gods come to offer advice. Rather, the two Dubliners must fight a solitary battle against external enemies and internal impulses, which devour parts of them without the hope of reward or escape.

*Ulysses'* tenth episode, "Wandering Rocks," explores unavoidable complications and entanglements. In the *Odyssey*, so dangerous are the wandering rocks that Odysseus receives advice to avoid them in favor of Scylla and Charybdis. The Wandering Rocks are external obstacles. In *Ulysses*, the metaphorical equivalents of the rocks are both internal and external obstacles. Father Conmee falls prey to memories of playing fields and communion wafers as he tries to say his office. Even more so, the narrative serves as a series of obstacles for readers of this episode who come to the novel with, and even after nine chapters still have, conventional expectations for character development and narrative focus. Stephen and Bloom do receive some character development in the episode; however, the chapter's focus lies elsewhere as well. The network of other characters reminds the reader of the intricate web of lives Stephen and Bloom touch or come across and how each of these lives can distract from the story's primary foci. Moreover, for the characters of this section, missing things involves not getting what they wanted or needed. The Dedalus girl receives only a portion of the money she wanted from her father. Another character misses seeing the cavalcade, whereas in the *Odyssey*, avoiding the rocks becomes a blessing for Odysseus and his men. In the most obvious parallel to the Wandering Rocks, the narrator traces the path of the Elijah throwaway as it floats on the Liffey to Dublin Bay. The paper itself reminds the reader of several themes not to be avoided. Specifically, the flier emphasizes Bloom's role as savior, as wanderer, and as outsider. Essentially, the rocks are complications in the plot and in the lives of the characters. Avoiding them, as Odysseus avoids his Wandering Rocks, does make things easier but far less textured and rich.

*Ulysses'* eleventh episode, titled "Sirens," focuses on seduction. In the *Odyssey*, Odysseus orders his men to plug their ears with wax so the sirens' song will not cause the boat to go astray and destroy itself on the treacherous shore. Odysseus, however, wants to hear the song. Therefore, in order not to destroy his boat, he commands his men to lash him to the mast and to ignore his orders, however persistent. In *Ulysses*, men do not manage to avoid entanglements with the closest parallel to the sirens, the barmaids. In fact, all fall under their spell to one extent or another. In clear contrast to the sirens' songs in the *Odyssey*, which developed exotic themes, the songs in *Ulysses* are popular and patriotic ballads, which all have heard before.

Also in contrast to Homer's story, unlike Odysseus who cannot control his impulses, Bloom does take control, to some extent, of his circumstances and even contributes his own music to the sirens' song, his flatulence. Joyce's *Ulysses* represents ideals of love and war yielding to ordering impulses and the delights of ordinary life. Epic love and battle come across as exaggerated and sentimental. Humor counters danger as ordinary sounds become the cause of celebration and relief.

The twelfth episode of Joyce's epic, with the Odyssean title "Cyclops," develops themes of love and anger. In the *Odyssey*, Polyphemus, a one-eyed giant, devours some of Odysseus's men. Odysseus defeats the cyclops by getting him drunk on wine, inducing sleep. Odysseus then blinds him. Joyce's tale serves up numerous points of intersection but with significant thematic variations. Specifically, in *Ulysses*, Bloom gets the citizen drunk with rage and anger, which blinds him. Odysseus's act involves violence. In contrast, Bloom blinds by preaching love and tolerance, which insights rage. Moreover, Odysseus leaves Polyphemus's cave hiding himself among the sheep, whereas Bloom reveals himself as a Jew and as a lover of peace. Odysseus does, ultimately, reveal his identity but only in the end, which brings down a curse. Bloom, likewise taunts the citizen, which nearly brings ruin in the form of a biscuit tin, but manages to avoid any lasting effects of the citizen's rage. Odysseus also manages to escape with his crew, who will die, whereas Bloom escapes with a microcosm of Irish society, including an Orangeman, that will survive. The people of Ireland, like the citizen, who mock one another rather than live together, Joyce's text indicates, become like a race of self-devouring cyclopes. Bloom, in contrast, offers humanity and love. Indeed, Bloom's offer enrages his cyclops; however, Bloom's action manages to unite, if even temporarily, the various strands of Irish society. Bloom defeats an external enemy and an internal enemy, responding with kindness and love to rage and hate.

"Nausicaa," the draft title of Joyce's thirteenth episode, explores issues of human contact and empathy. *Ulysses* and Homer's text offer interesting parallels. In the *Odyssey*, Odysseus finds himself washed ashore, naked, battle weary, and alone. Bloom also finds himself on the shore, emotionally weary after speaking with Dignam's family and after a day of contemplating and dreading Molly's act of infidelity. Princess Nausicaa offers Odysseus aid. Gerty also offers Bloom aid. However, the parallels between the texts end here. Odysseus and the princess speak directly to one another. Gerty and Bloom never speak, perhaps because of propriety. Societal conventions and standards also offer a contrast between the two women. Nausicaa comes to the shore to do her laundry. Many Dubliners in 1904 would consider such an act to be beneath a gentlewoman. Gerty, who has no royal blood, labors only in her imagination and aspires to a life of romance and privilege. Moreover, Odysseus's behavior demonstrates that he values emotional rather than physical contact, whereas Bloom and Gerty both, separately, place a primacy on sexual exchange. Odysseus also gains help for his return home, whereas Bloom must continue his solitary journey. Joyce humanizes the Odyssean story of Nausicaa by allowing his characters' behavior to comment on the lack of human contact and interaction in 1904 Dublin. Bloom and Gerty, consequently, satiate their needs temporarily with lonely self-gratification, whereas Odysseus communicates directly with other people and achieves an actual escape from his wanderings.

"Oxen of the Sun," the Odyssean title of Joyce's fourteenth episode, explores issues of responsibility and excess. In the *Odyssey*, Odysseus's men slaughter and eat Helios's, the sun god's, cattle, ignoring warnings to the contrary. Consequently, they die. Likewise, Bloom tries to warn Stephen about his companions but to no avail. Stephen also seems doomed. The nurse warns the group of medical students and others about their boisterousness. However, they ignore her warnings, continuing to joke and talk loudly despite the proximity of Mrs. Purefoy and her extended labor. In fact, her labor, an act of fertility, parallels the sun god's cattle, symbols of fertility. The crowd, with their rude behavior, allegorically destroy fertility in the same way Odysseus's men destroy fertility. Moreover, Stephen's creativity wastes away in the company of Mulligan and his companions. In another parallel with the *Odyssey*, just as Odysseus absents himself from his crew to pray for relief, Bloom comes to the hospital hoping to discover the relief of Mrs. Purefoy's labor pains. However, in contrast to Odysseus who falls asleep, Bloom remains vigilant. Essentially, Odysseus's lapse dooms him to isolated wandering through various hazards; he must journey again past the monster and whirlpool, alone and floating on a miserable craft. Bloom must also endure hazards but comes to them not in isolation but as Stephen's companion. Indeed, Bloom could avoid many hazards by avoiding Stephen. Both Bloom and Odysseus accept responsibility for their irreverent companions. Both endanger themselves to be with them; however, Bloom's fate is not the same type of isolation Odysseus must endure. Bloom offers companionship to Stephen, who ultimately rejects the offer, leaving Bloom alone. Both Bloom and Odysseus become vulnerable. However, Odysseus's vulnerability comes as a consequence of external forces destroying his companions. Bloom's vulnerability comes as a consequence of his kindness and desire for companionship.

Joyce's fifteenth episode, "Circe," by creating parallels with Homer, focuses on confronting and controlling desires. In the *Odyssey*, Circe turns Odysseus's men into swine. Likewise, Bloom sees before him Dubliners and foreigners animalized by their most base tendencies. In contrast to Homer's text, Odysseus, protected by a magic herb given to him by Hermes and armed with Hermes' advice, avoids transformation and rescues his men. Bloom armed with no protective herbs and no advice becomes transformed but not by an external power. Bloom's subconscious desires and impulses transform him. He comes to terms with them and, ultimately, takes control of them. Similarly, Odysseus saves his men from their fate just as Bloom tries to save Stephen. However, Bloom cannot fully protect Stephen and must allow Stephen to make his own mistakes. Furthermore, Circe offers Odysseus advice on his return journey. In *Ulysses*, Bella Cohen, the Circe figure, functions as a catalyst for many of Bloom's subconscious impulses, but Bloom's journey is his alone. In addition, Bloom chooses to leave, demonstrating that he does not come under Cohen's spell, whereas Odysseus's men must convince him to leave. Essentially, Circe functions as a type of mother goddess for Odysseus, leading him through temptation to illumination. Bloom discovers the temptations of Bella Cohen; however, he discovers illumination by coming to terms with and not discarding his subconscious desires. The strength he discovers, as a consequence of this process, he carries with him. By confronting his impulses, Bloom integrates them into his conscious personality so they become sources of strength rather than of weakness.

"Eumaeus," the sixteenth episode, examines issues associated with vulnerability and intimacy. Common themes to both the *Odyssey* and *Ulysses* involve the return of the wanderers and disguise. Odysseus, arriving in Ithaca, meets with Eumaeus, a faithful swineherd. Bloom and Stephen, on their way to Eccles Street, meet with a coffee house keeper and a sailor who are faithful to protecting themselves but certainly not to Bloom and Stephen. In fact, their various tales include likely fabrications and lies woven with half-truths so that any truth becomes obscured. Bloom and Stephen must guard their own interests. In the *Odyssey*, Athena advises Odysseus to disguise himself as an old man so that his wife's suitors will not kill him. Similarly, Stephen tries to avoid recognition, but Corley spots him and begs Stephen for money. Contrary to both Odysseus and Stephen, Bloom reveals his plans and desires to Stephen. Unlike Odysseus who tests his son, who had come separately to Eumaeus's hut before revealing himself, Bloom makes a gesture of trust, making himself vulnerable. In terms of a return home, the journey for Bloom and Stephen involves more of a metaphorical journey than it does for Odysseus, who literally arrives on his home soil. Bloom and Stephen return to intimacy and paternal/filial love rather than the variety of rejections each has suffered during the day. However, rather than become united in mutual recognition like Odysseus and Telemachus, Bloom and Stephen operate on parallel courses, not quite intersecting. Stephen does not appear ready to fully accept Bloom's intimacy, although he, significantly, does not pull away from Bloom at the end of the chapter. W.B. Murphy, a returning sailor, offers another counterpart to Odysseus. Murphy conceals his identity with layers of stories and through metaphors; the tattoos on his body tell the story of friendship lost. Murphy never reveals himself to anyone and remains isolated at the chapter's end. The episode suggests that Bloom returns to himself, discovers his identity by dropping his disguises and revealing himself to Stephen. The disguises and repressions offer some protection, but they block true self-understanding. Intimacy can lead to pain; it may be rebuffed. However, even in rejection, intimacy reveals an individual's identity at least to himself.

*Ithaca*, the seventeenth episode, focuses on self-reliance. In the *Odyssey*, father and son stand united and violently eliminate Penelope's suitors. In *Ulysses*, Bloom stands alone when confronting the memory of Molly's various suitors. He too defeats them by himself, but through equanimity and love rather than violence. Stephen leaves Bloom by himself before the end of the chapter, rejecting his intimacies. The father and son figures in Joyce's text find division through insult and disagreement initiated by Stephen, whereas in the *Odyssey*, father and son unite in battle. Left to himself, Bloom must confront not only his wife's adultery but also his life. He orders it through lists and budgets and through systematic examination. If Stephen had stayed, Bloom could not possibly have achieved the same level of self-examination and order in his life. He needs to move through more violent sentiments, such as anger and envy, before arriving at equanimity. Whereas Odysseus and Telemachus needed to use violence to expel an external threat, Bloom understands, when he is alone, that although his marriage might be threatened, his identity relies on his individual character and not on external sanction. In the *Odyssey*, the suitors position themselves for Penelope's favor by attempting to string Odysseus's bow. None can, and when Odysseus strings it with ease, he receives public sanction for his thinly veiled phallic display. Bloom, conversely, looses all contests of display to Boylan but conquers himself and controls his emotions and his response to his wife's suitors. In the *Odyssey*, external proofs of loyalty, bravery, and power restore order. Bloom restores order in his life through internal means. He recognizes that the furniture changed place and takes note of the changes, accepting them. He reviews his possessions. *Ulysses* indicates that external sanction, the kind achieved by Boylan and Mulligan, does not last. Internal self-sanction through recognition, on the other hand, offers the possibility of emotional and psychological peace.

*Ulysses'* final and eighteenth episode, titled "Penelope" after Odysseus's faithful wife, explores Molly's faithfulness and unfaithfulness. In the *Odyssey*, Penelope's sexual loyalty to her husband is the measure of her integrity and, to a large extent, her identity. Conversely, a reader comes to understand Molly's own integrity and identity, in part, through a litany of infidelities. Molly reveals that her desires and impulses, as they naturally express themselves, measure her identity. She reflects through an association of words and ideas on her life, weaving and unweaving her tapestry of experience, keeping at bay chains of doubt and repression that might divert her from contemplating her true self. Honesty and candor function as her antidote to disloyalty to self. She does not require external sanction nor does she measure her value as a person in terms of external proofs or demonstrations of sexual faithfulness. In contrast, Penelope weaves a tapestry by day and unweaves it at night to keep her suitors at bay, measuring her faithfulness to herself through sexual loyalty to her husband and through the external symbol of the weaving and the unfinished tapestry. Interestingly, despite Odysseus's heroic return, Penelope does not recognize him until he discloses the secret of their bed; it is immovable. Molly's bed jingles, rather excessively, but she recognizes her husband immediately, knows that he ejaculated that day, and sees that something about his experiences made him more confident. Molly and Bloom do not make a perfect couple in the same way Penelope and Odysseus make an ideal couple. They end their odyssey by telling one another their stories. Molly ends *Ulysses* by telling herself the stories of her life. Molly, however, communicates truly with herself through self-revealing memory. In this light, aspects of her repeated "yes" measure her self-questioning, self-probing, and self-discovery on various levels, including sexual, psychological, emotional, and intellectual.

By creating explicit connections between his text and the *Odyssey*, Joyce makes a gesture of timelessness, not only for his book but also for the characters on which *Ulysses* bases itself—the people of Dublin at the turn of the last century. Precisely because their lives offer no obvious external heroic example, they serve as models for all human experience and endeavor. Joyce indicates that heroism and allegorical journeys of self-discovery are possible in the ordinary circumstances of ordinary people. However, individuals who would choose to confront their demons, their subconscious desires, their vulnerabilities, and their less-than-perfect natures are indeed heroes of epic rarity and proportion. Consequently, Bloom and Molly function as types of epic heroes, not in their perfection (they certainly are not perfect) but rather in their effort, their gestures of self-reflection. This impulse elevates the ordinary to the extraordinary level and makes an effort at timelessness for the lives of ordinary people.

## POLITICAL THEMES

Joyce wrote *Ulysses* while in exile from the land of his birth over a period of years in numerous places, including Trieste, Zurich, and Paris. He knew what it was like to be a wanderer, to be one of the dispossessed. He knew also about dissatisfaction with his homeland, dissatisfaction with its paralysis and its malaise. He also knew about frustration with a war-torn Europe. Existence and experience seemed fluid and ever changing, and the old stabilizing forces, such as empire and the church, seemed unable to counter the flux. Joyce could also see the dissatisfaction and uncertainty of many mirrored in his experiences. Emigration and violence affected millions across Europe and particularly in Ireland. The world seemed a world of exiles, and the Irish Diaspora, like the ancient Hebrew Diaspora before it, could be a symbol for all peoples, driven from their homes to lands and places they did not know. Dublin in 1904, in this sense, stands as a microcosm for not just an Irish experience but for a world experience. However, the novel is set in Ireland, and it is the Irish experience of violence and dispossession that is paramount and that must be understood in order to come to terms with the full force of the colonial themes in *Ulysses*.[6] Individuals faced with the affects of colonial forces, Joyce's novel suggests, must come to terms with the marks of imperial possession, must work through their wounds and incorporate the effects of colonial trauma into their personalities. Doing so enables them to move on with a new identity independent of the trauma of their experience. Molly and Bloom stand as examples of this self-refashioning. However, most individuals never come to terms with their trauma in a healthy way. Most, like Stephen Dedalus, never escape the debilitating effects of colonialism. Others, like the citizen, hide their victimization inside masks of anger and violence.

In addition to Stephen, Deasy, a range of other characters, and the Catholic church offer examples of individuals and institutions who never escape the forces that victimize them. Specifically, Deasy's school's philosophy embodies the English notions of learning and instruction as logographic history, meaning a recitation of facts, names, and places without regard to the meaning behind these facts, names, and places. Deasy's school also embodies the notions of a school's playing fields and classrooms as the training grounds for an empire. Deasy's curriculum trains the body and mind to carry out orders, rather than to question inquisitively. The school models itself on the standards of English public (private) school instruction. In an equally unquestioning and unyielding way, the church, *Ulysses* notes, did not question a limiting ideology when it condemned Parnell. The Irish Catholic establishment chose a narrow set of principles modeled on the standards of British-Victorian morality rather than a broad-based identity. Outside of institutions, several individuals stand as examples of victims of colonialism that measure their identity by imperial standards. Simon Dedalus, Stephen's father, embodies several aspects of the stage Irishman. Essentially, he embodies many aspects of the anti-Irish stereotype when he avoids work to focus on drinking and singing. In addition to the elder Dedalus, the students in the maternity hospital yield to drinking and loud noise. Furthermore, Bloom, in "Lestrygonians," recalls student protesters who become violent, protesting British violence in South Africa, the students feeding the anti-Irish stereotype of a people impulsive, contradictory, and out of control. In addition, the barmaids, in "Sirens," embody not so much anti-Irish stereotypes as antifemale stereotypes, begging for the attention of men while simultaneously despising it. Unknowingly, and in Deasy's case perhaps knowingly, many characters and institutions in *Ulysses* embody the negative stereotypes and deleterious principles of an anti-Irish hegemony.

One very significant aspect of Stephen Dedalus's character involves internalizing oppressive stereotypes and even mimicking them, to the disadvantage of himself and those around him. Specifically, in the beginning of the novel, Stephen chooses to live in a Martello tower with Mulligan and Haines. The tower allegorically represents the role of British colonizers in Ireland. The British built Martello towers to prevent a successful French invasion in support of the Irish Republican cause.[7] Within this literal structure, Joyce establishes other metaphorical components. Mulligan, who mimics the mass at the novel's outset, stands for the Catholic church. Haines, an Oxford student studying a fanciful version of Ireland, stands for English oppression. Within the tower, these two oppressive forces stand together against Stephen. Beyond the metaphorical level, the Catholic church and the British state also established historical alliances against Ireland. In 1155, Nicholas Breakspear, Pope Adrian IV, issued a papal bull, or proclamation, granting England rule over Ireland. In addition to his living arrangements, which he tries to escape, Stephen exhibits qualities of the anti-Irish stereotype. Upon initial consideration, the conventional and negative representation of the Irish as nonintellectual creatures, who are overfanciful and imaginative, certainly does not apply to Stephen. However, when his thoughts become so complex as to obscure any grasp he might have of reality, as in "Proteus," he embodies the ultimate final representation even if not the components of the anti-Irish stereotype. Stephen, moreover, despite his physical absence from the tower, appeals to colonial-like forces for approval. In the National Library, he espouses a theory he does not wholly believe in in order to win the favor of a certain portion of Dublin's literary establishment. Most significantly, Stephen demonstrates that he has internalized colonial values when he returns Bloom's kindness with an anti-Semitic song. Stephen, in his act, embodies the forms of the oppressor. He echoes Deasy's anti-Semitism and rejects kindness in favor of disdain. By rejecting Bloom's hospitality, Stephen, weary and homeless, dooms himself to wander into the night. He becomes the agent of his own oppression, modeling the forces that dominate him.

Not all the characters and institutions in the book remain so obviously victims of colonial hegemony. Some do attempt to fashion a means of escape. However, for those characters and institutions, their means, whether literary or political, often still function as reflections of the colonizing power. Specifically, practitioners of the Celtic Twilight saw a romantic, dreamy Ireland as a bucolic alternative to the industrialized colonial power. However, in embracing such an ideal, they actually reinforce the colonial view of Ireland as a place of retreat from the real world and of the Irish as incapable of industry. In particular, George Russell embraces a mystical spiritualism as a source of vitality. In doing so, he contrasts his epistemology with a hyperlogical English Protestantism, which served the expansion of empire and its ethos. However, he also legitimized English notions of the Irish as being in need of logical and reasoned spirituality to discipline an intellect too ready, in the English view, to embrace the mystical and spiritual. Also in the Irish society represented in *Ulysses*, the heroes of the past and dead martyrs have an immediate and imminent presence. In "Hades," the mourners recall Parnell, O'Connell, and Emmett. The men recite the names of these political/historical figures without recalling the totality or even a significant portion of their deeds. The men pass by the monuments to these figures and even visit their graves and markers. In doing so, the mourners make the heroes and heroic dead a presence in their then-contemporary lives, but the presence is not a living presence. The heroes exist as a calcified remnant of the past. The graves and memorials offer a mute response to the challenges of the living and because of the way the mourners interact with the memory of these heroes. The men in the newspaper office, detailed in "Aeolus," exhibit a similar love for the dead past. They dwell on legends and tales of long-gone heroic deeds rather than live in the present. The literature of the Gaelic Revival and the history of Irish martyrs and rebellions far too often involves a seeming rejection of colonial forces. However, the method of rejection and the forms of identity embraced serve a colonial epistemology and a colonial ethos and purpose.

The citizen epitomizes the colonized individual who limits growth by embracing an epistemology as destructive as the colonial paradigm. Specifically, intolerance of foreigners and angry confrontation characterize the citizen's views and behavior. Similarly, intolerance of foreigners and angry confrontation also characterize English-colonial methods. Essentially, in his effort to define an identity outside of the colonized territory, the citizen makes himself into an image of the colonizer. In further reflection of the dislocating colonizing force, the citizen lives in the house of an evicted tenant. Moreover, the citizen, like the characters from "Hades" recites an Irish history that is a history of death and heroic loss. It speaks to only an identity of loss, offering doomed formulas for resistance. Essentially, the citizen's epistemology depends on an oppressor, someone or something to resist. Without the oppressor, his identity would disintegrate. Therefore, he can never fully emerge from oppression without the risk of losing his identity. By connection, Ireland, ironically, must remain under colonial dominance for his image of Ireland to survive. Basically, the citizen adopts a mask of identity, which enables him to project an image of power and control. Indeed, he appears in control of the discussion, directing its tone and its movement from topic to topic. However, he ultimately loses control. In the end, Bloom escapes unharmed and triumphant. Therefore, Ulysses indicates that the citizen's mask of power may be effective, to an extent. However, the mask eventually frustrates those who adopt it because it cannot answer the demands of an ever-changing environment. Like historical models and statues that do not come to life, the citizen's ideology cannot function in a truly living environment. Therefore, in order to survive with his ideology in tact, the citizen must destroy the agents of change or difference. The act of destruction, if it is successful, ensures that change will not occur. Consequently, the colonial paradigm will continue.

Significantly, Ulysses, in addition to the limited ideology of the citizen and the perpetual victimization of Stephen Dedalus, presents alternative identities that are more equipped to embrace an ever-changing environment. Such forms of identity include the colonizer, in the form of a daughter of a British soldier. They include outsiders, like a converted Jew, the son of an immigrant father. Molly and Bloom serve as examples of characters who escape both the agents of colonial oppression and the agents of seeming resistance that are, in actuality, oppressive forces. Molly and Bloom free themselves from the limited forces around them by embracing the totality and complexity of their identities. Specifically, Bloom falls victim to an anti-Semitism and an Irish provincialism that refuse to accept him. In response, Bloom preaches a gospel of love, the true Christian gospel, pointing out that Christ, like himself, was a Jew. Moreover, Bloom sees himself as having both masculine and feminine qualities, an attitude that would have been met with derision and disdain by both the hypermasculine colonial male and the manly ideal of Irish Republican resistance. Bloom, ultimately, uses his feminine and masculine personae not so much to do battle with these forces, although he does engage the citizen with a rather masculine taunt and a stereotypically feminine attitude toward violence, but to fashion a combined identity for himself, especially after "Circe," in order to live beyond narrow definitions and limiting ideologies. Similarly, Molly writes her own history not as a linear or logographic history, like that of Deasy's classroom, but rather, telling her tale, as one that moves in and out of time with no concern for linearity. Nor does she place a primacy on details of time and place and person. Her focus involves coming to terms with the essence of her emotional experience. Her history is a narrative history. Moreover, late-Victorian ethos posited an ideal female figure who must stand as a bastion of nonsexual/sensual virtue and propriety. Molly, in her monologue, dismisses such notions as prudish and deeply explores her sexual and sensual responses. The diversity of Bloom's and Molly's sometimes seemingly self-contradictory impulses and narratives reconcile themselves in each character's final self-image and identity. Molly's monologue recognizes the oppressive forces in her life. She moves beyond them. Just as Bloom recognizes and moves beyond the forces that oppose him. Both move beyond the limits of their environment, embracing complex identities that take multifarious forms.

Critics and casual readers alike observe that *Ulysses* provides an accurate image of Dublin at the turn of the last century. Joyce himself, legend has it, wanted to present a picture of a Dublin so detailed that, if the actual city were destroyed, his book could be used to rebuild it. In his portrait of Irish society in 1904, Joyce provides not only realistic details but a diversity of characters, including the daughter of a British soldier, British soldiers themselves, Catholic priests, Ulster Presbyterians, Irish nationalists, mystical writers, drunkards, lazy fathers, flirtatious young women, prostitutes, lost young men, and wandering Jews. By providing a portrait of Dublin so detailed and accurate, Joyce confounds in his diverse representation the limiting colonial stereotype of both the Irish and Irish Revival notion that there exists a supposedly pure Celtic identity that can revitalize the country. Conversely, Joyce's *Ulysses* posits multifarious Irish identities, encompassing the totality of Irish experience.

## PARENT/CHILD THEMES

Parent and child themes[8] in *Ulysses* focus around issues of continuity, meaning, in part, a sense of belonging to a community that transcends time and the vicissitudes of the present. Like Irish politics and colonialism, the ideal of continuity involves adaptation to change and, in the end, survival. The individual, himself or herself, stands as symbol of the adaptability and the survival of his or her ancestors. By adapting and changing, the individual also makes a gesture to the future. Importantly, not all the characters in *Ulysses* make such a gesture to the future, nor do they all come to terms with their past in a way that enables them to better survive in the present. Some characters, including Stephen, see their past and their culture's past and future, in whole or in part, as a calcified presence or possibility, unchangeable and immutable. Joyce traces the search for a sense of continuity through numerous characters, including not only Stephen but also Bloom, Molly, Dignam, Deasy, and others. Joyce also focuses on themes of religion and nation as they stand for images of the parent or of the child.

A study of a variety of parent and child themes in *Ulysses* reveals a diversity of relationships and perspectives. Those that offer promise focus on adaptability and change. After Stephen and Bloom, one of the primary father/son metaphors involves Stephen's theory regarding Shakespeare and Hamlet. One aspect of Stephen's theory presents Shakespeare using his art to establish a connection with his dead son, which indicates that Shakespeare creates a continuity through artistry that real life had severed. His uses art to revise circumstance. Another aspect of Stephen's theory indicates that artistry can give voice to a sense of severed continuity. In giving voice to the broken connection, art imaginatively reestablishes that severed contact. Specifically, Shakespeare and his wife, Stephen's theory suggests, experienced difficulties. By giving voice, through *Hamlet*, to a sense of tragedy and loss involving betrayed love, the play becomes a living, speaking, and breathing vessel of lost relations, imaginatively compensating for lost physical contact and emotional intimacy. The story of Reuben J offers a contrast to Stephen's theory of Shakespeare and Hamlet. Reuben J failed to see his son as a living presence. Reuben J's son's near-death metaphorically stands for the father's rejection. Moreover, the father negates his son's resurrection by treating him as a priceable commodity. In another example of father/son relations, Bloom's and Cunningham's efforts to give Dignam's son a sense of a secure financial and educational future indicate that they attempt to establish a living legacy of the father in the future prospects of his surviving child. In terms of Molly's relationship with her father, she recalls her father's life and military service, linking it to her memories of Gibraltar and to her early memories of romance. She weaves her father into her ever-changing reminiscences, making him a continuing living presence in her life. However, Molly initially struggles with the image of her daughter, in part, seeing Milly as a sexual rival. Ultimately, Molly links Milly to her memories of developing sexuality, allowing for a sense of continuity. Artistry, imagination, and memory have the potential to ensure continuity by demonstrating adaptation through literal and imaginative progeny.

Stephen's imagined and actual relationships with his paternal figures offer a far less promising vision of adaptability and continuity. In relation to his mother's memory, to his personal spirituality, and to female images of Ireland, Stephen cannot grow beyond a sense of loss and severed connection. Throughout *Ulysses*, memories of his dead mother haunt Stephen. He does not wash, avoiding water since her death. Moreover, his sense of guilt, associated with his actions at the time of her death, continually obscures his thoughts. Stephen refuses to embrace the memory of his living mother, only thinking of her suffering and dead, even to the point of imagining her rotting corpse coming before him. By associating water with her memory, Stephen metaphorically rejects life and the possibility of purgation of guilt. He cannot reach beyond the reality of her absence to embrace himself, the symbol of the continuing presence of her life. He neglects himself physically, intellectually, and emotionally, giving his body and spirit a dead reality to mirror his mother's corpse. Moreover, because Stephen refuses to pray at his mother's deathbed, he links not simply his lost Catholic faith but also any spirituality to the memory of his lost mother. Specifically, Stephen persists in rejecting an emotional engagement with his spirituality. He does embrace the intellectual elements of his religion, using Jesuit-taught logic and reason to battle Mulligan and others. Ultimately though, his personal spirituality fails him just as his thoughts become clouded on Sandymount Strand. Significantly, Stephen in this episode also tries but fails to write a poem, thinks of, but then rejects the idea of visiting his mother's family, and misperceives cockle pickers as midwives carrying a misbirth. Moreover, Stephen also experiences a sense of betrayal when he comes to terms with an allegorical figure representing Ireland. He feels slighted by the milk woman, who treats his rivals, Haines and Mulligan, with deference. Stephen, obviously, wants more from her than she can or will give him. Rather than deal with someone who is essentially a stranger to him on polite terms, Stephen judges her harshly for failing to give him what he thinks he needs from her. He cannot see beyond himself and, within himself, discovers only pain and loss. Stephen persistently refuses to grow beyond his mother's death, freezing his emotional and creative development and contributing to the deterioration of his physical condition.

Likewise, Stephen rejects a series of father figures, refusing to grow beyond a sense of betrayal. Specifically, Stephen accurately recognizes the myriad of his father's failures. Simon Dedalus relinquishes his paternal and financial obligations to his family. However, Stephen cannot overcome or grow beyond his father's failures. He cannot live his life without his father's behavior haunting him. Stephen decides not to visit his mother's family, in part because he imagines his father's ridicule. Further, he cannot sing or play music without thinking to adopt his father's mannerisms. Similarly, Stephen, while perceiving the failings of other father figures, like Deasy, remains under their influence. Stephen recalls Deasy's words about money, models his anti-Semitism, and delivers his letter to the paper. In fact, Stephen uses the bottom of Deasy's letter to write his attempt at a poem, juxtaposing both of their creative works. Just as he physically separates himself from his father, Stephen physically removes himself from Deasy's presence by resigning. However, just as Stephen remains haunted by his father's presence, he remains haunted by Deasy's presence. Stephen continues his pattern of rejection with Bloom, even though the elder man offers potential compensation for Stephen's failed father figures. Specifically, Bloom offers Stephen a home and the potential for financial security. Bloom also offers the possibility of having Stephen pursue teaching and his artistry through singing. In rejecting Bloom, Stephen demonstrates that he rejects the possibility of growing beyond the limited paternal examples of his father and Garrett Deasy. Stephen marks his relationships with paternal figures with acts of rejection. He physically separates himself from his father, Bloom, and Deasy. However, in separating himself, Stephen actually embraces the limited voice of his two negative father figures while spurning the potential for growth offered by Bloom.

In sharp contrast to *Ulysses'* representation of Stephen Dedalus's failed efforts to come to terms with his paternal figures, the novel offers a Leopold Bloom, who can come to terms with the sudden deaths of a father and a son. *Ulysses* also offers a Bloom who comes to terms with these losses by embracing possibilities for future growth. Bloom's father's suicide has the potential to destroy a paternal sense of continuity. Indeed, the trauma consequent of his father's death haunts Bloom, calcifying the memory of the father for Bloom. However, Bloom overcomes the difficulties related to his father's absence by embracing two symbols of paternal inheritance, his heritage as a Jew and being the son of an immigrant. Bloom's Jewish heritage has the possibility to limit him, casting him as an outsider and making him vulnerable to prejudice. Certainly, Bloom encounters prejudice and is excluded. However, he compensates for his exclusion and for being the object of derision by embracing his heritage and by integrating it into the more mainstream, for Ireland, Christian tradition. Bloom preaches a gospel of love and points out that Christ was a Jew. Bloom does the same with his immigrant heritage, transforming what many use to isolate him into a source of pride. Bloom aligns himself with Arthur Griffith, who looked to the land of Bloom's ancestors, Hungary, for a model for Irish sovereignty. Conversely, Bloom does let the death of his son haunt him. Rudy's loss inaugurates a prolonged period of sterile relations between Molly and Bloom. He, essentially, rejects the promise of future life, freezing his creative-sexual production at the time of his son's death. However, with Stephen, Bloom embraces life, making a gesture of vulnerability and openness. Even though Stephen ultimately rejects him, Bloom imagines a future as a steward of Stephen's growth and potential. Bloom imagines a place where Stephen can develop his talents. In this imaginative gesture, even though it may not come to fruition, Bloom opens his mind to a possible future that had been sealed with Rudy's death. Bloom also changes his attitude toward his daughter. As the novel progresses, Bloom begins to see Milly more and more as his heir. Ironically, Stephen's anti-Semitic song further raises the possibility of Milly as heir in Bloom's mind as the song engages Bloom's empathy for his daughter. Ultimately, Bloom overcomes his sense of rupture, consequent of his son's and father's death, by imaginatively embracing a potential future with Stephen as a filial figure and by coming to terms with Milly's presence.

*Ulysses* offers two models of parent/child relations. On the one hand, the story of Reuben J's and Stephen's failed relationships with their paternal figures indicates that the sense of continuity inherent in mother-child and father-child relations can be rejected if tragedy and loss become the focus of relationships. Stephen and Reuben J, essentially, reject their life in their various acts of paternal rejection. Conversely, Molly and Bloom struggle with loss and rejection but eventually overcome these negative tendencies and embrace the life-giving potential inherent in imaginative and literal regeneration. Ironically, Stephen too intellectually understands his life-giving potential; he attempts a poem and tells the story of Shakespeare's compensations. However, Stephen cannot act to save himself.

## ECCLESIASTICAL THEMES

*Ulysses* offers a counterpoint between Stephen's and Bloom's engagement with ecclesiastical themes.[9] In an analysis of Stephen Dedalus's behavior, concepts of consubstantiation and transubstantiation, gleaned from his experiences and education as a Catholic and student of Jesuit spirituality, offer models of negation and an active choice not to achieve a sense of transcendence or communion. On the other hand, in an analysis of Bloom's character, concepts of metempsychosis and parallax, learned from popular spirituality and mysticism, offer models of acceptance, transcendence, and a sense of oneness. Significantly, as separate and unlike as Stephen's and Bloom's reactions and spiritual training are, the metaphors through which each experiences physical, creative, and spiritual potentialities for communion and transcendence are actually quite similar. Specifically, consubstantiation and metempsychosis both imply a sense of belonging to a community or vitality (that is, God or omphalos) beyond the self. Consubstantiation literally means a simultaneous separate consciousness or identity and a merged or unified consciousness or identity. The Holy Trinity is a Catholic theological example. Metempsychosis suggests the return of one thing as another, reincarnation, or the memory of a separate and unique identity inside another identity. Transubstantiation and parallax both imply regenerative transformation. Transubstantiation, as in the Catholic Eucharist, indicates the metamorphosis of one substance into another. Parallax involves the concept of perceived transformation of one object into two separate objects.

Stephen consistently perceives his connectedness, his sameness (his consubstantiality), with others but also consistently rejects acting to validate that connection. Specifically, in the initial stages of the "Proteus" episode, Stephen considers the navel cord, in part likening it to a telephone cord, linking him to previous generations and through them to an Eden. Stephen's facetious reflection suggests a discomfort with the notion that he somehow has a physical/mystical connection with the past. Moreover, that the joke focuses on Eden directly links his discomfort to the religious implications of the connection and represents a rejection of spiritual engagement. Also in "Proteus," Stephen imagines a sexual oneness with the sea, likening the movements of its waves to the sensual motions of young girls. However, immediately Stephen recalls a Latin phrase he links to Saint

Ambrose, regarding repentance and wrongdoing. Stephen rejects the fertility of the sea and, by extension, of himself by associating sensuality and sexuality with sin and repentance. Elsewhere in the "Proteus" episode, Stephen considers the books he planned to write with letters as titles. He thought to send them to the great libraries of the world and imagines commentary on each of the titles. Stephen dwelling, even self-depreciatingly, on titles of books and on imagined critical commentary indicates not an emphasis on the creative process of artistry, the subjective product of labor, but on the objective product of fame. Essentially, Stephen privileges the ostentatious trappings of artistry rather than the subjective value created as a consequence of establishing a sense of oneness with individuals who will review the created work. Stephen's choice represents a negation of art. Despite accurately perceiving the possibilities inherent in spiritual, creative, and sexual gestures of unity and commonality with a larger human community, Stephen does not act to establish them, choosing instead to destroy the possibilities of unity through superficial, derisive, and satiric thought.

In contrast to Stephen, Bloom does embrace the transcendent possibilities inherent in metempsychosis, his counterpoint to Stephen's consubstantiation. Bloom recognizes, acknowledges, and acts to ratify his sense of oneness with a larger community by embracing spirituality, creativity, and sexuality. In the "Calypso" episode, Bloom defines the concept of metempsychosis simply and clearly for his wife, explaining it as the continuation of life transcending death. Bloom's seriousness, serving as counterpoint to Stephen's facetiousness, demonstrates a respect for the concept of life beyond the corporeal. Moreover, in choosing to define metempsychoses in positive terms, as the continuation of life, Bloom generates respect for the concept in others who hear his definition. His action of spoken seriousness, respect, and optimism lends credibility to his concept, demonstrating that Bloom embraces the spiritual impact of transcendence and makes it more likely that someone else will accept the transcendent possibilities that the concept of metempsychosis articulates. Furthermore, as Bloom falls asleep at the end of the "Nausicaa" episode, he half dreams about a variety of the day's events, including considering Molly and her infidelity, Gerty and her sexuality, Eastern visions of paradise and retreat, and Spanish/Eastern sexuality. In addition, as a bat flies around him, Blooms hears a clock chiming "cuckoo." Bloom's sense of oneness in this episode comes as his conscious and subconscious minds merge; he only half sleeps and half dreams. Therefore, his thoughts are not entirely random. He exercises a certain amount of volition in relation to them. In this state, Bloom unifies the fanciful and the real. He associates an imagined Levant with his wife's Spanish heritage.

Moreover, his volitional mind merges creativity and sexuality in his half-conscious associations. Even the flying objects around him carry their normal associations with creativity and spirituality but also death and humiliation. Bloom, therefore, accepts the possibilities that life, sexuality, and creativity continue in other forms after their death in his life and consciousness. By embracing the totality of his experiences in his unified visions on Sandymount Strand and through his earlier and respectful commentary on metempsychosis, Bloom ratifies the life-continuing potential inherent in death, embracing a community that includes himself, Gerty, an unfaithful Molly, and the man who cuckolds him, Boylan.

In contrast to Bloom, Stephen, just as he rejects the possibilities of sexual, spiritual, and creative communion with a larger human community, repeatedly rejects the regenerative spiritual, physical, and creative potentialities of transformation (transubstantiation) that offer themselves to him. Early in the "Telemachus" episode, Stephen juxtaposes images of the sea and his mother, essentially transforming one into the other. However, rather than embrace the transcendent possibilities of such an association, including the potential of his mother's spirit transformed from the material realm to the immortal realm of the sea, Stephen unconsciously associates the waters below him with an image of his mother's corpse, imagined in graphic and ghoulish detail. Moreover, he then consciously recalls the image of her vomited bile. Both Stephen's conscious and subconscious minds reject the possibility of his mother's spiritual transformation, despite the allegorical opportunities presented by the proximity of the sea. In "Proteus," Stephen consciously rejects an imaginative transformation. As he recalls Kevin Egan's stories of Irish rebellion and of his lost, handsome youthful form, Stephen rejects the reinvigorating potential of imagination and dwells instead on what he perceives to be Egan's forgotten and desolate exile. Stephen refuses to accept that Egan's stories animate his life in exile. By consciously rejecting the positive aspects of Egan's stories, Stephen likewise rejects the potential of transformative imagination. Fittingly, Stephen's own creative efforts on Sandymount Strand fail to come to fruition. Additionally, at the end of the "Proteus" episode, Stephen self-consciously places some of his snot on a rock on the shore. His act offers the potential embrace of his body's natural processes of transubstantiation. The color of the snot even matches the color of the sea. However, given the chance to reflect on his body's action, Stephen looks around to see if anyone perceives him. He cannot consciously grasp the metaphorical implications of his body's unconscious transformation. Indeed, he attempts to hide it. Just as he rejected the potential of consubstantial union, Stephen rejects the potential of transubstantial reinvigoration.

In moments of insight involving parallax, the counterpart to Stephen's transubstantiation, Bloom consciously transforms the substance of negative associations to positive associations. His thoughts focus on themes of sexuality, creativity, and spirituality. In his correspondence with Martha Clifford, Bloom transforms himself not only into Henry Flower but also into a literary man and sexual adventurer, countering his wife's infidelity and his failed ambitions. Specifically, in the strict definition of parallax, Bloom divides himself in two simply by changing perspective, now carrying a romantic name and identity. Leopold Bloom becomes Henry Flower, an artist who needs a special woman's assistance to bring his work to fruition. Bloom, himself, does not avoid the sexual associations of his created identity. Rather, he relishes them, playing her mildly sadomasochistic comments over and over in his mind. In addition, Bloom becomes a type of artist in his act of creating an alternate identity. In truth, he lies to Martha about his literary standing, but he does "write" for her a new persona, creating Henry Flower the artist. Essentially, Bloom changes himself, makes himself over, by exploring imaginative possibilities. Further, in the "Lestrygonians" episode, Bloom actually uses the word "parallax" while observing the time ball on the Ballast office. In a chapter that focuses on eating, Bloom's observations of transformation comment directly on the body's material processes of transformation. Unlike Stephen, who through self-consciousness and guilt rejects his bodily processes, Bloom embraces the body's transformative power. Before looking at the time ball, Bloom feeds the birds, embracing a traditional symbol of spirituality and creativity. He also considers rats, floating and bloated on porter, which recalls his earlier observations regarding the large rat transforming dead bodies into sustenance. He also considers advertisements, his personal form of creative regeneration. Most significantly, however, Bloom, at the chapter's outset, reads his name in a throwaway flier that proclaims Elijah and the Blood of the Lamb. Bloom, essentially and unconsciously, transforms himself into a type of messianic figure, later functioning as Christ distributing communion, in Bloom's case, to the gulls. Bloom, for his part, embraces the transformative potential of the human body, not only in sexual terms but in digestive terms. In addition, he consciously dwells on his unconscious associations of life in death, focusing on rats eating dead bodies and themselves dying from porter. The latter image recalls eucharistic wine. Ultimately, he unconsciously associates himself with prophets and messianic figures and, subsequently, performs an act of regenerative kindness.

Bloom and Stephen's separate but similar models, methods, and results of communion and regenerative transformation actually have a commonality. Both men, either instinctively or because of spiritual training, utilize a similar process through which to experience the sexual, creative, and spiritual potentialities of their existence. Both Stephen and Bloom come to terms with their worlds through a process of reflection, discernment, and action; the process has its roots in Jesuit spirituality. Both men actively perceive the world around them and link those perceptions to their life experiences. Both men come to understand which acts and reflections bring them growth and satisfaction and which acts and reflections do not help them mature and achieve a sense of contentment. Moreover, both men act on their reflections and discernments. Stephen acts in a negative way, consistently making choices that leave him discontented. Bloom, conversely, acts in a consistently positive way. Bloom chooses to engage with a community greater than himself, and Stephen chooses not to engage, rejecting kindness and humanity in himself and others.

## COMIC THEMES

It would be a mistake to read *Ulysses* as a wholly serious novel, stressing significant and important themes such as religious issues, parent/child relationships, and the epic only in the most solemn and ardent of terms. On the contrary, Joyce's novel utilizes comedy partly to reinforce and partly to undermine the more serious themes.[10] Four comic theories facilitate an understanding of Joyce's technique. Specifically, an analysis of *Ulysses* using the principles articulated in Grotjahn's *Beyond Laughter* reinforces the heroic nature of Leopold Bloom but, significantly, allows a reader to see Simon Dedalus sympathetically and also allows a reading of Stephen Dedalus as a type of comic hero in connection with the novel's more series themes, particularly parent/child relationships. In addition, the comic theories outlined by Henry Fielding in his preface to *Joseph Andrews* allow a view of *Ulysses* both as a traditional mock epic and as a heroic epic. Furthermore, utilizing Bahktin's principles of the comic, that he uses to analyze the folk humor of the Middle Ages, allows a reading of Joyce's text that reinforces the representation of Bloom as a hero. Finally, David Krause's comic theories further illuminate *Ulysses'* complex exploration of ecclesiastical themes, particularly in relation to the established Catholic church in Ireland.

Two concepts from Grotjahn's *Beyond Laughter* are useful for an examination of James Joyce's *Ulysses*. The first is the connection between wit and aggression, and the second is his definition of the clown. According to Grotjahn, wit facilitates aggression by disguising the object toward which an individual or group wishes to express aggression. The disguise inhibits inner resistance and opposition to the focus of aggression. Simply put, people feel comfortable facing the aggression if it is disguised. Further, people do not feel threatened by the aggressive force when it is disguised. Consequently, an individual's pent-up energy is released in laughter. The aggressive force is conquered and people feel free. Grotjahn outlines a clear, three-part process. First, an aggressive idea is represented. Second, the aggression is conquered when it is comically portrayed. Finally, the aggression is removed from the conscious mind to the unconscious. The aggression is disguised through exhibitionism, nonsense, and play on words. Moreover, for Grotjahn, the clown represents a depreciated father figure. Essentially, the clown represents a situation that happens in every man's life. He grows up. He finds himself becoming stronger than his father and feels guilty about this. However, through comedy, the father can be harmlessly emasculated because he is made into a buffoon. Aggression toward the father is vented when the father is disguised. Therefore, the father must be overthrown because he is ineffective. Consequently, the son is not so much rebellious as victorious. It is the father who becomes impotent, castrated, and conquered.

Grotjahn's theories can be usefully and effectively applied to Joyce's text. Within the text, Stephen not only throws off the authority of his biological father, but he also throws off the authority of two colonizing fathers—the Catholic church and England—and throws off the authority of Leopold Bloom, a metaphorical father figure (the Ulysses to Stephen's Telemachus). Each of these figures is made into an impotent object of derision, shown to be powerless, and then discarded by Stephen. Simon, Stephen's biological father, cannot support his family. He spends his days socializing and drinking. His lack of financial prowess could be interpreted as a form of allegorical impotence. Within the context of the story then, Stephen's biological father is transformed into an ineffectual buffoon. Indeed, it is Stephen's books his sisters sell in order to feed the family. More important, however, is Stephen's overthrow of the colonizing fathers. Initially, Buck Mulligan, the representative of the Catholic church, and Haines, the representative of British colonialism, seem victorious. They seize Stephen's home from him. As a tower, this too could be seen as a phallic object. However, after their initial display of potency, each is revealed to be a comic representative of an impotent father. The tower, itself a remnant of English efforts at fending off a French invasion in support of Irish Republicans, becomes a useless relic. Mulligan, the priestlike figure whose words open the book, demonstrates his seeming power. He takes Stephen's key and receives invitations to literary meetings. Mulligan also physically beats Stephen. However, Mulligan does not succeed in destroying Stephen, and Stephen successfully mocks the literary circle that accepts Mulligan. As for Haines, the English scholar who comes to Ireland speaking the Irish language with his English accent, he too is initially triumphant. He too wins the tower. However, he too is made into a buffoon. He has dreams of a black panther, an obvious phallic image, devouring him. Further, he remains isolated from the symbols of ancient Ireland, unable to communicate with the milk woman. Finally, both Buck Mulligan and Haines rely on Stephen for financial support for their rent and milk. Most significantly, however, Stephen conquers the image of his metaphorical father, Leopold Bloom. Ultimately, while accepting his hospitality, Stephen sings an anti-Semitic song and refuses to stay with Bloom. Further, throughout the book, Bloom becomes an image of impotence. His wife has an affair. People snicker at him behind his back. He abandoned his religion in favor of his wife's faith, but he does not truly understand the intricacies of the Catholic church mistaking the meaning of INRI and IHS. Further, in a sense he abandons his country by marrying the daughter of a British soldier. Finally, he looses his key. Consequently, he is made into a buffoon before Stephen emasculates him finally by rejecting him.

However, Joyce's text does illuminate some problems with Grotjahn's theories, most notably sympathy for the father. Although Bloom is placed in situation after situation that should rob him of his dignity, he remains sympathetic, as does Simon. Essentially, Simon is not entirely an image of a degraded clown. In the end, he appears more as a kind but ineffective figure, not to be discarded but to be pitied. Bloom too is pitiable but also powerful despite his repeated castration episodes. He does consummate a type of relationship with Gerty McDowell on the beach, with bells ringing in the background. She does allow him contact and sympathy. Further, Molly's affirmation in the end suggests that Bloom may win out over Blazes in the contest for Molly's affection. Certainly, it is Bloom that ultimately goes to sleep with Molly at the end of the day as Bloom discards the potted meat from the bed. Finally, Molly dismisses Blazes' aggressively intimate gesture and embraces Bloom's decency. Essentially, Grotjahn's theory does not allow for sympathy with the father figure that mitigates a sense of guilt and aggression. Comedy may disguise the aggressive components of the father figure; however, it does not disguise the sympathetic components.

Henry Fielding argues, in his preface to *Joseph Andrews*, that the novel is a comic epic poem in prose. Essentially, the novel's characters and plot line would employ techniques similar to those of the epic. However, those epic characters would be placed in comic situations and circumstances. The comedy of those situations would be naturalistic in the sense that it highlights vanity, hypocrisy, and affectation. Significantly, Fielding also argues that sympathy must be discarded before the comic can truly achieve its full force.

Initially, Fielding's theory reads like a blueprint for Joyce's *Ulysses*. Indeed, the title and the chapters are modeled on an epic. The characters themselves find a resonance with the Homeric heroes and characters. By placing these epic characters in then-contemporary circumstances, Joyce apparently achieves the dual goals of the mock epic. He degrades the object of satiric attention, the contemporary world, and upgrades the classical ideal by comparison. Certainly, Penelope's faithfulness achieves a hollow resonance with Molly's infidelity. Telemachus remains the faithful son and helps his father secure the kingdom, whereas Stephen mocks Bloom and leaves him. Bloom, himself, simply journeys around Dublin as opposed to Ulysses, who managed journeys to the known boundaries of the world. Further, Bloom's journey lasts only a day, whereas Odysseus wandered for years. A cursory examination of the incidents in *Ulysses* compared with the incidents in Homer's epic suggests that Joyce achieves Fielding's idea of the mock epic poem in prose.

However, by using sympathy to help draw the comic situation, Joyce, in actuality, uplifts the contemporary and makes the epic seem bland and affected by comparison. Joyce achieves his sympathy through naturalistic detail. His figures are not superhuman; rather, they are all too human, with human weaknesses and failings. This technique achieves an audience's sympathy and creates a modern epic in prose, Fielding's model for the novel, not by disparaging the contemporary but by creating empathy with it. Bloom's journey may only last a day and it may only be around Dublin; however, within the course of his wanderings, he encounters real-life monsters and humiliations. Joyce causes his readers to identify with Bloom by using the same naturalistic techniques Fielding suggested in order to distance readers' sympathy from characters. Bloom is chased from a bar. He surreptitiously watches women, has imaginative liaisons, and is humiliated by his wife's affair. All are normal human happenings. All could and do happen to everyone. Certainly, the fact of these events distances Bloom from the heroes of ancient epics, but the circumstances and the method of representation create a sympathy for Bloom and make him into a modern hero. Stephen does not remain faithful to his father. Certainly, in this, Stephen is unlike Telemachus. However, like Bloom, Stephen's struggles and his thoughts arouse sympathy and identification, so that, despite Stephen's inhospitable and caustic nature, a reader can see in him a model for a method of struggle and not simply an image of victory. Molly, herself, does not inspire complete confidence, as does Penelope. However, when she speaks for herself, discarding the accepted rules of a novel-like prose, she draws a reader into not simply her actions but her thoughts and feelings. By drawing a reader into herself, she gains sympathy for her motives not simply judgment for her actions. Ultimately, Joyce's model for the novel does find a resonance with Fielding's model. However, rather than distance from the characters by comparison with ancient forms, Joyce achieves identification through sympathy.

In his study of the folk humor of the Middle Ages and the Renaissance, Bahktin argues that laughter was not valued in official discourse. However, he also suggests that it received the primary role in unofficial forms of discourse that actually were the most prominent forms in the lives of "common" people. Specifically, he explores folk carnival humor in which all people participated. Within these ceremonies, the hero was both derided and elevated, people participated rather than simply observed events, the world was symbolically destroyed and then revived, and the clown was not seen as an eccentric or dolt but rather as a representative of a form of life simultaneously real and ideal. Essentially, the clown, or grotesque, embodies the contradictions of both the "base" and the "ideal," the "upward" and the "downward" but not in a way that is wholly derisive; rather, the clown represents the ideal fusion of these two halves of the human whole.

Bahktin's theories of the comic help illuminate many aspects of *Ulysses*. Specifically, Bloom, the hero of the text, is simultaneously derided and elevated. He is a cuckolded figure whose true fidelity serves as a model for husbandly behavior. He is mocked and considered an outsider because of his Jewish ancestry and birth, but his behavior marks him as the most wholly Christian figure in the book. He is rejected by Stephen but, at the same time, the narrative values Bloom's efforts to save Stephen from Nighttown and from hunger and loneliness. Further, the narrative style and naturalistic content of *Ulysses* cause the reader to be drawn imaginatively into the narrative. The technique does not so much relay events as it attempts to reproduce something of the experience of living through the events of the book within the reader's mind. Further, within the text, the world is symbolically destroyed and then revived. On the most basic level, the story begins in the morning, the narrative then passes through the day and into the night, and culminates in the early hours of the next morning. Further, the story begins with the destruction of Bloom's world. He wanders, exiled from his home and as an outsider. He journeys throughout Dublin seeking affirmation, which, for the most part, eludes him. Ultimately, however, after the hour in which Blazes meets Molly, Bloom's fortune begins to change. His world revives. He gains the upper hand in the bar. He receives solace from Gerty. Finally, he returns home, and although rejected by Stephen, he does achieve something of a communion with him. Finally, he returns to his bed next to his wife. In addition, Bloom embodies both the "higher" and the "lower" human processes. Allegorically, he integrates himself into the world through his waste and discharge. He ingests, digests, and gives back through bodily elimination the totality of experience (sensory perception, understanding, communion, and integration). Visually, he sees Gerty's beauty despite her handicap and ejaculates acknowledging her beauty and his response. He reads the story in the paper and then communes with the story by wiping himself with it. He urinates both into the sea and with Stephen, reinforcing his union with both. Further, he sits on the lemon soap he purchased for Molly while in the funeral car. He creates an aroma of sweet lemon within the car. Not surprisingly, many of Bahktin's theories of the comic find a resonance with the characters and events of *Ulysses*.

However, it would be a mistake to see *Ulysses* as simply a representation and endorsement of Bahktin's carnival. Incidents and characters within the context of *Ulysses* reveal weaknesses within the totality of Bahktin's argument. For example, Bahktin argues that the comic is separate from "official" discourse, and, although the comic parodies the official discourse, the "official" discourse can exist outside of the comic. Certainly, Joyce's text suggests that the comic is always present in official discourse. For example, the initial chapter parodies the Mass. Mulligan serves as priest coming to the alter of God and blessing an imaginary congregation. However, in an actual Mass, Bloom inserts a genuine comic element. His misinterpretation of signs and gestures reinforces his isolation. However, he also echoes popular misunderstanding. He thinks that INRI means "Iron nails went in" rather than meaning "Jesus of Nazareth, King of the Jews." Further, many at the library take Stephen's parody of literary criticism as "official" discourse. Further, Deasy's misinterpretation of history makes him a mock Nestor figure. However, his misreading actually exists as the "official" discourse of the most extreme Ulster Unionists. Essentially, Bahktin distinguishes between the carnival and the official, whereas Joyce makes no such distinction.

In *The Profane Book of Irish Comedy*, David Krause argues that comedy is like myth in that both restructure and release unconscious aspirations. In terms of comedy, repressed and suppressed desires and emotions find an outlet within the comic tradition. Krause goes on to argue that comic mythmaking finds its archetypes in the folk memory of the Irish people. Within this tradition of myth merged with the comic, Krause identifies a trait that he sees as characteristic of Irish comedy. Specifically, he argues that comedy is a type of liberation from colonial and colonizing powers, such as the Catholic church, English imperialism, devotion to commerce at the expense of native traditions, or narrowly defined cultural nationalism. Comedy, for Krause, is a type of liberation in which the power and the virulence of these forces is temporarily suspended within the laughter of the comic situation.

In terms of the Catholic church, Krause suggests that Irish characters must reject the guilt associated with renunciation as the means for eternal life. The comic situation temporarily suspends guilt and weakens the force of the church. Nowhere is this better illustrated than in Buck Mulligan's parody of the Catholic Mass at the beginning of *Ulysses*. Mulligan's character represents indulgence rather than renunciation. He is plump and graceless. He sets himself up as the priest speaking Latin and re-creating the sacred gestures and rituals, even performing a mock transubstantiation with the shaving cream and the shaving bowl. By aligning Mulligan with the Catholic church in comic parody, Joyce indicates that the church, like Mulligan, is not an agent of ritual but of indulgence. Within Mulligan's foibles and abuses, a reader can see the foibles and abuses of the church; he can discern hypocrisy. Humor frees the people, even temporarily, from Catholic guilt, demonstrating that guilt and renunciation are not the omnipotent forces that they pretend to be. Humor then functions as a type of counterritual in which the characters on stage or within a text temporarily free themselves from the consequences of sin.

*Ulysses'* comic elements both reinforce and contradict the more serious themes of the novel. The comedic elements present a counterreading of Stephen Dedalus, presenting him as a type of hero, devaluing the pretensions of many individuals and institutions in his society. Comedic themes also allow a sympathetic reading of Simon Dedalus while reinforcing the heroic nature of Leopold Bloom. Together with the more serious Odyssean themes, ecclesiastical issues, parent/child relationship, and political themes, the comedic elements present a text rich in its diversity of representations and characterizations, providing a depth of understanding.

## NOTES

1. The most comprehensive list of themes and motifs in *Ulysses* can be found in William Schutte's *Index of Recurrent Elements in James Joyce's* Ulysses (Carbondale: Southern Illinois University Press, 1982).

2. Of the many studies of Joyce and Homer, the most recent and important include Reed Way Dasenbrock, "Ulysses and Joyce's Discovery of Vico's 'True Homer,'" *Eire Ireland: A Journal of Irish Studies* 20:1 (Spring 1985): 96–108; Lillian Doherty, "Joyce's Penelope and Homer's: Feminist Reconsiderations," *Classical and Modern Literature: A Quarterly* 10:4 (Summer 1990): 343–349; Richard Ellmann, "Joyce and Homer," *Critical Inquiry: A Voice for Reasoned Inquiry into Significant Creations of the Human Spirit* 3 (1977): 567–582; Barbara Hardy, "Joyce and Homer: Seeing Double," *James Joyce: The Artist and the Labyrinth*, ed. Augustine Martin (London: Ryan, 1990); Margaret Mills Harper, "Fabric and Fame in the Odyssey and 'Penelope.'" *Gender in Joyce*, ed. Jolanta Wawrzycka and Marlena Corcoran (Gainesville: University Press of Florida, 1997); Margaret Mills Harper, "*Taken in Drapery*': Dressing the Narrative in the *Odyssey and Penelope*," *Molly Blooms: A Polylogue on "Penelope" and Cultural Studies*, ed. Richard Pearce (Madison: University of Wisconsin Press, 1994); Cheryl Herr, "'Penelope' as Period Piece," *Molly Blooms: A Polylogue on "Penelope" and Cultural Studies*, ed. Richard Pearce (Madison: University of Wisconsin Press, 1994); James McDonald and Norman McKendrick, "The Telemacheia in *The Odyssey* and *Ulysses*," *International Fiction Review* 16:1 (Winter 1989): 3–10; Donald Palumbo, "Death and Rebirth, Sexuality and Fantasy in Homer and Joyce," *Colby Library Quarterly* 20:2 (June 1984): 90–99; Shirley Clay Scott, "Man, Mind and Monster: Polyphemus from Homer through Joyce," *Classical and Modern Literature: A Quarterly* 16:1 (Fall 1995): 19–75; Fritz Senn, "Remodeling Homer," *Light Rays: James Joyce and Modernism*, ed. Ehrlich Heyward (New York: New Horizon, 1984), 70–92; Craig Stanley Smith, "Eros in the 'Nausicaa' of Homer and Joyce," *Researcher: An Interdisciplinary Journal*, 13:3 (Spring 1990): 53–61; and Constance Tagopoulos, "Joyce and Homer: Return, Disguise, and Recognition in 'Ithaca,' " *Joyce in Context*, ed. Vincent Cheng and Timothy Martin (Cambridge: Cambridge University Press, 1992).

3. James Joyce, *Letters*, vol. 1, ed. Stuart Gilbert and rev. by Richard Ellmann (New York: Viking Press, 1966), p. 145.

4. Joyce, *Letters*, vol. 3, p. 154.

5. Richard Ellmann, *James Joyce* (Oxford: Oxford University Press, 1982), p. 611.

6. For a fuller discussion of colonial themes in Joyce, see the following: Derek Attridge and Majorie Howes, eds., *Semicolonial Joyce* (Cambridge: Cambridge University Press, 2000); Susan Bazargan, "Mapping Gilbraltar: Colonialism, Time, and Narrative in 'Penelope,' " *Molly Blooms: A Polylogue on "Penelope" and Cultural Studies*, ed. Richard Pearce (Madison: University of Wisconsin Press, 1994); Vincent Cheng, *Joyce in Context* (Cambridge: Cambridge

University Press, 1997); Vincent Cheng, *Joyce, Race, and Empire* (Cambridge: Cambridge University Press, 1995); Seamus Deane, *Celtic Revivals: Essays in Modern Irish Literature, 1880–1980* (London: Faber and Faber, 1987); Hunt Hawkins, "Joyce as Colonial Writer," *College Language Association Journal* 35:4 (1992): 400–410; Mary King, "Hermeneutics of Suspicion: Nativism, Nationalism, and the Language Question in 'Oxen of the Sun,' " *James Joyce Quarterly* 35:2–3 (Winter-Spring 1998): 349–71; Carol Scholoss, "Molly's Resistance to the Union: Marriage and Colonialism in Dublin, 1904," *Molly Blooms: A Polylogue on "Penelope" and Cultural Studies* ed. Richard Pearce (Madison: University of Wisconsin Press, 1994); and Tracey Teets Schwarze, "Silencing Stephen: Colonial Pathologies in Victorian Dublin," *Twentieth Century Literature: A Scholarly and Critical Journal* 43:3 (Fall 1997): 243–263.

7. Declan Kiberd, *Inventing Ireland* (London: Jonathan Cape, 1995), p. 327.

8. For a detailed discussion of parent/child themes, consult Diana Arbin Ben Merre, "Bloom and Milly: A Portrait of the Father and the 'Jew's Daughter,' " *James Joyce Quarterly* 18:4 (Summer 1981): 439–444; Sheldon Brivic, "The Father in Joyce," *The Seventh of Joyce*, ed. Bernard Benstock (Bloomington: Indiana University Press, 1982); P.P.J. van Caspel, "Father and Son in the Lotus-Eaters Episode of Joyce's *Ulysses*," *English Studies: A Journal of English Language and Literature* 60 (1979): 593–602; John Dixon, "Ecce Puer, Ecce Pater: A Son's Recollections of an Unremembered Father," *James Joyce Quarterly* 29:3 (Spring 1992): 485–509; Robert Frumkin, "*Ulysses*: Stephen's Parable of the Plums," *Colby Quarterly* 28:1 (March 1992): 5–18; Cheryl Herr, "Fathers, Daughters, Anxiety, and Fiction," in *Discontented Discourses: Feminism/Textual Intervention/Psychoanalysis*, ed. Marleen Barr and Richard Feldstein (Urbana: University of Illinois Press, 1989), pp. 173–207; Theodore Holmes, "Bloom, the Father," *Sewanee Review* 79 (1971): 236–255; Colleen Lamos, "Cheating on the Father: Joyce and Gender Justice in *Ulysses*," in *Joyce in Context*, ed. Vincent Cheng (Cambridge: Cambridge University Press, 1992), pp. 91–99; Jean-Michel Rabate, "A Clown's Inquest into Paternity: Fathers, Dead or Alive in *Ulysses* and *Finnegans Wake*," in *The Fictional Father: Lacanian Readings of the Text*, ed. Robert Davis (Amherst: University of Massachusetts Press, 1981); Frances Restuccia, *Joyce and the Law of the Father* (New Haven: Yale University Press, 1989); and Christopher Roper, "God, Joyce, Derrida: The Father, the Son, and the Holy Deconstructed," *Inter-Action* 1 (1992): 132–145.

9. More detailed exploration of these themes can be found in the following: Barbara DiBernard, "Parallax as Parallel, Paradigm and Paradox in *Ulysses*," *Eire Ireland: A Journal of Irish Studies* 10:1 (1975): 69–84; Ursula Harrigan, "Ulysses as Missal: Another Structure in James Joyce's *Ulysses*," *Christianity and Literature* 33:4 (Summer 1984): 35–50; Barbara Stevens Heusel, "Parallax as a Metaphor for the Structure of *Ulysses*," *Studies in the Novel* 15:2 (Summer 1983): 135–146; Garry Leonard, "'A Little Trouble about Those White Corpuscles:' Mockery, Heresy, and the Transubstantiation of Masculinity in 'Telemachus.' " in Ulysses

*Engendered Perspectives: Eighteen New Essays on the Episodes*, ed. Kimberly Devlin (Columbia: University of South Carolina Press, 1999); Myra Glazer Schotz, "Parallax in *Ulysses*," *Dalhousie Review* 59 (1979): 487–499; Fritz Senn, "Met Whom What?" *James Joyce Quarterly* 30:1 (Fall 1992): 109–112; and J.W. Wheale, "More Metempsychosis? The Influence of Charles Dickens on James Joyce," *James Joyce Quarterly* 17 (1980): 439–444.

10. For a more detailed discussion of comedy in Joyce, consult Robert Bell, *Jocoserious Joyce: The Fate of Folly in Ulysses* (Ithaca, NY: Cornell University Press, 1991); Zack Bowen, *Ulysses as a Comic Novel* (Syracuse: Syracuse University Press, 1989); Edward Kopper, "*Ulysses* and James Joyce's Use of Comedy," *Mosaic: A Journal for the Interdisciplinary Study of Literature* 6:1 (1972): 45–55; and Joseph Voelker, "Clown Meets Cops: Comedy and Paranoia in Under the Volcano and *Ulysses*," in *Joyce/Lowry: Critical Perspectives*, ed. Patrick McCarthy and Paul Tiessen (Lexington; University Press of Kentucky, 1997).

# 6　Narrative Art

Joyce, in *Ulysses*, utilizes challenging literary forms in order to reveal subtleties of character and theme. Specifically, Joyce begins his text with conventional narrative techniques and with innovations carried forward from his earlier works, providing readers with, at least initially, a sense of narrative stability and continuity prior to his later, more innovative and unconventional narrative practices. However, Joyce also weaves into the first several chapters of his story narrative techniques, which he will expand on later in his book, that undermine traditional narrative representations. Indeed, Joyce's narrative techniques ultimately concede that literary forms cannot adequately express ideas in conventional ways. Rather, the expression of ideas and emotions requires a disruption of traditional literary forms. Joyce, raised in an environment that embraced oral culture and in a society that witnessed the near destruction of its native language, understood the essential fragility of language forms and written language's inadequate ability to express the totality of individual and cultural experiences. Joyce's characterization further emphasizes the themes of an inadequate written form of expression of the individual's experience and of a culture's vitality. In terms of characterization, Stephen Dedalus, the artist of Joyce's earlier work, cannot grow beyond his sense of desperation and loss. The heroes of the novel include a mediocre advertising salesman, who expresses himself sometimes in clichés and in received forms, and his wife, who reads romance novels. However, they have an ability to come to terms with their emotional and intellectual subtleties that eludes Stephen. Essentially, *Ulysses* stands as a work of artistry that advocates the disruption of conventional artistry as a form of expression and aspiration.

## LANGUAGE AND STYLE

*Ulysses* functions simultaneously as a work of supreme and intricately wrought literary craftsmanship and also as a work of literature that values the spoken word over the written word.[1] As Karen Lawrence observes in *The Odyssey of Style in* Ulysses, the text begins with a certainty in the literary form but then continues, with each subsequent chapter, to value more and more the spoken word.[2] Critics generally agree that the first eleven episodes of *Ulysses* follow a common literary pattern and that each subsequent chapter adopts a new pattern more radical than its predecessor and more reliant on the spoken or aural word than on the written word.[3] Indeed, the "Oxen of the Sun" episode parodies a history of the written word and the "Penelope" episode functions as a written version of thought and word without any traditional literary pretext.

Specifically, Lawrence explains the traditional narrative techniques that Joyce incorporated into his text, including familiar uses of character development and narrative style and voice. The novel begins by focusing on the voice of the artist, Stephen Dedalus. *Ulysses* essentially picks up where *A Portrait of the Artist* left off. Stephen considers writing and artistic creation. However, his efforts stall in the complexity of his thoughts and reflections that form the heart of the "Proteus" episode. Consequently, Joyce, even though he leads readers to an unexpected conclusion of the growing futility of Stephen's artistic aesthetic, leads readers to this point in a conventional way. Specifically, Lawrence cites Joyce's use of third-person narration, dialogue, and the dramatization of scenes as examples of his use of traditional novelistic elements. She further observes that Joyce continues his own narrative innovation, the stream-of-consciousness technique, but that the revolutionary nature of this device is now familiar to readers of Joyce's texts.[4] Moreover, Lawrence takes note of the other narrative conventions that Joyce carries forward, at least in the novel's first eleven episodes.

In particular, Lawrence notes that the narrative voice that carries the reader through *Ulysses'* early episodes functions simultaneously as a unique and autonomous narrator and as a voice that adapts to certain situations. Specifically, the narrative voice will often assume the diction and use of language particular to the character the narrator observes, melding the stable narrative voice into a new form that functions as a hybrid voice, enhancing characterization while advancing plot. The technique, once again, carries forward an innovation first advanced in Joyce's earlier work. A *Portrait of the Artist*, for example, makes use of what some critics call the "Uncle Charles principle," which notes that the narrative voice in Joyce's first published novel often adapts itself to the characters that are the focus of certain chapters or sections of chapters, including Uncle Charles. Essentially, Lawrence notes, these various narrative techniques, more or less revolutionary in practice, essentially carry forward narrative innovations or traditional narrative forms familiar to readers of Joyce's earlier works. They give the reader something to hold on to, a familiar and stabile ground that enables readers to adjust to Joyce's more radical narrative innovations. Moreover, the familiar narrative technique provides a sense of continuity between the early episodes of *Ulysses* and between *Ulysses* and Joyce's earlier works, including *A Portrait of the Artist as a Young Man* but also the more realistic narrative style of *Dubliners*.

Lawrence, however, also notes several narrative innovations that prepare the reader for the text's later, more radical, style, including the use of a comic narrative voice, the juxtaposition between Bloom and Stephen, narrative omissions, and simple language.[5] Lawrence notes that as the narrator adopts characteristics of Bloom's comic voice, the narrator lays the groundwork for the narrative insurrections of later chapters. Essentially, because comedy is an act of rebellion or at least inversion or reorganization, Bloom's narrator's comic voice and tone begin to unsettle the traditional narrative structures that stabilized the text. In addition, Lawrence observes, the juxtaposition between Stephen's rather esoteric thoughts and observations and Bloom's more mundane and libidinal preoccupations further emphasizes the comic nature of the text and stretches the range of the narrative voice. In order to carry forward the pattern of narration and adaptation, the narrator must not only change but change in a radical way to accommodate the diverse nature of Stephen's and Bloom's multifarious reflections and preoccupations. Therefore, the comedy inherent in Joyce's laying side by side such diverse characters calls into question the notion of narrative consistency between characters and chapters and of narrative reliability.

Moreover, Lawrence points to Hugh Kenner's critical observations regarding narrative omissions, articulated in "The Rhetoric of Silence," to buttress her arguments. Kenner notes that the narrator leaves out certain relatively vital details of the conversations between Molly and Bloom.[6] Specifically, Molly most assuredly tells Bloom at some point that Boylan will visit her at four in the afternoon. Bloom, for his part, tells Molly, at some point, that he plans to go to the theater that day and also that he will dine out that evening. However, the text does not record the conversation, even though Bloom later alludes to the details of such a dialogue with his wife. Kenner notes that the absence of a narrative record of the conversation serves two purposes.[7] On one level, the technique reveals much about Bloom's character. The narrator may have suppressed the telling of the scene because it must have been painful for Bloom to make arrangements for his wife's infidelity. The narrator, assuming characteristics of Bloom, then also represses a painful incident. The repression further reveals elements of Bloom's nature regarding his wife's dalliance with Boylan; the incident is painful enough to necessitate repression and forgetfulness. However, as Lawrence and Kenner also note, the narrative omission raises questions about narrative fidelity. What else are readers not hearing? Can readers trust the narrator? What components of the story remain incomplete or even distorted as a consequence of narrative adaptation to individual characters? Reinforcing the idea of narrative fragility, Lawrence also points to the simple language used to begin the text.[8] Joyce uses basic structures and elemental sentence patterns to start his story. On one level, the beginning parallels the opening of A *Portrait*, in which readers see the world of the novel through a child's eyes. However, Lawrence observes the simple structures also undermine traditional forms of written expression, laying the framework for later more obvious disruptions of conventional modes of writing. Indeed, even as Lawrence notes the intricate literary techniques that emphasize Joyce's mastery of the craft of writing, she points to several other literary devices that undermine the integrity of literary craftsmanship and the stability of traditional written forms of expression.

Declan Kiberd, in his editor's introduction to *Ulysses*, focuses, in large part, on the reasons behind Joyce's revolutionary techniques while exploring some additional linguistic and stylistic forms in the text.[9] Specifically, Kiberd considers Joyce's dissatisfaction with English-language forms and examines his dissatisfaction as it manifests itself in terms of the characters' abilities of articulation and self-expression, in terms of Joyce's writing as the manifestation of Irish history and culture, and in terms of literary representation in the context of scientific advancement. Specifically, Kiberd cites Joyce's use of a pastiche of styles as evidence of his dissatisfaction with any single form. Moreover, Kiberd argues that *Ulysses'* technique culminates in the end of literary technique; Molly's monologue escapes from the strictures of traditional literary representation. Kiberd goes on to attribute Joyce's dissatisfaction with traditional modes of written English to his experiences as a young man growing up in Ireland. Not only did Joyce experience a largely oral literary and cultural tradition, he also inherited a community whose language disappeared in favor of English in the previous century. However, Joyce's dissatisfaction with written forms does not mean that he shared the aspirations of the Irish-language revivalists, who sought a pure Irish culture in reclaiming the Irish language. On the contrary, Kiberd argues, Joyce uses Irish-language elements in the text precisely to demonstrate the inadequacy of all written forms. The islandwide loss of Irish as a language of everyday commerce and culture, with some notable exceptions, simply reinforced Joyce's understanding of the fragility of language. Indeed, Kiberd goes on to note that the Irish characters in *Ulysses* speak fluently, suggesting that the problems associated with expression do not stem from English rather than Irish. Rather, the problem lies in forms of expression themselves. For as fluent as many of these characters are, they remain, Kiberd notes, inarticulate. The characters who do manage to articulate their ideas clearly, and Kiberd concedes that *Ulysses* does contain numerous characters that do articulate ideas in a clear way, do not become articulate because of their grasp of English or Irish. Rather, articulation, Kiberd suggests, comes with the loss of feeling. Therefore, to extend the logic of Kiberd's argument, if Joyce's narrative were conventionally articulate, then his text would have no feeling. Moreover, emotional integrity or wholeness cannot be articulated in any rational way.

Indeed, Kiberd reads *Ulysses*, in part, as the expression of concession. Literary form cannot master rational thought in the same way that scientific knowledge and technical innovation can master the rational and be understood through empirical means. Kiberd proceeds to point out that scientific enquiry and technical innovation marked, in societal terms, the progress of civilization for many in the nineteenth and twentieth centuries. Joyce's text, then, is literature's answer to that measure of progress. Literature and art, according to Kiberd's reading of *Ulysses*, cannot articulate the rational. Indeed, culture through art articulates something quite different from the rational and the empirical. It articulates the inner thoughts, feelings, and aspirations of individuals and communities. Characters may talk around each other. They may not be able to use language to express to one another the full measure of their thoughts and feelings. Bloom never tells Molly that he forgives her. Molly never speaks to Bloom. She speaks to his sleeping form. However, *Ulysses* proves that the inner consciousness of the individual does exist and is vital precisely because the text communicates so much of the inner nature of individuals despite the fragile and limited nature of communication. Essentially, the literary nature of *Ulysses*, in its destruction of conventional and more naturalistic forms of expression, reveals that without these traditional modes of communication something indeed exists. In other words, the sign may be an inadequate expression of the signified, but the signified reveals itself despite the limited sign.

## MAJOR CHARACTERS

*Ulysses* primarily focuses on the lives of three major characters: Stephen Dedalus, Leopold Bloom, and Molly Bloom. Other chapters within this study concentrate on Stephen Dedalus and Leopold Bloom. Consequently, the current chapter explores them only in brief detail, devoting most of the discussion to Molly Bloom.

As *Ulysses* opens, Stephen Dedalus, now twenty-two years old, has fulfilled little of the personal and artistic ambitions that surrounded his character in A *Portrait of the Artist as a Young Man.* He returned from Paris, receiving notice of his mother's imminent death, without producing the major work of art he thought would come of his journey abroad. Moreover, he manifests, at the beginning of *Ulysses* and throughout the text, symptoms consistent with depression. He does not wash. He eats and sleeps little. He cannot focus on his work. He indulges in drinking, temporarily satisfying his desire for forgetfulness but ultimately revealing bitterness and disgust with his life and family. Indeed, he remains emotionally isolated from his father, physically separated from his siblings, and distant from people he meets in the novel. He makes himself vulnerable to the attacks of his roommates and rejects the well-intentioned affections of Leopold Bloom by modeling the worst prejudices of his former employer, Mr. Deasy, and the worst behavior of his roommates.

In terms of Stephen's relationship to art and to his self-image as artist/creator, his aesthetic has grown from the objective relationship between artist and the product of artistic labor articulated in A *Portrait* to a highly subjective model. Stephen offers a reading of Hamlet that relies heavily on biographic details and psychological complexities. However, Stephen also reveals that he does not fully believe his own theories, and, indeed, he wallows in intellectual complexities and aesthetic theories at the expense of his own artistic production and at the expense of his relationship to real people. He so imagines the world around him that, in the third episode, he misreads the activities and professions of individuals on the beach and imagines rather than interacts with his mother's family.

Stephen's aesthetic theories and his sense of loss, isolation, and depression relate directly to his sense of rootlessness. His views his father with scorn, seeing in his laziness the cause of his wife's early death and his family's poverty. Critics observe that the inept father figure is consistent with Irish writing throughout the twentieth century,[10] ranging from Synge's creation of a brutish father in *The Playboy of the Western World* to Frank McCourt's representation of the drunken and lazy father in *Angela's Ashes*. Critics relate the inept father to Ireland's situation under colonial rule, arguing that the impotent colonized father relates directly to the powerless predicament of a colonized people. In addition, Stephen's mother's long-suffering relationship with her husband and her early death can also be related to Ireland's colonial circumstances. In the tradition of the aisling,[11] Stephen watches as a woman wastes away because of deprived and desperate circumstances. Stephen, like many Irish patriots and literary figures, fled Ireland to discover freedom and the opportunity for self-expression. However, the desperateness of his familial circumstances forces Stephen's return, and he becomes trapped by those same forces he sought to escape. As *Ulysses* comes to an end, Stephen remains trapped within the limited circumstances of his environment, rejecting the opportunities offered by Bloom for escape and independent development.

Leopold Bloom, on the other hand, escapes from similarly limiting circumstances, using his imagination and a natural optimism to free himself from depression and isolation. Bloom too is beset by images of a failed father who committed suicide and died owing money as a consequence of failed business ventures. Moreover, the tragic death of his son shakes Bloom's own sense of paternity and masculinity. Further, most of the characters in the novel either openly and cruelly mock Bloom, such as Stephen and the citizen, or treat him only with polite deference. Bloom has few intimates. In addition, the female figure in his life torments him with an infidelity with his business and social rival. In business, Bloom also cannot find complete success. He, despite devoting hours to researching an advertisement and canvassing for its sale, does not fully consummate the business deal. Nor does Bloom fully consummate his sexual relationships. He spends time watching the bottoms of statues and following the figures of passing women on the street. He does actively indulge in a masturbatory sexual relationship with a woman on the beach, in which she participates. However, he does not directly communicate with her nor does he achieve any lasting contact. In addition, Bloom's status as the descendent of immigrants and his Jewish heritage make him vulnerable to the ridicule and disdain of many throughout the novel. His lack of knowledge of basic Catholic traditions and practices also marks him as an outsider. Nevertheless, Bloom, by the end of the novel, manages to avoid despair.

However, *Ulysses* offers clues that Bloom's optimism only occurs at the novel's conclusion. He, after all, has failed to engage in fully integrated sexual activity since the death of his son. Moreover, the image of a suicidal father also haunts him years after his father's death. Therefore, *Ulysses* details Bloom's recovery from depression and despair. Bloom finds comfort in small acts of kindness and in human interaction. He imaginatively transforms his somewhat limiting experiences by accentuating their positive content. He creates a meaningful relationship with the girl on the beach. He assumes that his acquaintances do not fully intend to harm him. Moreover, he assumes the best about them. In addition, he asserts his own theories of love and deference in the face of violent opposition. He also fashions his own aesthetic, indulging in fantasies of the East and of sensual pleasure. His fantasies value his "Oriental" heritage in the face of prejudice and hatred. However, he recognizes the limits of his created impressions of the East, consequently achieving the benefit of imaginative escape along with the realistic knowledge of the limits of intellectual and imaginative fancy. Further, in the psychologically complex fifteenth episode, he comes to terms with his father's death, his son's death, and his wife's infidelity. He accepts his daughter as his heir, makes himself emotionally vulnerable to Stephen, confidently asserts his (Bloom's) presence in his relationship with his wife, and processes many of his own personal and psychological demons. Bloom, as he approaches middle age (he is thirty-eight at the novel's outset), finds himself coming to terms with the difficult circumstances of his youth and early adulthood.

Molly Bloom's character occupies relatively little of the narrative.[12] She appears in the fourth episode, makes a cameo appearance in another episode, and finally emerges as a clearly defined figure only in the final episode. However, her behavior and faithfulness to her husband become a preoccupation of his thoughts throughout the day. Essentially, even though she seems to occupy only the margins of the text, she is really central to the narrative. Indeed, in more than this way, Molly is a marginalized figure made central. She is the daughter of a British soldier, raised in a colonial outpost, who lives in the heart of the Irish capital. She is also a woman with relatively few career options and limited educational possibilities who manages to help support herself, at least partially, through her singing and also actively pursues imaginative escapes through literature, albeit popular and sexually charged romance novels. Moreover, many characters in the text notice only her physical and sexual attributes and potential. However, she manages to not limit her own self-perceptions; she sees herself as more than a sensual, pleasure-giving machine.

On a symbolic level, she values the former periphery culture without losing her essential identity. However, she, because her monologue operates as private revelation, does not "transform" the dominant society. Specifically, the "Penelope" episode takes a reader through both an emotional and an intellectual series of revelations in which Molly in turn comes to terms with a larger community of women, her personal history, and a sense of communion with the sublime that leads her to a greater understanding not only of the oppressions that limit the intellectual and emotional development of herself but of all women. Molly, as critics have suggested, is a contradictory figure. However, she is contradictory not because she is feminine or marginal and not because Joyce attempts to "moralize" about loose women.[13] Molly is contradictory because she represents a transition from oppressive and limiting discourse to a more liberated discourse. She articulates the principles of liberation but does not yet act on them.

In the course of her monologue, Molly Bloom details the story of a woman who "poisoned her husband" because she was "in love with some other man" (613).[14] Initially, Molly responds with revulsion seeing the murderess, a Mrs. Maybrick, as "the downright villain" (613). Certainly, this is the way Molly is supposed to respond if she is to fulfill the expectations of Dublin's middle-class community. Specifically, that stratum of society would have seen that a woman, by killing her husband, destroys not only an individual's life but also strikes out against the institution of marriage and, consequently, challenges one of the most fundamental organizational structures of society and consequently, threatens the very stability of the society itself. Marital traditions, cultivated in turn-of-the-century Ireland by the values of not only the Catholic church but also of Victorian morality, posit the ideal union of a man and a woman, suggest a power dynamic within a marriage that restricts women to roles of subservience and submission to the male will. Certainly, Joyce's choice of the name "Mrs Maybrick" suggests both the romanticized image of the pure May bride and a debilitating solidity that hangs "like a brick" around the neck. However, Molly, defying the traditional societal convention, soon develops a sense of empathy for Mrs. Maybrick, refusing to dissolve the bonds of identification between herself and another woman and refusing to link her repulsion for murder with a repulsion for the woman who committed the murder. Consequently, Molly implicitly rejects both the traditions of Victorian morality and the teachings of the church. Further, the manner of identification explicitly seeks to justify Mrs. Maybrick's actions while simultaneously deriding men and, by connection, the chain of revulsion that seeks to encourage Molly to reject any sense of community with women who, like Mrs.

Maybrick, find themselves trapped in a not entirely fulfilling union. Molly admits that

> of course some men can be dreadfully aggravating drive you mad and always the worst word in the world what do they ask us to marry them for if were so bad as all that comes to yes because they cant get on without us white Arsenic she put in his tea off flypaper wasnt it . . . she must have been madly in love with the other fellow to run the chance of being hanged. (613)

Molly transfers the repulsion she initially felt for the act into repulsion for men who can "drive you mad," drive you to a state where you have no choice but to kill. Molly universalizes Mrs. Maybrick's plight by referring to all women in marriage as "us," unites in a common victimhood all women who suffer "the worst word" at the hands of their mates. Further, Molly empowers women by admitting that "they [men] cannot get along without us." In short, Molly forms an emotional bond with Mrs. Maybrick, empathizes with and universalizes her plight. Molly perceives the connection between one woman's marriage and the entirety of male/female relations. In short, Molly is able to make the marginalized place central in her imagination, is able to move beyond condemnation to emotional identification. However, Molly's power to project this central vision of women's worth and power is necessarily limited. Her monologue is a monologue after all. She does not communicate her ideas to others and, consequently, help to transform society. However, she does experience a personal sense of empowerment, is able to escape, however temporarily, from the bonds of her marriage, not through murder but through infidelity. It is true that hers is a private insurgence, but it does grant, at the very least, a personal sense of liberation that can perceive the like oppression of all married women, can form an imaginative emotional bond with them, and make central, in a very personal way, the previously marginalized sense of women's experience.

Molly moves from a sense of emotional community with women to a sense of personal emotional rehabilitation and onto an experience of revelation concerning the underlying violence present in some male/female interactions. She recalls the history of her passionate involvement with men and metaphorically and rhetorically links that continuity to violence revealing, on an imaginative level, the same sense of emotional identification with herself that she achieved with Mrs. Maybrick and the community of married women. However, just as Molly begins her section of the monologue devoted to Mrs. Maybrick by parroting societal repulsion against the

act of murder, Molly reinforces the conventional stereotype of the emotional female when contemplating her younger self: "at last he made me cry
of course a woman is so sensitive about everything I was fuming with myself
after for giving in only for I knew he was gone on me and the first socialist
he said He was he annoyed me so much I counldnt put him into a temper"
(612). Molly uses the expression "of course" to describe her "sensitive" response, characterizes that type of reaction as typical of "a woman." In addition, Molly echoes another stereotypical characterization of women and
passionate love. Significantly, the romantic sentiment she inspires is
linked to madness—"he was gone on me." The words recall both insanity
and absence, imply love lost as soon as won, and suggest that she causes her
partners madness. Both representations of women as a source of overly
emotional response and as a catalyst for insanity fit the caricature of the
feminine perpetuated by turn-of-the-century popular novels, the same
novels Leopold brings home to his wife. However, Molly's recollections
also subvert the caricature.

> I put him off letting on I was in a temper with my hands and arms full
> of pasty flour in any case I let out too much the night before talking of
> dreams so I didnt want to let him know more than was good for him
> she used to be always embracing me . . . afterwards though she didnt
> like it so much the day I was in fits of laughing with giggles I couldnt
> stop about all my hairpins falling out one after another with the mass
> of hair I has youre always in great humour she said yes because it
> grigged her because she knew what it meant. (612)

A cursory review of these lines suggests that Molly once again places herself
in a traditional role of womanhood—"my hands and arms full of pasty
flour" and her "hairpins [are] falling out." However, a rehabilitation of her
self in her memory, the sense of liberation, is present. Molly chooses to remember not simply details that summon a two-dimensional image of her
younger self but rather portray an individual who is "always in great hu-
mour" because of her sexual experiences. Molly Bloom was not embarrassed or hesitant regarding her physical interaction with men. On the
contrary, she allows her sense of freedom to permeate her emotional being,
to overflow in confident and all-encompassing giggles that extend from
herself to consume the impressions of those who surround her.

Subsequently, Molly remembers "the brutes of men shouting bravo toro
sure the women were as bad in their nice white mantillas ripping all the
whole insides out of those poor horses I never heard of such a thing in all my

life" (622). Significantly, Molly's private recollection also links romantic memories to violence. No longer is amorous attention associated with a young girl's giggling fits. Rather, Molly places men and women in the context of a bullfight associating interaction between the sexes with violent ritual. Both groups enjoy the spectacle, are mesmerized by it. Further, Molly's rather vivid description juxtaposing the "nice white mantillas" with the "ripping all the whole insides out of those poor horses" comes directly after her description of women being "as bad" as the men. It is as if the women's elaborate hats and the men's cheers mutilate the horses. Through imaginative association, Molly recognizes the violence inherent in certain societal conventions associated with romantic interaction. Her memories liberate her consciousness from a caricature of male-female interaction, demonstrate her ability to recognize the subtleties that exist beyond stereotypical representations. However, as is the case with Molly's sense of community with Mrs. Maybrick and women in marriage, Molly's sense of personal emotional revelation remains personal, with the exception of her ebullient laughter. It is not likely that the recovery of her personal memories, even in such detail, will transform Dublin society. However, she does achieve a significant revelation, does establish a continuity of liberation tracing itself from her youth in Gibraltar into her contemporary recollection. It is true that it remains a personal revelation, but it is a revelation nonetheless.

The monologue, in addition to establishing an empathetic bond with an ostracized woman and a sense of personal emotional reclamation and revelation, expresses an intimation of communion with some sublime or even overtly religious celestial force. Once again, Molly initially focuses on a rather conventional, almost caricature, portrayal. In this case, it is a representation of divine transcendence. She recalls that "till that thunder woke me up God be merciful to us I thought the heavens were coming down about us to punish us when I blessed myself and said a Hail Mary like those awful thunderbolts in Gibraltar as if the world was coming to an end" (611). The selection associates thunder with childhood images of retribution for perceived sin; associates the sign of the cross and a prayer to the blessed virgin with charms designed to ward off punishment, almost certainly for sexual transgression; and associates "the heavens" with anger, omnipotent control of nature, and seemingly capricious appeasement. The scene recalls Stephen Dedalus's images of hell and, certainly, the type of strict Catholic upbringing reflected in Molly's representations permeates turn-of-the-century Irish culture. However, Molly also communicates sublime sensations associated with the source of sacred penalty—sexuality.

Molly declares that she "liked the way he made love then he knew the way to take a woman when he sent me the 8 big poppies because mine was the 8th then I wrote the night he kissed my heart at Dolphins barn I couldnt describe it simply it makes you feel like nothing on earth" (615). Molly draws a picture of ritualized courtship. The poppies, a symbol of death, and the dolphin, a symbol of sexuality, provide the setting for intimate physical contact, provide the setting for sensation "like nothing on earth." Sexuality becomes a method to escape transience, a pathway to a secular religious association with forces that can elevate the human experience.

In a later section of the monologue, Molly provides a litany of earthly pleasures, allegorically associated with sexuality and physical delight, and establishes an association between these forces and the Christian God. She submits "that would do your heart good to see rivers and lakes and flowers all sorts of shapes and smells and colours springing up even out of the ditches primroses and violets nature it is as for them saying theres no God I wouldnt give a snap of my two fingers for all there learning" (643). The reproductive power of nature manifest in water alternatively running and still, certainly suggesting male and female sexuality, combines with images of flowers and colors and "all sorts" of "shapes and smells," recalling not only the natural world but also a very human experience of physical intimacy, to create an impression of the earth alive with physical ebullience, alive with the presence of a celestial power that, like Molly's earlier sensation, can transcend the forces of mortality. Significantly, the force does not carry the associations of a negative Catholic God, but Molly does unquestionably associate these images and impressions with a "God" whom intellectuals reject. Molly suggests that intellectual scepticism separates humanity from the true divine force, even if that divinity is represented by organized religion, the most likely object of scholastic rejection. Moreover, Molly declares that she "wouldnt give a snap of my two fingers for all there learning" reaffirming her personal experience with the divine and rejecting the interpretation offered by patriarchal philosophy. Certainly, Molly liberates herself from restrictive associations that seek to purge the sublime from the world and that also seek to discredit an emotional response to experience. However, once again, personal liberation does not necessarily translate into public transformation. Molly does assert the value of her individual consciousness and its emotional experience with women, her personal history, and heavenly powers. However, in the end, it remains a personal revelation.

Significantly, Molly's reflections, although they value the emotional, are not exclusively emotional. She does display considerable intellectual powers. In the initial stages of her monologue—just as in the emotional scenes in which she established a sense of community, continuity, and communion with the sublime only after an instinctual endorsement of tradition and traditionally oppressive societal standards—Molly cloaks a scepticism about a community of women, formed only in opposition to men, in an impulse of jealousy. She considers an old rival and "wonder[s] what shes got like now after living with that dotty husband of hers she had her face beginning to look drawn and run down the last time I saw her she must have been just after a row with him" (613). Certainly, Molly's remarks fit within the conventional standard of women deprecating one another privately, and in clearly physical terms, because of a deeply felt sense of rivalry. By instinctually attacking her acquaintance in terms of her less than ideal physical appearance, Molly lends value to the physical, sees it as a measure, perhaps the most important measure, of a woman's worth and meaning. Sexuality, then, and its power to enrapture men, becomes the means through which women become rivals, through which they rupture a sense of community. However, in the very next line of her monologue, Molly sarcastically represents her rival's impulse to practice yet another traditionally stereotypical view of women—their supposed impulse to form a sense of community only in opposition to men. Molly acknowledges that she "saw on the moment she [her former rival] was edging to draw down a conversation about husbands and talk about him to run him down" (613). Significantly, Molly refers to her rival's attempt as an effort to "draw down a conversation," to degrade discourse, to bring it to a lesser level. Molly also characterizes her rival's efforts as "a conversation about husbands," not simply one particular husband. By generalizing the discussion, Molly's rival releases herself from responsibility for her condition, yields power to men in that she wants to establish the notion that all "husbands" behave this way, that women cannot escape an oppressive relationship. Later in her monologue, Molly too will characterize male behavior, but not in universal terms. She reflects that "if I only could remember the 1 half of the things and write a book out of it the works of Master Poldy yes and its so much smoother the skin much an hour he was at them Im sure by the clock like some kind of a big infant I had at me they want everything in their mouth all the pleasure those men get out of a woman" (621). Here, Molly refers to "those men," and only to those men who behave like "a big infant" and constantly want for oral gratification. Her sarcasm characterizes a certain class of men as ridiculous, represents their impulses as absurd. In addition, her characterization follows an expressed desire to "write a book" detailing her observations. Literally, she empowers herself, reaffirms her intellectual capabilities, not in opposition to all men, not in a desire to denigrate all "husbands" but in an assertion that certain behavior is inappropriate and absurd. Significantly, as the monologue progresses, Molly articulates her desire that she would "love to have a long talk with an intelligent well educated person" (641). Unlike her emotional desire to establish a community only among women, her rational impulse is to form a community regardless of gender identification. In doing so, she values her intellect, values her ability to satisfy someone regardless of the sexual or emotional satisfaction she might grant. Like her personal emotional sense of community with women, Molly's assertion of her intellectual capabilities and her desire to communicate on a nonphysical level has its limits. She does not yet communicate her ideas to another. However, at the end of her monologue, she is able to understand that she needs more than sexual or sentimental contact with the world. She wants a reflective, rational community with another, needs such contact to discover fulfillment.

In addition to her desire to establish a more intellectual relationship with someone, Molly proceeds to reflect on her past, her personal sense of continuity, and through sarcasm, to reclaim herself. She intellectually asserts dominance over the men whom she has sexually engaged. Unlike her emotional reclamation of her past, Molly does not simply reject the negative aspects of male behavior. Rather, she declares her consciousness, projects her rational will into her past. In the initial stages of her monologue, Molly focuses on her most recent sexual encounter. Perhaps a bit disturbed by the brazen manner Blazes left her room, with a pat on her backside, she describes his sexual organ as "that tremendous big red brute of a thing he has I thought the vein or whatever the dickens they call it was going to burst through his nose" (611). She rhetorically separates his penis from his body. She does not call his penis, his penis. Rather, it is something he owns, a possession or tool; it is not part of his being, his consciousness. In doing so, she not only empowers herself through ridicule—certainly, a man who takes such seeming pride in his sexual ability as Blazes does would want a more admiring characterization of his sexual organ—she recognizes that her lover's sexuality *is* at a part removed from his consciousness, that his penis *is* simply a tool, that the encounter for him *is* simply an opportunity to exercise not his sexuality, which would imply an emotional as well as a physical engagement, but his sexual organ. She intellectually regains control over the encounter, blithely dismissing him in the same manner, but with more imaginative a gesture than he earlier used to dismiss her. Shortly after her characterization of her "well-endowed" lover, Molly imaginatively recalls her early experiences with sexuality, in its fully integrated emotional and intellectual state. She remembers that

> he used to be a bit on the jealous side whenever he asked who are you going to and I said over to Floey and he made me the present of lord Byrons poems and the three pairs of gloves so that finished that . . . I know plenty of ways ask him to tuck down the collar of my blouse or touch him with my veil and gloves on going out 1 kiss then would send them all spinning. (612)

Unlike her most recent encounter, Molly controlled the entire dynamic of an earlier involvement. Rather than succumb to a "tremendous big red brute of a thing," she realizes that her potential lover is "a bit on the jealous side." Consequently, she manipulates him, compels him to give her not his sexual organ but poetry and gloves. Each gift acknowledges a different component of Molly's identity. The gloves complement her physical being with subtlety and grace. The poetry acknowledges an intellectual and emotional component to her personality. Further, she, unlike Blazes, realizes the value of simple gestures of intimacy rather than simply an animalistic exchange of fluids. She allowed her potential lover to "tuck down the coller" of her "blouse," or she would give him "1" kiss and flirt with him. She realizes that sexuality involves a slow process, a building. Her intellectual reclamation of her past, coming as it does so soon after her encounter with Blazes, clearly offers her an imaginative alternative to her most recent lover, offers an image of subtlety and grace to imaginatively regenerate her sexuality. She explores her recollection to empower herself, to once again give herself a sense of control. Just as in her emotional reclamation of continuity with her personal past, Molly, in an intellectual and imaginative reclamation, establishes a continuity of liberation tracing itself from her youth in Gibraltar into her contemporary experiences. Once again, her memory is a personal revelation not likely to deliver an entire community from slavery from sexual and intellectual bias. However, Molly is able to rehabilitate her personal self-image, initially through sarcasm, a practice she will use again and again to describe many men, even Bloom: "Id rather die 20 times over than marry another of their sex of course hed never find another woman like me to put up with him the way I do" (613). Ultimately, Molly moves beyond ridicule to personal intellectual sanction, reclaims her past to establish an imaginative continuity with her sexuality.

Significantly, Molly does not simply use sarcasm to regain a sense of intellectual and emotional continuity with herself. In many ways, the device becomes her expression of a personal creativity, an imaginative contact with some sublime force. In addition, Molly demonstrates considerable intellectual skills in fashioning a relationship with creative expression, either directly through sarcasm or indirectly through another's creative talents. Unlike her emotional contact with the divine, Molly, in her intellectual expression of some celestial force, relies less on received images of the divinity—traditional religious characterizations—and more on contemporary human creative impulses that seek to discover the sublime within each individual. Initially, she mixes outright insults with more clever expressions of disdain. Referring to her most recent lover, she reflects that "thats no way for him has he no manners nor no refinement nor no nothing in his nature slapping us behind like that on my bottom because I didnt call him Hugh the ignoramus that doesnt know poetry from a cabbage thats what you get for not keeping them in their proper place" (638). Importantly, she not only completely disassociates his sexual being from his consciousness, she reveals that he has no consciousness; he has "no manners nor no refinement nor no nothing." He is a nothing without his sexual organ. Subsequently, Molly reinforces her characterization by exclaiming that he has no knowledge of poetry revealing the man's faults in a creative way, certainly,—"Hugh the ignoramus that doesnt know poetry from a cabbage"—but she also reveals that she values poetry and artistic expression. At this point in her monologue, she does not create any formal artistic representation, but she does, most certainly, create portions and brief expressions of formal creative worth. However, as the monologue progresses, her sarcasm combines with a more traditional poetic description not only lending valuable insight into her personal experience with art and formal representations but also revealing subtle truths and insights into "accepted" forms. She observes that men are

> like that Indian god he took me to show one wet Sunday in the museum in Kildare street all yellow in a pinafore lying on his side on his hand with his ten toes sticking out that he said was a bigger religion than the jews and Our Lords both put together all over Asia imitating him as hes always imitating everybody I suppose he used to sleep at the foot of the bed too hes big square feet up in his wifes mouth. (634–35)

She humanizes both religious expression and artistic devotion. She reveals a truly natural component to the Indian Buddha, sees him as a man and not as simply a god. Further, she values the feminine partner of this particular celestial representation, tells his story, as it were, from her perspective, feminizes the representation by personally identifying herself with the Buddha's partner. Although her characterization remains quite powerful, it is also a clear expression of her personal need for empathy. Obviously, she feels neglected; she initially sees herself as the sexual partner of the Buddha, significantly not as an equal partner, but as one whose husband fixates on a limited physical aspect of her body to satiate his sexual needs. She gets his feet in her mouth and derives little intimacy from the experience, whereas he becomes physically stimulated by her ass. The true limits of her contact with formal artistry and her contact with men become clear after studying her fantasy involving Stephen. She reflects that she "can teach him the other part Ill make him feel all over him till he half faints under me then hell write about me lover and mistress publicly too with our 2 photographs in all the papers when he becomes famous O but then what am I going to do about him though" (638).

Although it is true that she reverses the traditional muse relationship from passive to active, puns hell empowering herself by suggesting immortality rather than damnation for sexual promiscuity, reverses the inevitable scandal to her advantage, and, finally, comes back to earth allowing her fantasy to be her artistic creation, she remains essentially at a part removed from direct artistic expression. Her physical form remains her primary method of interaction between herself and men, her primary method of creative endeavor. Certainly, Molly's experience with imaginative expression is limited. She yearns for a creative escape from transience. However, she sees her greatest opportunity within the creative world of another. She can never really come to terms with her own expression, never really values her own considerable creative gifts. Clearly, sarcasm is an articulation of frustration, of bitterness. In many ways, Molly expresses the fate of women in turn-of-the-century Ireland; thwarted by convention and unable to communicate their own creative drives, they yield their impulses to another. However, Molly's experience through Stephen is, in a very limited sense, a liberation. She realizes that her physical pleasure must have an intellectual component, that her infidelity served to humiliate her and restrict her growth because she became involved with a partner, who, like Bloom, although an exaggeration of Bloom, values her most for the sexual pleasure she can give. Again, she will not transform the world, and her expression is limited; however, her revelation is an important gesture to herself and her abilities.

## MINOR CHARACTERS

*Ulysses* focuses attention on numerous minor characters who impact the lives of the novel's three major characters. Molly's father never actually appears in the text, but both Molly and Bloom refer to him frequently. He was a major, or sergeant-major in the British army, stationed in Gibraltar when Molly was born. Joyce fictionalized his military exploits, placing him at Rourke's Drift during the Zulu Wars. He also has many similarities with the stage Irish caricature; he was hard drinking, had a temper, and smoked. Blazes Boylan also impacts Molly's life. They engage in sexual intercourse in the afternoon. Boylan promotes singers and boxers, has organized a concert tour in which Molly is a featured participant, and does some successful advertising work. He also fancies himself a ladies' man, is a flashy dresser, and taps Molly on the backside after their encounter.

Various members of Stephen's family either make an appearance or figure prominently in his thoughts. Specifically, his mother, May Dedalus, haunts his thoughts, coming before him as a corpse. Stephen returned from Paris, hearing news of her imminent death, but refused to pray at her bedside. She died about eight or so months prior to the start of the novel. Stephen has not bathed since her death. Stephen's father, Simon Dedalus, entertains other characters throughout the text with his sense of humor and fine singing voice but neglects his family. He brings in little or no money and drinks to excess. Three of Stephen's sisters also appear in the text: Boody, Dilly, and Maggy. Boody mocks her father's inability to provide for his family. Maggy tries to sell her brother's books to pay for food, and Dilly buys a French primer in an attempt to educate herself.

A number of Stephen's father or mentor figures also make appearances. Garrett Deasy, who runs the school in Dalkey, offers Stephen advice, instructing him in anti-Semitism and stinginess. Deasy is a Presbyterian from Ulster. Father John Conmee, S.J., the former rector at Clongowes and the Jesuit who arranged for Stephen's scholarship at Belvedere, also appears but in a much more sympathetic light than does Deasy or Simon Dedalus. Readers meet him as he prays his office and wanders across Dublin on an errand of mercy. Stephen also thinks about his relationship with Kevin Egan, an exiled Irish patriot he met in Paris. Stephen meets with the derision of various members of Dublin's literary establishment, including John Eglinton, an essayist, and George Russell, the poet and mystical philosopher.

Stephen's roommates in the Martello tower are Buck Mulligan and Haines. Mulligan is a medical student who mocks Stephen and Bloom during the course of their day. Mulligan also receives the attention of members of the literary establishment. Haines is an Oxford research student studying the Irish people and the Irish language. He has bad dreams and treats Stephen and others in a patronizing manner.

The characters that have the most impact on Bloom's day include various female figures. Bloom often considers his daughter, Milly. She is fifteen years old and is apparently attractive, if a bit heavy. Martha Clifford functions as Bloom's paramour by correspondence. She writes him mildly suggestive letters and functions as the object of his fantasies. Gerty MacDowell functions as a more immediate object of sexual attraction for Bloom. He considers her as she sits on the shore playing with a friend's children and watching fireworks. She is physically handicapped. Bella Cohen runs a house of prostitution that Bloom visits in order to protect Stephen. She functions as a key to unlocking Bloom's repressed fantasies and desires. Bloom also thinks of his son and father. Rudolph Bloom immigrated to Ireland and changed the family name from Virag to Bloom. He committed suicide in 1886. Rudy Bloom died in 1893, just eleven days after he was born. Other characters that figure prominently in Bloom's day include Paddy Dignam. Bloom attends Dignam's funeral and tries to help his family. Martin Cunningham also tries to help the Dignam family and treats Bloom with kindness and consideration.

Cunningham's human response to his environment, taken into consideration with Bloom's and Molly's embrace of their humanity in the face of hatred, anger, and derision, points to an overall theme in Joyce's text. *Ulysses*, in its characterizations and in its narrative forms, suggests that a coming to terms with self and society that does not embrace the psychological complexities of individual nature and of an individual's emotional depth cannot adequately equip individuals to understand themselves or their society. Indeed, Stephen cuts himself off from growth, losing himself in a morass of intellectualizations and physical indulgences while expressing cruelty in response to Bloom's kindness. Stephen, the conventional hero of the conventional novel, gives way to unconventional heroes and to subjugated forms of expression. In terms of narrative form, Joyce follows a similar pattern. Initially, he facilitates the reader's interaction with *Ulysses* by presenting his material in conventional ways, offering stability. However, he ultimately purges his text of traditional forms of expression and representation in favor of more revolutionary narrative techniques. Essentially, Joyce embraced radical departures of language and characterization and character development because he understood, perhaps as Declan Kiberd argues because of his experiences growing up in Ireland, that language cannot adequately express the totality of human experience. *Ulysses* stands then as a supreme expression in literary form of the supreme inadequacy of literary forms.

## NOTES

1. For a more thorough discussion of Joyce's narrative style, consult the following: Harold Baker, "Rite of Passage: 'Ithaca,' Style, and the Structure of *Ulysses*," *James Joyce Quarterly*, 23:3 (Spring 1986): pp. 277–297; Shari Benstock, "Who Killed Cock Robin? The Sources of Free Indirect Style in *Ulysses*," *Style* 14:3 (Summer 1980): 259–273; Joseph Bentley, "The Stylistic Regression in *Ulysses*," in *James Joyce and His Contemporaries*, ed. Diana Ben Merre and Maureen Murphy (Westport, CT: Greenwood, 1989), pp. 31–35; Monika Fludernik, "The Dialogic Imagination of Joyce: Form and Function of Dialogue in *Ulysses*," *Style* 20:1 (Spring 1986): 42–57; Mark Gapia, "Culture, Anarchy, and the Politics of Modernist Style in Joyce's 'Oxen of the Sun,' " *MFS: Modern Fiction Studies* 41:2 (Summer 1995): 195–217; Andrew Gibson, "'Broken Down and Fast Breaking Up': Style, Technique and Vision in the 'Eumaeus' Episode in *Ulysses*," *Southern Review: Literary and Interdisciplinary Essays* 17:3 (November 1984): 256–269; Hugh Kenner, " 'O, an Impossible Person!' " in *James Joyce: A Collection of Critical Essays*, ed. Mary Reynolds (Englewood Cliffs, NJ : Prentice Hall, 1993), pp. 96–107; Karen Lawrence, "*Ulysses*: The Narrative Norm," in *James Joyce: A Collection of Critical Essays*, ed. Mary Reynolds (Englewood Cliffs, NJ : Prentice Hall, 1993), pp. 118–129; Vicki Mahaffey, *Reauthorizing Joyce* (Cambridge : Cambridge University Press, 1988); Lesley McDowell, " 'Just You Try It On': Style and Maternity in 'Oxen of the Sun,' " in *Re: Joyce: Text, Culture, Politics*, ed. John Brannigan and Geoff Ward (New York: St. Martin's Press, 1998); Patrick McGee, "Joyce's Nausea: Style and Representation in 'Nausicaa,' " *James Joyce Quarterly* 24:3 (Spring 1987): 305–318; John Somer, "The Self-Reflexive Arranger in the Initial Style of Joyce's *Ulysses*," *James Joyce Quarterly* 31:2 (Winter 1994): 65–79.

2. Karen Lawrence, *The Odyssey of Style in James Joyce's "Ulysses"* (Princeton: Princeton University Press, 1983), p. 42.

3. Ibid., p. 43.

4. Ibid., p. 41.

5. Ibid., p. 52.

6. Hugh Kenner, "The Rhetoric of Silence," *James Joyce Quarterly* 14 (Summer 1977): 383.

7. Ibid., p. 382.

8. Lawrence, *Odyssey*, p. 52.

9. Declan Kiberd, "Introduction," in *Ulysses*, James Joyce (London: Penguin Books, 1992), pp. ix–lxxx.

10. Declan Kiberd, *Inventing Ireland* (London: Jonathan Cape, 1995), pp. 380–394.

11. Breandan O Buachalla, *Aisling Ghear* (Baile Atha Cliath: An Clochomhar Tta, 1996).

12. A more detailed listing and discussion the critical dialogue surrounding Molly appears in the subsequent chapter.

13. Richard Kain, *Fabulous Voyager* (Chicago: University of Chicago Press, 1947), pp. 99–100.

14. All textual citations reference the Gabler edition of *Ulysses* (New York: Vintage Books, 1986).

# 7   Reception

James Joyce's works, particularly *Ulysses* and *Finnegans Wake*, often serve as a testing ground for new and innovative critical approaches to literature. The complexity and revolutionary quality of his later works offer fruitful ground for practitioners of a variety of critical epistemologies, including semiotics, deconstruction and poststructuralism, structuralism, Marxist theory, feminism, and psychoanalytic theory. Readers coming to *Ulysses* for the first time may find the complexity of these various critical approaches confusing. Moreover, the abundance of material loosely classified as critical theory functions as an impediment to accessing many of the illuminating theories and revelations contained in these writings. A number of critical studies and guides are particularly useful in helping readers sort through the plethora of critical material. This chapter relies heavily on three guides. Bonnie Kime Scott's *James Joyce*[1] sorts through the variety of feminist approaches to Joyce's work. In particular, she offers many of her own insights into Joyce's writings and *Ulysses*. Margot Norris's *A Companion to James Joyce's* Ulysses[2] provides a summary of various critical theories and offers representative essays for the more important critical approaches to Joyce's text. Finally, Alan Roughley's *James Joyce and Critical Theory*[3] offers the most concise and illuminating summary/evaluation of a variety of the most important critical studies of Joyce's work.

## SEMIOTICS

One of the basic concepts of semiotics can help illuminate Joyce's use of self-referential techniques.[4] Specifically, *Ulysses* demonstrates the hollowness of certain narrative forms. Barthes, in *Mythologies*, defines a concept that can help illuminate Joyce's technique. Particularly, Barthes identifies the first and second orders of signification. The first order of signification involves the denotative meaning of a text (that is, plot, narrative, setting, objective characterization), whereas the second order of signification involves connotative meanings. Joyce will often, through manipulation of the appearance of the text or through character's comments, draw attention to the second order of signification. His technique helps reveal the connotative meanings' disconnectedness from its intended purpose. Specifically, Joyce utilizes the self-referential process to demonstrate the potential hollowness of certain forms of communication, particularly of logographic and of epic history (ethos). Joyce's technique also points to narrative history, not so much to highlight weaknesses potentially inherent in this form of telling but to highlight the fictive nature of all forms of history and telling.

In "Ithaca" and in "Nestor," Joyce demonstrates the problems associated with logographic forms of history and communication. Essentially, logographi attempts to apply scientific, rational standards to history and narration. Its origins lie in the fifth century B.C. with the Greek historian Hecataeus. Subsequent historians, such as Thucydides, sought to introduce a search for moral ideals into traditional logographic historiography. More recently, Macauly, the English historian, sought to explore the most particular details of English history while simultaneously tracing into his histories a metaphor of England as a new Israel, sowing into his explorations the motifs of England in slavery, in exile, and in the promised land. Deasy, in conversations with Stephen, echoes Macauly's specific metaphors of Ireland as the new Israel. More significantly, however, Stephen tutors his students in history and mathematics under a curriculum that privileges the memorization of facts and specific dates over deeper understanding and illumination. Stephen's conversation with one particular boy, whom Deasy sent to Stephen to check mathematical figures, demonstrates a self-reverential shallowness potentially inherent in logographi. Specifically, Stephen asks the boy if he understands the concepts behind the figures he just copied. The boy does not understand. The boy grasps the objective facts associated with mathematics but does not grasp the concepts underlying the external facts. The scene in "Nestor" suggests, therefore, that scientific and rational forms of relating events and concepts have limitations in that they may not always reveal underlying truth. Similarly, in "Ithaca," Joyce structures his narrative to resemble a scientific or rational exploration of Stephen and Bloom's interaction. A reader understands, as a consequence of the detailed and empirical analysis of events precisely what occurred between Stephen and Bloom. However, Stephen's motivations and Bloom's responses elude a reader's understanding, revealing the limits of logographic discourse. *Ulysses* then attracts attention, through the structures of its narrative and through character's comments, to the disconnectedness between the objective goals of logographic history and the subjective aims of scientific and logical exploration. Utilizing Barthes's terminology, the boy at Deasy's school and the reader's of "Ithaca," understand the denotative meanings of the text or math problem. However, the deeper connotative meanings elude both the boy and the reader. Moreover, Deasy's imposition of ideology onto his recitation of Irish history distorts his facts, creating a gap between the first and second orders of signification.

In the "Eumaeus" episode, Joyce demonstrates some problems potentially associated with epic forms of history and telling. Characteristic of epic history is an appeal to ethos, an appeal to an ideal society or an ideal form of behavior. Specifically, Plutarch, in his *Lives*, posits heroes and heroic deeds as models for human action and interaction. Similarly, Carlyle wrote his histories as the tale of "Great Men" moving the course of time and progress of humanity toward an ideal end. *Ulysses*, in a sense, can stand as a counterepic when taken as a whole. Particularly, W.B. Murphy, the sailor in "Eumaeus," highlights specific problems with a moral or goal influencing the telling of personal history. The sailor carries an obvious parallel to Odysseus. Both returning mariners tell the story of their travels before returning to their wives. Murphy, significantly, does not consciously associate himself with the Greek hero. However, a reader cannot help but see the common motifs of exile, suffering, and return between Murphy and Odysseus (Ulysses). Joyce, by creating the obvious parallel and by having Bloom point out the tenuous nature of the truth in Murphy's tales, draws attention to the fictive nature of epic telling. More importantly, Joyce draws attention to the difficulty in following a model form of behavior if that model exists only as fiction. The sailor, Plutarch, and Carlyle all posit their histories as factual representations. All posit certain forms of behavior within those factual presentations as model behavior. For Murphy, his friendship with Antonio, as told in tattoos, serves as an ideal friendship. However, when the fictive nature of the presentation becomes clear, when it becomes obvious that the writer/teller of epic history lies, then the model becomes corrupted. Bloom observes that Murphy may have killed Antonio, an observation that certainly places doubt on Murphy's ability to detail an ideal friendship. Utilizing Barthes's vocabulary, Murphy, like the writers of epic history, relays a series of events, an example of the first order of signification. In addition, Murphy, like Carlyle and Plutarch, places an ideal connotative meaning within those events, the second order of signification. Joyce, through self-referential narrative techniques, places doubt on the veracity of Murphy's histories and, by extension, his authority to describe a model or ideal form in his histories. By connection then, Joyce reveals potential problems inherent in all aspects of epic forms of telling.

In the "Penelope" episode, Joyce highlights narrative forms of telling. Narrative history emphasizes conveying not so much the facts of an incident but the emotional impact of events on an individual. Emphasizing an appeal to pathos, narrative or oral history has its roots in storytelling and in nineteenth-century forms of religious witness, in which the penitent declares a litany of sins and behavior to a congregation. A minister then imposes an ethical matrix onto the details of the witness. In Joyce's experience, he would have come across forms of narrative history in the Catholic sacrament of confession, in which an individual penitent privately relays his life story to the priest, who then imposes an interpretation on the stories so as to instruct and, ultimately, forgive the penitent. In *A Portrait of the Artist*, the adolescent Stephen rushes into a confessional and tells the tales of his sexual debaucheries, which the priest judges for him. In *Ulysses*, Molly's final monologue serves as an example of narrative history. Joyce draws attention to her personal confession mode of telling in the structure or lack of structure in the episode. He uses very limited forms of punctuation and paragraphing, placing a signpost for the reader that the final chapter involves a different type of communication than that practiced in the previous chapters or found in other forms of literature. Molly's dialogue, the form of the words on the pages indicates, will not be logical, will not be concerned with the denotative details of more conventional discourse. Rather, Molly's monologue will focus on connotative meanings. To utilize Barthes's vocabulary, "Penelope" does not focus on the first order of signification but rather on the second order of signification. Indeed, reading Molly's monologue does successfully make denotative details obscure. Her use of masculine pronouns, for example, purposely blurs references to Bloom, Boylan, and others. One event fades into another. The particular details of her narrative become less important than the emotional impact of her testimony. Because details and the objective truth of her history are not as important as the subjective effect of events on her life, the fact that she may not tell the denotative truth or that she might obscure the objective happenings of her life becomes less important than the fact that she addresses issues associated with sexuality, jealously, betrayal, and motherhood. Indeed, many critics point to her testimonial as an indication of her importance as a narrative voice. That she deemphasizes objective details humanizes *Ulysses* and, thus, reinforces the novel's function as a counterepic or alternate discourse. Indeed, Molly's monologue can be read in this way. However, her use of narrative confession may also be read as an example of the potential deleterious consequences of a discourse that purges the rational from the emotional. Essentially, is it possible for Molly to communicate the emotional impact of events when she communicates with no one? Molly's discourse is so personal that it is indeed private. She shares her life and thoughts with no other character. However, the reader comes to understand the intricacies of her character in all the more detail. Joyce then uses self-referentiality to point out the fictive nature of his text and the fictive nature of the novel form. Essentially, then, Joyce demonstrates the unreality, the disconnectedness from reality, of all forms of history and telling, whether they are logographic, epic, or narrative.

## DECONSTRUCTION

Deconstruction and poststructuralism[5] are synonymous, to a large extent. However, so pervasive is the influence of Jacques Derrida that a specific and detailed reading of his particular interpretation of *Ulysses* should prove valuable to students. In "*Ulysses Gramophone* Hear Say Yes in Joyce," Derrida argues for a reading of Joyce's text as an open text. Certainly, deconstruction argues for many texts to be read as open texts in the sense that deconstruction looks for readings of texts that offer contradictory and random associations "open" to various interpretations. However, Derrida further suggests that *Ulysses* offers aural and visual clues that invite random readings and associations, that Joyce writes not simply a novel that deconstructs itself. According to the deconstructionist theory, all works of art deconstruct themselves. Moreover, Joyce writes a text that invites readings that deconstruct other readings, that invites, through textual puns and clues, readers to bring their own associations to the text. Derrida focuses on notions of paternity, telephonic communication, postcards, and audible and visual affirmations.

In terms of paternity, Derrida offers examples of Stephen's relationship with Ireland and with Bloom that favor choice and individuality over biological paternity and obligation. Stephen, Derrida points out, makes a distinction between belonging to Ireland and Ireland belonging to him. Derrida considers it significant that Stephen reverses the traditional relationship with paternity. The former association suggests that an individual owes something to his country, whereas the latter distinction indicates that not only does the individual not owe anything to his country but that the country owes him something. Derrida immediately considers Stephen's relationship to Bloom, suggesting a sympathy between them, a sympathy that argues for choosing parents, in this case a stepfather, over biological parents. Derrida sees Stephen's choices as an example of *Ulysses* being a novel that deconstructs traditional relationships and the assumptions that convention carries with it.

Derrida also considers nontraditional articulations of narrative, writing, and myth in *Ulysses*, indicating that they, like Stephen's relationships with paternal figures, reverse traditional assumptions and expectations. Making a general observation about Joyce's text as similar to a postcard, Derrida observes that each chapter resembles a series of postcards representing the private thoughts and assumptions of individuals both written for public consumption and intended for public consumption. Simultaneously, none of the chapters has a specific audience in mind but rather a series of nonintended audiences and nonintended readers who carry to the text their own assumptions and associations. Derrida makes particular reference to Bloom's incompletely addressed postcard and offers it as an example of a text that will be read and interpreted by many but, significantly, not its intended audience. Moreover, Derrida goes on to note, it becomes impossible to trace the exact path of the postcard, of all the card's readers, and, therefore, it is impossible to measure the true impact of the text. In addition, according to Derrida, it is impossible to trace an original intent in the postcard's author and sender. Derrida specifically considers the message to Breen, for which he seeks monetary compensation through legal means. The message has numerous possible senders, and Joyce offers many tantalizing but no definitive clues as to its point of origin. In addition, the message itself remains obscure, offering Molly, Bloom, Mrs. Breen, the boys in the pub, and Breen various interpretations and meanings. Some of the interpretations relate not to the message but to the presumptive target of the message—Breen. Some of the meanings relate to Bloom's relationship to his wife. Derrida then observes that Bloom considers writing down his experiences more than once. Derrida makes specific mention of Bloom's intended short story about the cabman's shelter and Bloom's desire to write an erotic tale, which he thinks about while relieving himself. Derrida notes the alimental associations of the latter example and deduces that Bloom's writing would be composed of random associations with not intended meaning but with revealing layers of interpretation, sometimes contradictory layers of interpretation, and not just for Bloom but also for all his readers. A reader of Derrida's article can infer, then, that he makes an equivalence between Joyce's text and Bloom's intended text. Both, according to Derrida, privilege association and contradiction over specific themes and meanings. Ultimately, Derrida relates Bloom's intended text and *Ulysses* to Odysseus, arguing that, like the seaman in the "Ithaca" episode, the Greek hero, Bloom, Stephen, Joyce, and all their various readers and audiences embark on a circular journey in reading Joyce's text and in their writing of it into their lives and experiences, returning to the original text with their own revisions and extrapolations that may or may not have been the intended effect of the original text. Derrida, essentially, argues that *Ulysses* functions as an open text, urging readers to explode the limited world of the novel and carry into it their experiences and readings.

Subsequently, Derrida focuses on telephonic communication, suggesting that it too becomes a type of open-ended communication, revealing significant associations. Specifically, Derrida argues for the gramophonic broadcast impact of telephone conversations, observing that such conversations, overheard in part or in whole by various individuals, multiply meanings and associations far beyond the intention of the call's initiator. Derrida makes specific mention of Bloom's random associations between a typesetter, writing the paper backward, Bloom's intent to phone about a newspaper advertisement, the name of the newspaper, Bloom's memory of his father reading his prayer books from right to left, and the Hebrew prayer that summons Israel and God the father. Derrida argues that these associations, although random, point toward significant associations in Bloom's mind regarding paternity, inheritance, faith, career, and others. His act of considering a call summoned these random associations together. The call gives them temporary meaning through their association. Derrida goes on to observe various other forms of communication, which he groups under the title of Aeolian sounds. These sounds include dental floss, a reference to battle sounds, a ringing telephone, and parts of an overheard conversation. A reader of Derrida's article can infer, from his reference to the Aeolian harp, that Derrida points out random sounds that carry elements of interpretive meaning because of their random association. The inner voice, private voice, combines with various other private voices to multiply meanings and associations exponentially. Derrida concludes his observations regarding the telephonic theme by pointing out the association between Bloom and Elijah. Derrida observes that Elijah becomes, at the end of the world, the focus and magnification of various voices, human and divine. Elijah, according to Derrida, gathers together and broadcasts the multiplicity of voices, creating associations and meanings and nonintended results as a consequence of his position. Derrida's observations regarding telephonic multiplication reinforce the deconstructionist epistemology in the sense that they argue for a reading of *Ulysses* in general and Bloom's character in particular as types of open texts, to which readers bring their own associations and meanings, reading themselves and their experiences into both Bloom's and Joyce's text. Therefore, not only are various interpretations valid but, according to Derrida, welcomed by the structure of Joyce's verbal constructions.

Derrida also focuses throughout his article on a variety of forms of affirmation, ultimately considering Molly Bloom's forms of assent. Derrida suggests that the various forms of affirmation, both obvious and not so obvious, reinforce a reading of *Ulysses* as an open text that welcomes personal engagement and individual interpretation. Derrida begins his series of observations by pointing out that the word "yes" appears numerous times, not only in Molly's monologue but also throughout the book. In terms of Molly's monologue, she focuses her affirmations, according to Derrida, on her marriage and Bloom's acts of betrayal. Molly's affirmations, Derrida observes, do not simply validate her marriage nor even confirm that Bloom betrayed her. More significantly, Molly's affirmations confirm her interpretations of Bloom's actions, validate her own individual reading and response to her husband's behavior. Derrida goes on to observe that Molly's affirmations, both verbal and physical (the movements of her eyes), offer themselves to her husband asking for confirmation of his request for breakfast in bed. She asks for validation of her understanding. Ultimately, Derrida focuses on Molly's final affirmation, which he points out can only truly be understood if read; the first letter is capitalized. Visually the affirmation carries more meaning than it does audibly. Moreover, the meaning draws in the human eye, relating it to a pun on sight, or reading. Derrida, throughout his piece, argues for *Ulysses* not simply as a text that carries contradictory meanings but as a text that welcomes contradictory readings and interpretations.

## POSTSTRUCTURALISM

Poststructuralism is a convenient term used to represent a multiple of critical perspectives and dialogues. Simplifying such diverse theorists and philosophies doubtlessly distorts the nuances of each individual author and piece of criticism. Consequently, it is important to note that poststructuralism involves much more than the notion that a text undermines itself, that it offers conflicting and even contradictory readings of characters, events, and themes. Texts offer only shifting ground for readers and critics determined to demonstrate the validity of a single critical perspective. *Ulysses* offers poststructuralists a text that seemingly invites such scrutiny and even validates its own disintegration under critical scrutiny.

Stephen Heath, in "Ambiviolences: Notes for Reading Joyce,"[6] argues that *Ulysses* destroys the old assumptions of novel writing and reading, dissolving into fragments the solid methods of engagement. Plot, narrative distance, and character become established in new ways, Heath asserts. Readers of Heath's article can make an easy connection between Joyce's writings and the paintings of Picasso and even Dali. These artists, like Joyce and others, represented the explosion, sometimes literally, of societal assumptions and conventions. They explored the interior self and its impact on the exterior self and, in turn, its impact on the environment and on society at large, including the reader or viewer.

Jean-Michel Rabaté, in "Le Noeud Gordien De ((Penelope)),"[7] explores the distinction between Molly's name and Bloom's name. Rabaté points out that Bloom's name can also stand as a verb and functions to act on or to place action onto Molly. Molly, on the other hand, possesses a name that becomes, in her relationship with her husband, a noun. A reader of Rabaté's article can easily determine how Molly and Bloom work against each other in this way, serving to deconstruct and undermine each other's actions.

André Topia, in "The Matrix and the Echo: Intertextuality in *Ulysses*,"[8] focuses on Leopold Bloom's interior monologues and dialogues. Topia explores how Bloom's thoughts become grafts combining his ideas and external stimuli. Topia's reading of Bloom offers a contrast to nonpoststructuralist readings of *Ulysses* and other texts in that Topia sees Bloom's allusive dialogues not as two or more separate texts juxtaposed against one another but as a combined new text.

Topia focus on Joyce's use of interior monologue, with its ready associations from the external and internal worlds of the speaker, as a prime example of the process of creating a new text. Essentially, the conscious mind receives stimuli from the external world. The subconscious mind then creates associations with the external stimuli, associations not always logical or expected. The mind then incorporates the interactive associations not as separate texts but as a new text with grafts of associated material comprising its whole.

Topia discusses the consequences of such interactions and associations, pointing out that the reaction, to borrow a term from chemistry, does not arrest itself at the time of speaking or articulation but rather continues. Both the interior mind and the perception of the external stimuli continue to interact and transform their combined form. The result can prove to be disorienting if a reader or speaker places absolute faith in the notion of stable origins. Nonetheless, the result can also yield insights into the speaker's mental processes and life experiences.

Topia emphasizes the parodic potential of such interaction. If a reader or speaker privileges one discourse over another, then, inevitably, the new text, the grafted text, deflates the privileged discourse by presenting a new degraded version of its former self. The process reveals the weakness of the privileged discourse. Parody works even if neither discourse seems privileged by conventional standards, if a reader or character privileges the notion of a pure discourse. Parody, in this sense, Topia asserts, varies from classic notions of the parodic in that the new text need not follow any conventional standards of juxtaposition, method, or form. Indeed, Topia's definition of parody argues the language itself becomes the ultimate degraded form, or, more correctly, the grafted text once recognized degrades the old assumptions regarding the stability of language.

The new text, in addition, has the potential to displace the old textual original as the original. Essentially, a reader or, more likely, the speaker may not recall exactly what an original text read, substituting the grafted version for the original. The substitution is not necessarily an act of will. Unconsciously, the grafted version rewrites the image of an original text onto a reader's mind or a speaker's mind.

Analysis, more specifically literary criticism, can then focus on the distortion of the original text, the subconscious material used to revise and alter the original, the new created text, and the ongoing processes of transformation. All these factors inform, Topia asserts, the living nature of a character's discourse and representation.

Topia focuses specifically on Bloom's interior monologue in the "Lotus Eaters" episode, arguing that Joyce represents a montage of texts in Bloom's reflections. The texts include not only immediate stimuli and remembered associations but also involve the continued creation and revision of the new text and additionally involve a wide variety of remembered actions and reflections and old-new texts also constantly revised. The many voices revised and received and, subsequently, revised produce themselves simultaneously in Bloom's conscious thoughts. In particular, Topia explores Bloom's extended reflections that begin with a quotation regarding an advertisement for Ceylon Tea. Topia emphasizes Joyce's choice not to place quotation marks around Bloom's use of the advertisement's quoted material. Topia argues that the absence of quotation marks indicates that the advertised material does not exactly correspond to the original advertisement but rather represents Bloom's processes of revision. Topia then focuses on Bloom and not the advertisement, asserting that Bloom's spoken phrase argues for the disintegration of Bloom's consciousness and the gradual elimination of identity. Topia asserts that the processes of creating the new text corrupt both the original advertisement and Bloom's individual consciousness. Even though Bloom's consciousness and unconsciousness reform the external idea, Topia dismisses such a process as the confirmation of Bloom's identity. Rather, because the reformations take on the character of clichés and standard utterances, Topia argues that Bloom's new text is simply a montage of previous advertisements. Topia goes on to explore Bloom's contemplation of an Eastern or Levantine paradise as, itself, further evidence of Bloom's conscious thoughts encompassing nothing more than a collection of clichés. Bloom's superficiality, as Topia represents Bloom's character, becomes a type of index file in which clichéd expressions organize themselves under topic headings and appear when external stimuli summon them. Topia acknowledges that Bloom's consciousness and his subconscious are largely, although not entirely, computerized output patterns. Significantly, Topia does not recognize or acknowledge Bloom's own commentary on his thoughts that clearly comprise portions of his interior monologue. Bloom repeatedly observes that his collection of advertising and other clichés may not represent the reality of the East or the Levant. Bloom's reflections in this regard, certainly, suggest a self-consciousness beyond the machine. In fact, Bloom's reflections indicate an awareness of the superficiality of clichéd discourse. Nevertheless, as Topia asserts, Joyce presents in *Ulysses* a text that invites scrutiny into its nature and identity as a text. Joyce appears to solicit, to use the Bloomian advertising terminology, individual reflection and revision of received textual material and to invite scrutiny into the superficiality of the word and the characters created by the word.

Topia proceeds to analyze the "Cyclops" episode utilizing the same critical perspective that comprised his analysis of the "Lotus Eaters" episode. He asserts that "Cyclops" simply expands on the patterns established in the earlier episode. Topia particularly focuses on the open conflict clichéd and superficial discourse creates between itself. Topia scrutinizes a chapter that focuses on conflict in order to demonstrate that the revision of discourse involves the coming together of various trains of thought. The variety of strains destroy themselves in the act of coming together, replacing the old forms of discourse with new forms. However, Topia argues, because the new forms themselves are simply recombined clichés with little reflective revisionary material, the new forms are fragile and subject to disintegration without viable substitutes of revisions. Essentially, the process of transformation breaks apart clichéd discourse along fracture lines established in the adaptation of solely clichéd discourse. Once again, Topia argues, Joyce's text invites such a disintegration, further moving it away from realistic novels. However, Topia asserts that Joyce's text demonstrates the very realistic fault lines present in what Topia perceives to be Joyce's representation of Dublin. Topia's argument, in this sense, is characteristic of poststructuralist readings of *Ulysses*. The poststructuralists emphasize Joyce's intentional creation of a text that deconstructs not only itself but the standards of discourse of its society by revealing the fragility and superficiality of language and other forms of representation.

## STRUCTURALISM

Structuralism essentially attempts to contextualize literature within conventional and established frameworks, metaphors, and structures. The structural elements explored by the variety of theorists and critics practicing within the matrix called structuralism explore elements ranging from the structure of language to the adopted structures of myth. Structuralist thought and theory that focus on *Ulysses* explore Joyce's use of and variation from received patterns.

The basic motifs contained in *Ulysses* include patterns associated with the *Odyssey* and the Roman Catholic Mass. The structural elements of the Mass present in *Ulysses* are the Liturgy of the Word, the Liturgy of the Eucharist, and the Closing. The Liturgy of the Word, in the Catholic service, includes the opening prayers, psalms and readings from the Old and New Testaments, the gospel reading, the homily, the Nicene Creed, and petitions. In Joyce's text, Mulligan performs a mock invocation; he parodies the opening prayers of the Mass. The "Nestor" episode includes many elements, like the stories Stephen tells his pupils, his riddles, and even the history lesson, that parallel the series of readings. In addition, Deasy delivers a homily to Stephen. In "Proteus," Stephen's interior monologue opens with clear references to the Nicene Creed. He continues with musings, parts of which could be considered petitions and even prayers. *Ulysses'* central twelve chapters, with their partial focus on eating and creative transformations roughly parallel the Liturgy of the Eucharist. Bloom even begins the section with an offertory; he delivers Molly her breakfast. The final three chapters roughly follow the Closing of the Mass, with Molly offering the final blessing. Significantly, although *Ulysses* follows a rough outline of both the Mass and the *Odyssey*, it is possible to make too much of these parallels or even to overplay the significance of any one element. Joyce's text, indeed, does follow numerous structural patterns. A proper understanding of the text includes acknowledging them and also realizing their limits, both in terms of organization and in terms of thematic association. In addition to these broader structural parallels, numerous smaller motifs recur throughout the text, including metempsychosis, parallax, potted meat, the smells of lemon soap, sexuality, celibacy, and even the man in the macintosh.

Joseph Kestner, in "Virtual Text/Virtual Reader: The Structural Signature Within, Behind, Beyond, and Above,"[9] explores *Ulysses'* relationship to its predecessors. Kestner considers the interaction between Joyce's text and the texts and structures on which *Ulysses* draws. Both the origin text and Joyce's text, Kestner observes, transform a reader's understanding of each other. Specifically, Kestner examines the creative processes at work in Joyce's mind as he considers writing and as he writes *Ulysses*, noting particularly Joyce's early fascination with Homer's hero. Kestner observes that the artist transforms the raw material of the alluded-to text in order to better adopt it to his means. Kestner also explores the evolving relationship between Joyce's texts, considering the view of the artist as articulated in *Stephen Hero, A Portrait of the Artist,* and *Ulysses.* Kestner likens Joyce's transformations of Stephen's aesthetic theory, in all its forms and through his evolving form, to the work of an alchemist transforming the substance of creative materials. In this sense, Proteus, the ever-shifting god of the sea, serves as the ideal metaphor because Proteus constantly revises his shape and form depending on circumstances. His omnipotent ability to adapt himself to circumstances can stand for the artist's ability to transform the raw materials of perception and the ability of Stephen (and Joyce) to alter his (their) creative interaction with the raw materials on which they draw. Specifically, Kestner observes Stephen's transformation from the artist in *Portrait* determined to write his country's national epic and the artist in *Ulysses*, who acknowledges that the epic has not yet been written; the latter artist may in fact have abandoned the necessary creative perspective required to write the national epic. Kestner notes that Stephen's transformation requires that readers perceive the Stephen from *Portrait* in a new light, as the artist of failed youthful, creative ambitions. For Kestner, Stephen uses the raw materials of his earlier artistic incarnations to build his new artistic epistemology, just as Joyce's draws on his earlier work and structures, myths, and forms outside of his work. The interaction creates a new dynamic that changes both the way readers come to terms with the new text and the way in which readers come to terms with the original text.

Robert Scholes,[10] drawing on the theories outlined by Jean Piaget in *Structuralism*, explores in "*Ulysses*: A Structuralist Perspective" various themes and patterns that, after careful and diligent scrutiny, offer insights into what Scholes considers to be the epitome of structuralist texts. Specifically, Scholes believes the three principles of wholeness, transformation, and self-regulation govern *Ulysses*. Essentially, larger frameworks, that include the *Odyssey* and the Mass, provide a unity to Joyce's novel, a sense of wholeness. Joyce's further use of a single specific location and condensing Odysseus's journey into a single day follow what many critics understood to be Aristotle's unities of place and time. Joyce's focus on numerous characters and perspectives functions as a type of improvisation or transformation on Aristotle's unity of action, providing Joyce a means through which, according to structuralism, he could express his own creativity. Further, Joyce varies the characters and scenes from the *Odyssey*. He does not strictly follow Homer's order nor do Bloom and Stephen and Molly follow the exact pattern of their Homeric counterparts. Ultimately though, the larger structures give *Ulysses*, Scholes contends, a mechanism through which Joyce disciplines his text. Essentially, structuralist analysis offers readers a way to come to terms with *Ulysses* through a matrix of understanding, giving the text the stability so many first-time readers find wanting.

Scholes examines the "Oxen of the Sun" episode along the lines through which he comes to understand the text as a whole. Indeed, the chapter utilizes numerous structural elements, including chronological literary references paralleling conception, gestation, and birth. These two elements offer an overall structure to the chapter. Joyce's variations include his parodies of various literary styles and writers and his choice of the elements of gestation on which he focuses. The characters themselves offer variations and transgressions from the overall established patterns; the medical students boisterously refuse to respect the birth process. Ultimately, however, the larger structures move the chapter and the text forward.

Scholes also examines the "Cyclops" episode, utilizing the structuralist's distinction between narrative prose and poetry. For the structuralists, narrative prose focuses on the advancement of plot and on characterization. Whereas, poetry, the structuralists observe, focuses on the metaphorical implications of language and the subtleties of sound and word placement.

Scholes focuses particularly on the scene in which Joyce describes a wedding, making heavy use of metaphors involving trees. Scholes demonstrates that the subtleties of language utilized in this scene focus less on narrative progression than on the symbolic implications of language. Scholes observes that not only do the names make reference to trees but that they also refer to sexuality and violence and sexual stimulation. Structuralism, as Scholes demonstrates, offers useful readings of both the "Oxen of the Sun" and the "Cyclops" episodes.

Another structural theorist, Seymour Chatman, in *Story and Discourse: Narrative Structure in Fiction and Film*,[11] explores the distinction in *Ulysses* between point of view and voice. Chatman asserts that characters and narrators offer points of view of a variety of other characters, nonhuman entities, and events. The narrative voice at these times, according to Chatman, disappears. Chatman's observations directly contradict observations of other critics who suggest that the narrative voice changes with the character on which the text focuses, the "Uncle Charles" principle; several critics note that in *Portrait*, the sections that focus on Uncle Charles utilize a narrative voice that closely resembles the voice of the character. Chatman argues his interpretation through Bloom's observation in the "Hades" episode. Bloom considers what the horse that draws the funeral car must be thinking. Bloom focuses on the vessels and straining muscles of the neck. Chatman asserts that the point of view is unquestionably Bloom's. Chatman additionally observes that the narrative voice disappears from the text at this point. The character's perspective takes over the narrator's voice. Essentially, Chatman, like many other structuralist theorists, focuses on Joyce's use of and variation from conventional patterns and structures, whether they be language structures, narrative structures, or broader motifs and patterns, such as Homer or the Mass.

## FEMINISM

Numerous articles and books discuss a variety of issues associated with feminism(s) and Joyce studies.[12] Although no single study or even a group of studies should be considered representative, Bonnie Kime Scott's *James Joyce* serves as an ideal introduction to the variety of feminisms and feminist themes present in Joyce's works in general and in *Ulysses* in particular. Scott focuses chapters on placing Joyce within a matrix of feminist theory, a chapter that also serves as a good introduction to feminism; reading Joyce's works in the context of challenging the male-centered literary cannon; exploring Joyce's writings and issues associated with gender, discourse, language, writing, and culture; and examining Joyce's works in the context of myths regarding female origins.

Scott, in her introduction, offers a number of themes that feminist critics develop in their readings of Joyce's works. Specifically, she focuses on the fact that feminists generally challenge the assumptions, the teachings, and the received traditions of culture and society that involve oppression and bias. Often times, Scott argues, the oppression and bias remain undetected by the masses and unnoticed by the intelligentsia. If noticed, those in power, most often male, tolerate the oppressive behaviors and patterns because they serve personal gender-based agendas. Scott also points out that feminist critics aim to recognize power-based paradigms present in critical theory and in literary criticism and practice, including their own writings and thoughts. She adds that feminist critics will attempt to change the oppressive patterns and practices. Feminism also, Scott observes, strives to recognize the common practices of related theoretical models and epistemologies, forging a conscious alliance with them to help disrupt dominant patriarchal models of discourse. Some feminists, Scott points out, may find difficulty with critical practice that focuses on Joyce because they feel that feminist energies should devote themselves to neglected female writers, giving voice to female traditions and cultures that patriarchy mutes and has muted. Scott counters that a study of Joyce proves beneficial because similar patterns of patriarchal thought and oppressive practices that dominated and attempted to diminish the value of women and their culture dominated, dominate, and attempt and have attempted to diminish Irish voices. Moreover, Joyce's work offers valuable insights into the roles and career paths women had open to them in Ireland at the turn of the last century. Feminism, Scott argues, functions as an ideal critical matrix through which to come to terms with Joyce's work.

Scott also raises the issue of *écriture féminine*, and, although she does not specifically examine in a detailed way its relation to the "Penelope" episode, readers can easily make the connections between the concepts that underlie and comprise "writing the feminine," and Joyce's final chapter. Specifically, *écriture féminine* seeks to develop new definitions of women that exist outside of those imposed on them by a patriarchal society. Certainly, Molly struggles against received impressions and strictures that limit her self-expression. In addition, Molly's monologue expresses, in a highly personal and unconventional way, her vision of the world in which she lives, another aim of *écriture féminine*. Molly also, in accord with the aims of "writing the feminine," explores issues associated with her unconscious. Indeed, her use of sometimes apparently random associations and, other times, more or less directed stream-of-consciousness thought suggests that Molly gathers her memories valuing her own organizational and expressive structures rather than those of the patriarchal Dublin or British military society. Moreover, Molly's monologue further values female sexuality, without the strictures of supposed and often times hypocritical male-dominated society. She readily and happily recalls a variety of her sexual experiences. She sometimes romanticizes her encounters, but she also realistically understands what attracts her to Boylan. She knows he does not fulfill her emotionally. She does not like the pat he gives her on her backside. However, she looks forward, at times, to a return visit because it will give her sexual joy. Her anticipation runs counter to societal conventions that indicate the pure and hospitable wife should wait faithfully for her husband's attentions. Most significantly, however, the form of the "Penelope" chapters belies conventional literary representation. With very little punctuation and conventional organization, Molly offers a narrative history of herself and her experiences, fulfilling many of the principle aims of *écriture féminine*.

Scott explicitly demonstrates that *Ulysses* provides useful insights into another feminist principle, that of "joissance." Joissance relates to the pleasure women can take and, according to some feminists, do naturally take in their developing sexuality. In contrast to women and their joissance, many feminists argue that men focus on power and loss in relation to sexuality. Scott focuses on *Ulysses'* revisions of myths and Stephen's Oedipal fixations in order to explore issues associated with joissance in *Ulysses*.

Specifically, Scott outlines *Ulysses'* expression of myths that value women's sexual joy. She specifically mentions Stephen's relation to the Virgin Mary, an object of his youthful spiritual devotion. Scott observes that, in *Ulysses*, one sign of Stephen's faltering involves his apparent transformation in his view of the Virgin. Stephen no longer sees her as the sexless, willing vessel of the messiah but rather sees her as an unsophisticated vessel for the will of God. Further, in Stephen's view, Scott points out, Mary experiences a joyless pregnancy. Although Stephen's new conception devalues Catholicism, it also devalues women's joyful experience with their bodies. Stephen still sees Mary as sexless, as simply a conduit of male will. Stephen also, Scott suggests, carries with him further images of women that represent patriarchal internatizations of the role and function of the female. Specifically, Stephen perceives women as existing outside of himself, as adversaries, or as the literary muse. Indeed, extrapolating on Scott's themes, in Stephen's anti-Semitic tale, a young girl tempts a young boy to his death. The sea, a symbol of motherhood, becomes for Stephen anathema. Moreover, Stephen's mother's death becomes for him a fixation on which he imposes his feelings of guilt and loss, not only regarding her but also his life in Paris and his relation with his father. The images of the mother's corpse coming before Stephen represent Stephen's metaphorical projections of his own state of mind onto a female form that disappoints, frightens, and haunts. Scott also discerns a positive representation of a woman in *Ulysses*. According to Scott, Joyce revises the myth of Circe by transforming her from an evil witch to a psychologically and spiritually healing figure. Circe, in her new form, according to Scott, delights in sexual and sensual pleasure and assists Bloom in his coming to terms with her guilt and his repressions. She helps Bloom liberate himself, whereas the Circe of the *Odyssey* performs only tricks of enslavement. *Ulysses* then offers Bloom and Stephen as counterexamples of *Ulysses*' revision of myth. Stephen revises feminine mythological representations but according to patriarchal paradigms, whereas a revised female mythological figure assists Bloom.

Scott further addresses Stephen's Oedipal issues, observing that he inherits his father's view of Irish nationalism and its relation to masculine loss and the female as a temptress. Specifically, an extrapolation from Scott's argument reveals that Stephen's father, as evidenced by his songs and stories that he sings in the "Sirens" chapter, values the received view of Ireland as a female figure and men as subjects who sacrifice their lives for her. It is the old aisling theme and, indeed, Stephen's creative aesthetic, as far back as *A Portrait*, tends to view women as distant muses ready and waiting for masculine sacrifice. Women then become the focus of male loss.

Scott also addresses issues of *Ulysses*' accurate representation of limited female roles. Apart from Molly, who tries to escape patriarchal representations, Scott offers Gerty MacDowell as an example of women in *Ulysses*. Gerty has aspirations but tends to express them in traditional and patriarchal masculine forms. An oppressive masculine discourse of romance novels permeates her thoughts, giving her little room for self-exploration and true self-expression. Moreover, she possesses a limp, a metaphor for her limited role in a masculine society. Other women in the text become faithful and suffering wives or prostitutes; all struggle against realistic oppressive forces present in Victorian Dublin.

## MARXIST CRITICISM

Defined concisely, Marxist criticism focuses on a work of art as both the product of the cultural, sociological, economic, and political ideology of its time and as a producer and reworker of these same factors.[13] Early Marxist criticism of *Ulysses* judges it along these lines and in terms of its conformity to a Marxist ideology, faulting and praising the text for its adherence to certain Marxist values. More recent criticism, on the other hand, functions less as a judging ideological force and more as analysis of the trends and values reflected in the text. Alan Roughley focuses his summary of Marxist criticism of Joyce and *Ulysses* on both the ideological critics and the more literary critics, among the latter being Eagleton and Jameson.

Roughley begins his critique of Joyce's Marxist critics by focusing on two Soviet reference book articles. Pieces by Ivan Kashkin and E.V. Kornilova[14] explore Joyce and *Ulysses* from an ideological perspective. Kashkin praises Joyce's text for its representation, as he sees it, of a country and a people defeated by historical and economic forces, including colonialism and capitalism. However, Kashkin finds fault with the text because it does not offer a counterpart to the defeated and defeating ideology. Moreover, Kashkin sees the Joyce of *Ulysses* as a prisoner of Catholic theology and aesthetics who represents Stephen as a heroically defiant figure, who is himself prisoner of Catholic theology and aesthetics. Kashkin does praise Joyce as an innovative prose writer but also observes that the innovations, themselves, parody and tear down the old forms without replacing them with new, presumably Marxist, forms. Kornilova also recognizes, in a positive way, Joyce's representation of a world defeated by mercantilism and colonialism but also regrets that Joyce does not counter these negative forces with Marxist, positive alternatives.

Alick West, in *Crisis and Criticism*,[15] also examines *Ulysses* from an ideological perspective but one that values not simply the ideas in the book but the transformative aesthetic form of the work. However, West faults *Ulysses*, citing the same type of difficulties Kashkin and Kornilova found. West regrets that Bloom and Stephen do not advance against the individuals and forces attempting to usurp their roles as, respectively, husband and resident in the tower. West compares the two characters' inaction to the lack of advancement, by Western workers, toward their, as West sees it, inheritance. However, West finds Marxist potential in Joyce's work, particularly in the shared experience of the Dubliners represented in the story. The characters, according to West, seem on the verge of surrendering their individual identities in favor of the advancement of society, along Marxist ideological patterns. However, Joyce, paralyzed, as West sees it, by the same forces that oppress his characters, cannot implement or demonstrate the proper Marxist revolution in *Ulysses*. In particular, West observes in Joyce an apparent rejection of the Catholic faith but, nonetheless, a continuing internalization of its values and philosophies, a valuation that leads Joyce away from the Marxist ideal. Presumably, West finds the Catholic church's emphasis on individual consciousness and responsibility the main obstacle to a societal consciousness, one of the goals of Marxism. Essentially, West and other ideological critics find potential in *Ulysses'* apparent rejection of many anti- and un-Marxist principles and ideologies. However, they also see *Ulysses* as a flawed text because it does not offer a Marxist alternative to the flawed, as they see them, non-Marxist principles.

In terms of less ideological Marxist approaches to Joyce's text, Alan Roughley points out that Terry Eagleton explores, in *Exiles and Émigés: Studies in Modern Literature*,[16] the relation of *Ulysses* to myth. Eagleton points out that nothing in Dublin society or Irish experience would suggest that *The Odyssey* would function as the most appropriate mythic parallel. Indeed, Eagleton argues, the fact that creative ingenuity created the parallels between Homer and early twentieth-century Dublin suggests that creativity and aesthetic ingenuity underlie all human experience with myth. No mythic or spiritual system then, if Eagleton's logic is carried foreword, functions independently of the human mind, including religious systems. Conversely, according to Eagleton, *Ulysses* debunks the myths of materialism, commerce, and the viability of Catholicism. Eagleton's argument counters early Marxist and ideologically based Marxists who argue that *Ulysses* offers no positive vision to counter the negative representation of capitalism and colonialism.

Roughley also identifies the work of Fredric Jameson as significant in connection with Marxist analysis of *Ulysses*. Jameson uses a musical analogy of position, opposition, and unity to explore Joyce's text. Specifically, Jameson observes the system functioning on a thematic level to bring each chapter into context with the novel as a whole. On a stylistic level, Jameson points out that *Ulysses'* variety of forms and patterns also combine in the unified form of the book and point toward a new, nonindividualistic style. Jameson also observes that the characters seem to come together but that, in reality, they retain their individual natures. Jameson also explores *Ulysses* in historical terms, emphasizing the importance of historical understanding, not only to comprehend the subtleties of Joyce's text but any literary or artistic work. Specifically, Jameson argues that historical factors place Joyce's work into a context without which a true understanding of the novel remains impossible. Jameson then focuses his critical inquiry not onto *Ulysses* but onto other critical interpretations of *Ulysses*. He particularly attacks psychoanalytic theory, myth criticism, and ethical readings. In his opinion, nonhistorically based analyses of the text distort the reality of

*Ulysses* to favor a personal, critical agenda. On the other hand, Jameson considers historical-based criticism most relevant to the text and the least subject to personal manipulation.

More specifically, Jameson points out that *Ulysses*, as part of the modernist literary tradition, focuses on the disconnectedness between man and society, as a consequence of a mass-produced environment. In order to accept Jameson's reading of the text, critics must assume that the Marxist view of history is the most objective reading of history. Moreover, unless Jameson be accused of hypocrisy, his view that *Ulysses* condemns the dissociation of man and his environment must be seen as less reinforcing Jameson's Marxist reading of history, as validating Jameson's ideology, than as a major focus of the text. Jameson also requires of his readers that they renounce the critical ideologies of previous interpretive schools in order to focus on not so much the primary reading of *Ulysses* but on, in Jameson's view, the only valid reading of the text.

Despite Jameson's sometimes all too virulent attacks on other critical schools, his work does yield valuable insights into *Ulysses*. Specifically, he focuses on the city's environment, its people, and its history. Jameson observes that city life takes people away from a direct connection with the products of their labor and with each other but that gossip brings the people together. Jameson, essentially, emphasizes the ideal of an unofficial discourse as the positive or unifying force more ideological Marxists find lacking in the text. Jameson attributes Dublin's powers of collectivity to its position on the periphery, existing both on the edges of the British Empire and on the edges of the established capitalist state. Because Dublin retains much of the characteristics of a village, it can, in Jameson's view, represent much of the nonindividualistic ideals of the preindustrialized society.

*Ulysses'* variety of narrative forms then, for Jameson, functions as proof of the gradual nonindividualistic sanction that the text posits. In terms of this reading, the "Ithaca" chapter, with its complete absence of a narrative voice, reflects the climax of the novel. Individual characterization and perspective, Jameson contends, are set asunder in the objective relaying of facts and events. Jameson's reading of the "Ithaca" chapter's focus and thematic, Marxist impact, supposes that the supposedly scientific narration of the chapter does not favor any individual character's perspective, that the questions asked and the choice of answers that the text offers do not establish individual characterization. Moreover, the "Penelope" chapter must not then, if Jameson's reading is to retain its full power, reestablish the individual. The latter condition remains problematic for numerous reasons, not the least of which is Joyce's choice in *Ulysses* and *Finnegans Wake* to end his text with individual female voices. All must be discounted as fruitless expressions of the individual in favor of the collective, nonindividual Marxist spirit, if Jameson's reading were to stand.

## PSYCHOANALYTIC CRITICISM

Simply put, psychoanalytic criticism applies various theories associated with the science of psychology to the study of literature. Early psychiatrists and psychologists, in fact, regarded literature as the expression of subconscious desire and impulses. Furthermore, many of Freud's writings seem like works of literary analysis. Later critics, using psychoanalytic theories, focus on literature not so much as the expression of subconscious desire but as consciously crafted specimens that express beliefs about the unconscious and its relation to the conscious mind and world. In terms of criticism that explores the totality of Joyce's works and *Ulysses* in particular,[17] Alan Roughley once again offers the clearest and most concise guide to psychoanalytic criticism and Joyce's text. Specifically, Roughley focuses, in general, on the work of numerous critics, including Coleman, Walcott, Shechner, and O'Brien. In particular and extended detail, Roughley emphasizes the writings of Kimball, Brivic, and Ferrer as their work relates to *Ulysses*.

In terms of writers who contribute to the interrelation between Jung and Freud and *Ulysses*, Elliott Coleman, in "A Note on Joyce and Jung,"[18] emphasizes Jung's theories of the male anima and the female animus as they apply to the "Circe" episode. Coleman even suggests that Joyce's text may have helped Jung develop his theories. William Walcott, in his "Notes by a Jungian Analyst on the Dreams in *Ulysses*,"[19] stresses what he sees as meaningful coincidences in various characters' dreams. In particular, Walcott argues that Stephen's dreaming of Haroun al Raschid anticipates Stephen's relationship with Bloom. Walcott also points out that the dream allows for greater understanding of Bloom and Stephen as individuals and of their relationship. Mark Shechner, in *Joyce in Nighttown: A Psychoanalytic Inquiry into "Ulysses,"*[20] observes that certain relationships between the conscious and the unconscious pervade *Ulysses*, including the expression of repressed wishes, their transformation into desire and longing, remnant longings from infancy and childhood, the formation of guilt and the subconscious mind, and the symbolic/allegorical nature of human actions. Darcy O'Brien, in "A Critique of Psychoanalytic Criticism, or What Joyce Did and Did Not Do,"[21] explores the nature of psychoanalytic criticism and *Ulysses*, questioning the intentionality of Joyce's representation of unconscious patterns. O'Brien would rather that readers of *Ulysses* focus on the facts as represented in the text. Other studies explore in greater detail some of the same themes and issues examined by these critics.

Specifically, Jean Kimball, in "Freud, Leonardo, and Joyce: The Dimension of a Childhood Memory,"[22] focuses on the similarities between Freud's discussion of the historical figure Leonardo and Joyce's created character Leopold Bloom. Specifically, Kimball traces out numerous similar traits and characteristics, arguing that the sheer number of similarities suggests more than coincidence. Among the convergent traits between Freud's Leonardo and Joyce's Bloom, Kimball cites their desire for peace and reconciliation of violence. The similarity is all the more remarkable, Kimball suggests, because both Leonardo's and Bloom's societies valued confrontation and violence. She also points out that Bloom and Leonardo, as represented by Freud and Joyce, share many sexual proclivities and characteristics. Kimball also observes the similarities between Stephen and Freud's Leonardo, remarking that both share an ambivalence toward mother figures. Moreover, Kimball argues, that Joyce consciously replaced Freud's emblem of the vulture, applied to Leonardo, with a bird, the hawk, applied to *Ulysses*. The difference, Kimball suggests, indicates an embrace of creativity and release rather than of death and imprisonment.

Daniel Ferrer, in "Circe, regret, and regression,"[23] argues that the "Circe" episode utilizes a technique similar to Freud's principle of the "uncanny." Essentially, Joyce presents, in the "Circe" episode, elements from the rest of *Ulysses* that are both strange and familiar. Extrapolating from Ferrer's suggestion and from his reference to totems (animals representing humans), readers are confronted with strange yet familiar elements that compel readers to question certainties. If humans behave as animals and in fact become animals, if young women from the beach become prostitutes, if Bloom can transform gender, then readers must abandon their assumption that they are reading a realistic novel and yield to unconscious associations. Indeed, Ferrer urges the reader to yield to his/her own associations, suggesting that he/she stand facing a mirror and that an image in the mirror is best understood from a distance, that a whole or gestalt image must be considered for true understanding to develop. The manner in which the unfamiliar weaves itself into the familiar, Ferrer points out, is also significant. Bloom and Stephen both come to terms with uncomfortable unconscious realizations. Bloom does so through the image of Shakespeare, whereas Stephen sees himself as a great man in degraded form. Ferrer's interpretation explains why Bloom emerges from the chapter stronger and why Stephen emerges in a weakened state. Bloom grows more comfortable with himself by accepting his unconscious. Stephen cannot come to terms with his unconscious and remains frustrated. In fact, Stephen's anger and frustration become more manifest.

Sheldon Brivic, in *Joyce Between Jung and Freud*, explores the varying influence of Jungian and Freudian elements in Joyce's works. Brivic makes numerous interesting observations. Notably, he observes in Joyce's work an emphasis on both the individual consciousness, a Freudian concept, and the collective unconscious, a Jungian principle. More specifically, Brivic notes that Jung's theories allow for religious and spiritual elements to enter into the formation of an individual's sensibility. Brivic takes particular note of the images that rise in the "Circe" episode. A decaying corpse in the form of his mother confronts Stephen, as Brivic notes, with images of castration and powerlessness. Moreover, Brivic observes, the paternal figures are equally threatening, and Stephen, although he attempts to destroy them with his ashplant, actually remains vulnerable, as his pathetic experience with the soldiers demonstrates. In addition, Brivic indicates that Stephen's Shakespeare theory suggests a sexual desire for the mother figure, complicated and accentuated because of his mother's recent death and his apparent disregard for her feelings. Reinforcing Brivic's view, Stephen has the mother figure within his Shakespeare theory damage the male figure, which represents not only a reversal of the archetype of father injuring mother but also represents an expression of Stephen's guilt regarding his feelings for his mother. Brivic also observes other Jungian-type patterns in *Ulysses*, notably the distinction between spirit and form. Brivic argues that Stephen, in this scenario, represents the spirit and Bloom represents form. Bloom, after all, eats regularly, engages in a type of sexual liaison, and indulges his senses, whereas Stephen refrains from eating, represses his sexual desires, and neglects his sensual nature. Brivic's theories in this regard do not take into account Bloom's more metaphysical side, his contemplation of metempsychosis and parallax. However, Brivic's observations do trace out numerous important parallels between *Ulysses* and Freudian/Jungian thought.

In addition to the distinction between matter and energy, Brivic notes that Freud's theories help illuminate the nuances of individual characterization, whereas Jung's theories reveal much about the interaction between characters and the characters' relation to the symbolic elements of the text. Specifically, Bloom's resourcefulness compared with Stephen's intellectually paralyzed manner of interaction with the world and events focuses attention on Bloom's similarity to Odysseus in that both are men of action. Moreover, Bloom's and Stephen's interaction functions as a symbol of noncompetitive male relations, according to Brivic. Although Stephen's final insult to Bloom might contradict Brivic's theory at least in part, it has much validity. Moreover, Brivic takes note of the less than perfect relations between the two, suggesting that the circumstances reveal that Stephen is a disturbed filial figure. In addition, Brivic notes that Bloom and Stephen share a great deal. Both have troubled psychological relationships with women, both are outsiders, both wander about Dublin, excluded from their homes. In this sense, Brivic notes Stephen becomes the rebel hero and Bloom, the submissive victim. The two characters juxtaposed reveal yet another Jungian-like archetype. Brivic's observations, taken in conjunction with the various psychoanalytic theories reveal subtleties of characterization and symbolization not available to critics who disregard these theories.

Indeed, it would be a mistake for students of Ulysses to disregard any theoretical model. All have something to offer regarding an understanding of Joyce's text. Taken as a whole, the variety of critical theories reveals numerous subtleties in the novel unavailable to readers not willing to consider a variety of critical perspectives. Even the contradictions and conflicts that various theories offer each other reveal nuances of the text and can spark individual interpretation and understanding.

## NOTES

1. Bonnie Kime Scott, *James Joyce* (Atlantic Highlands, NJ: Humanities Press, 1987).

2. Margot Norris, ed., *A Companion to James Joyce's Ulysses* (New York: Bedford Books, 1998).

3. Alan Roughley, *James Joyce and Critical Theory* (Ann Arbor: University of Michigan Press, 1991).

4. The most notable semiotic studies of *Ulysses* include Roland Barthes's *Elements of Semiology* (New York: Hill and Wang, 1980) and *Mythologies* (London: Jonathan Cape, 1972); Umberto Eco's *A Theory of Semiotics* (Bloomington: Indiana University Press, 1979) and *Foucault's Pendulum* (London: Secker and Warburg, 1989); Julia Kristeva's *Desire and Language* (New York: Columbia University Press, 1980); and Robert Scholes's *Semiotics and Interpretation* (New Haven: Yale University Press, 1982).

5. The most useful studies of poststructuralism and deconstruction, for an understanding of *Ulysses*, include Derrick Attridge's "Criticism's Wake," in *James Joyce: The Augmented Ninth*, ed. Bernard Benstock (Syracuse: Syracuse University Press, 1988) and *Poststructuralist Joyce: Essays from the French* (Cambridge: Cambridge University Press, 1984); Helene Cixous's *The Exile of James Joyce*, trans. Sally Purcell (New York: David Lewis, 1972); Jacques Derrida's "*Ulysses* Gramophone Hear Say Yes in Joyce," trans. Tina Kendall, with emendations by

Shari Benstock, in *A Companion to James Joyce's* Ulysses, ed. Margot Norris (New York: Bedford Books, 1998), pp. 69–90; Julia Kristeva's *Desire in Language*, ed. Leon Roudiez and trans. Thomas Gora et al. (New York: Columbia University Press, 1980).

6. See Atteridge's *Post-Structuralist Joyce*.

7. Ibid.

8. Ibid.

9. See *James Joyce Quarterly* 16:1 (Winter 1979): 27–42.

10. Robert Scholes, *In Search of James Joyce* (Urbana: University of Illinois Press, 1992).

11. Seymour Chatman, *Story and Discourse: Narrative Structure in Fiction and Film* (Ithaca: Cornell University Press, 1978).

12. The most important studies of feminism and *Ulysses* include Christine van Boheemen's *The Novel as Family Romance* (Ithaca: Cornell University Press, 1987); Sheldon Brivic's *Joyce's Waking Women* (Madison: University of Wisconsin Press, 1995); Suzette Henke's *James Joyce and the Politics of Desire* (New York: Routledge, 1990); Vicki Mahaffey's *Reauthorizing Joyce* (New York: Cambridge University Press, 1988); and Margot Norris's *Joyce's Web: The Social Unraveling of Modernism* (Austin: University of Texas Press, 1992).

13. The postcolonial section of the previous chapter considers much of the criticism classified under traditional Marxism. However, additional studies include Edna Duffy's *The Subaltern "Ulysses"* (Minneapolis: University of Minnesota Press, 1994); Terry Eagleton, Fredric Jameson, and Edward Said's *Nationalism, Colonialism, and Literature* (Minneapolis: University of Minnesota Press, 1990); and Cheryl Herr's *Joyce's Anatomy of Culture* (Urbana: University of Illinois Press, 1986).

14. Roughley, *James Joyce*, pp. 219–220.

15. Alick West, *Crisis and Criticism* (London: Lawrence and Wishart, 1936).

16. Terry Eagleton, *Exiles and Émigés: Studies in Modern Literature* (London: Chatto and Windus, 1970).

17. More detailed explorations of psychoanalytic criticism and *Ulysses* appear in Sheldon Brivic's *The Veil of Signs: Joyce, Lacan, and Perception* (Urbana: University of Illinois Press, 1985); Susan Stanford Friedman's *Joyce: The Return of the Repressed* (Ithaca: Cornell University Press, 1993); Frances Restuccia's *Joyce and the Law of the Father* (New Haven: Yale University Press, 1989); and Mark Shechner's *Joyce in Nighttown: A Psychoanalytic Inquiry into "Ulysses"* (Berekley: University of California Press, 1974).

18. Roughley, *James Joyce*, p. 170.

19. Ibid., pp. 180–181.

20. Ibid., pp.180–184.

21. Ibid., pp. 183–185.

22. Ibid., pp. 185–189.

23. Ibid., pp. 201–209.

# 8    Bibliographical Essay

Earliest criticisms of James Joyce's *Ulysses*, covering the first few decades of its publication, established the text as a classic work of fiction but only after considerable critical discussion and debate. Specifically, most of the controversy surrounded the book's revolutionary form and content. Many critics found it to be remarkably unfocused and not worth critical attention. However, studies by Stuart Gilbert and others established the text's critical and technical worth.

The earliest serious criticism of Joyce's text comes shortly after its publication. Specifically, Ezra Pound, in an essay titled "James Joyce et Pécuchet" published in *Mercure de France* (1922) and later translated for *Shenandoah* (1952), emphasized the realistic qualities of Joyce's text, placing *Ulysses* within the context of the French literary tradition, notably citing Flaubert. However, Pound also stressed *Ulysses'* variation from standard realism by emphasizing the book's variations from traditional literary realism, arguing that the text's focus on minute details particularized its broader themes. Moreover, Pound emphasized the text's musical structure, pointing out its use of counterpoint and rhythm in intertwining detail and themes throughout its structure. T.S. Eliot, in his highly influential essay titled "*Ulysses*, Order, and Myth" and published in *The Dial* (1923), explored *Ulysses'* use of the *Odyssey* as a unifying and organizing structure. Eliot stresses *Ulysses'* balance between the classical and the contemporary, using myth to order and structure the chaos of contemporary experiences by contextualizing humanity's actions and motivations. Eliot also explores the text's vast symbolic textures, all of which he uses to highlight Joyce's use of ancient and established elements to focus on what Eliot saw to be the formlessness and lack of direction present in early twentieth-century society. Eliot's and Pound's criticism gave a framework to many subsequent explorations of Joyce's text, notably from French and Continental critics and English critics who focused on Joyce's use of the French literary tradition. Specifically, Edmond Wilson (*Axel's Castle* [New York: Scribner's, 1969] ) and Valéry Larbaud (*The* Ulysses *of James Joyce* [Ann Arbor: University of Michigan Press, 1948] ) explored Joyce's literary antecedents. Wilson, like Pound, explores *Ulysses'* debt to Flaubert and the French realists and cites the influence of the French symbolist tradition with its use of individual perceptive and stylistic innovation to contextualize contemporary life. Larbaud explored the impact of Dujardin's stream-of-consciousness narrative technique on Joyce's work. Even Carl Jung (" 'Ulysses': A Monologue," in *Critical Essays on James Joyce,* ed. Bernard Benstock, [Boston: G.K. Hall, 1989], pp. 9–27) ventured a review of the book, admitting to rather conventional literary tastes, Jung nonetheless praises *Ulysses.* He begins by admitting his frustrations. Ultimately, however, admitting that it accomplishes wonders. Essentially, Jung answers his own concerns and other early critical concerns by seeing what many saw in the text's weaknesses as its ultimate strengths. However, despite the work of these and other critics, *Ulysses* fell prey to a number of influential and sometimes savage critical attacks.

Notably, Wyndham Lewis took exception to what he saw as the novel's formlessness. In *Time and Western Man* (London: Chatto and Windus, 1927) , Lewis openly condemned Joyce's use of literary influences and narrative techniques, arguing that *Ulysses* lacks any focus whatsoever. So influential was Lewis's interpretation that Joyce authorized and contributed to Stuart Gilbert's *James Joyce's* Ulysses (New York: Knopf, 1952). Gilbert's book focuses on what Lewis and other critics saw to be *Ulysses'* weaknesses. Gilbert devotes the early part of his study to tracing the various influences on Joyce's text, the book's themes, and Joyce's techniques. Gilbert then focuses, in the second part of his study, on how various themes and motifs repeat themselves throughout the text, particularly noting the Homeric Odyssean motifs in a chapter-by-chapter summary and analysis. Gilbert's study was not the first to emphasize the parallels with Homer and other major influences and motifs. In addition to Eliot's work, S. Foster Damon, in his essay titled "The Odyssey in Dublin" and published in *The Hound and the Horn*, explores not only the Homeric parallels but also the references to

*Hamlet* and to Dante's *Divine Comedy*. In addition, Paul Jordan, in *A Key to the* Ulysses *of James Joyce* (New York: Covici, 1934), also traced out the Odyssean motif. However, Gilbert systematically focused at length on each of the episodes in a way no previous critic had done, and he utilized the practical suggestions and advice of Joyce himself to such an extent that his guide still serves as a good introduction and supplement to the text, even if it does, at times, over emphasize the text's form and structure along allusive lines. Indeed, so valuable a plan did Gilbert provide that his work established Joyce's text as a classic in spite of the attacks of Lewis and other critics. Gilbert made the book accessible to many readers who found its forms and techniques inscrutable. Moreover, Gilbert literally made parts of *Ulysses* available to American readers while it was still under a censorship ban.

The other major critical work of the 1920s and 1930s, Frank Budgen's *James Joyce and the Making of* Ulysses (London: Oxford University Press, 1972), focuses on the biographical and human aspects of the text and its production. Budgen knew Joyce well while he was writing *Ulysses*, and Budgen's book draws on that personal knowledge to grant insight into Joyce's creative processes and the nuances of his art. Budgen's avoidance of a specific intellectual or critical perspective, such as that which informs Eliot's or Jung's approach, and Budgen's focus not on the text's industry or form, as in Gilbert's study, but on *Ulysses*' human dimensions and its quiet optimism make Budgen's analysis particularly valuable. A reader gets the sense that *James Joyce and the Making of* Ulysses meets the text and the author on their terms and not through a filter of an intellectual agenda, no matter how well motivated an agenda.

Another major opinion of Joyce's text was also not written by a professional literary critic. Judge John M. Woolsey wrote the opinion declaring *Ulysses* nonobscene and thus making the text legally available in the United States. Woolsey's decision, made in the case of the *United States of America v. One Book Called* Ulysses, became a landmark in case law in the United States, declaring that a work's artistic merits mitigate its supposed corruption. Woolsey's decision reveals that he carefully read the book and acknowledges that Joyce attempts something new within its pages. Woolsey also recognized the human dimensions of the text. Woolsey's decision, along with Gilbert's and Budgen's larger studies, established *Ulysses*' place in critical debate and laid the foundations for what would come to be called the Joyce industry.

However, it was not until the 1940s and 1950s that *Ulysses* began to find a home in academia. Joyce's entry into the literary mainstream corresponds with the publication of his final work, *Finnegans Wake*, and with his death. Harry Levin, in *James Joyce: A Critical Introduction* (London: Faber and Faber, 1943), advances the theory that Joyce's work combines naturalistic elements with symbolist techniques and, consequently, stands as a definitive modern text. Levin, a scholar whose area of expertise was Renaissance drama, might seem an odd choice to write the seminal academic critical study of Joyce. However, after he had written a brief review of *Finnegans Wake*, Joyce himself asked James Laughlin, the general editor of a series titled "The Makers of Modern Literature," to offer Levin the volume devoted to his (Joyce's) work. Levin's work contextualizes *Ulysses* within nineteenth-century and early twentieth-century novels and poetry from not only England but also the Continent, particularly France and America, noting Joyce's similarities to Hawthorne, among others. Levin also stresses the autobiographical elements in Joyce's text, noting the parallels between Joyce and Stephen Dedalus. Moreover, Levin down plays the Homeric parallels in *Ulysses*, preferring instead to emphasize the ways in which the text diverges from the *Odyssey*, deemphasizing earlier critical approaches that tended to trace out the intricate relations between Homer and Joyce, sometimes at the expense of other aspects of Joyce's work. In terms of Joyce's use of language, Levin stresses the realistic representation of human thought in contrast to the realist or naturalist novel. Levin explains that Joyce enters into the human mind and realistically portrays the manner in which individuals think and interact with their environments. Levin, a comparative literature professor at Harvard, did more than any other critic to establish Joyce and *Ulysses* in the academic world.

After Levin's work, the next major academic study of Joyce was Richard Kain's *Fabulous Voyager: James Joyce's "Ulysses"* (Chicago: University of Chicago, 1947). Kain focuses on the stylistic and naturalistic details that Levin highlighted and explores them in an intricate manner. One of the most striking details of Kain's study involves his lists. He indexes more than 500 references to Bloom, provides a character list numbering 150, offers a directory of addresses, and includes a motif index. He also emphasizes the novel's setting in Dublin and in Ireland, stresses the human elements of the characters, and explores the book's general themes of alienation and companionship. In particular, Kain, with the help of Trinity College's librarian, consulted newspapers from June 16, 1904, and maps from 1904, comparing textual references and allusions to these primary sources. Kain is the first critic to note that Sceptre and Throwaway actually ran in the Gold Cup and finished in the order Joyce records their finish in *Ulysses*. Kain also makes use of Thom's directory of Dublin and notes that 7 Eccles Street was vacant at the time. Kain also places, as does Levin, Joyce in context with his literary predecessors. However, Kain also explores *Ulysses'* debt to recent writers, such as Proust and Thomas Mann. Kain focuses particular attention, and for the first time sympathetic attention, on Leopold Bloom, emphasizing the character's humane approach to life and the obstacles with which he is confronted. Kain also explores Stephen's character, concluding that he fails to understand the human nuances of life and remains unsatisfied as a result. Kain sees that Molly, on the other hand, does grasp the fundamental lesson of life and is good-hearted. Ultimately, Kain sees *Ulysses* as an indictment of modern civilization, focusing on society's shortcomings and contradictory elements. Kain's work, coming out of one of the first college courses on Joyce and *Ulysses*, continues Levin's trend of subjecting the work to systematic academic scrutiny. However, Kain takes Levin's introduction to the text and offers, in addition to a general analysis of themes and techniques, a particular level of scrutiny of textual details that was without precedent in Joycean criticism and which laid the groundwork for numerous future academic articles and books.

The next major book focusing on *Ulysses* is Hugh Kenner's *Dublin's Joyce* (London: Chatto and Windus, 1955), which, like Kain's study, focuses on the minute particulars of Joyce's text within an Irish context, but Kenner also stresses the notable absences in the book. An academic work, written in a nonacademic style, *Dublin's Joyce* focuses attention on Joyce's treatment of a number of sophisticated issues in *Ulysses*. Specifically, Kenner establishes a balanced approach to the use of Homeric parallel in Joyce's text, arguing that the *Odyssey* functions as a rough outline to the happenings in the book but that too much emphasis on Homer distorts Joyce. Moreover, in his explorations of particular characters, Kenner notes subtleties. For example, he sees Bloom as a reflective individual but one whose reflections stop short of true insight and rarely last beyond a sentence or two. He also asks several relevant questions regarding Bloom's and Molly's conversations that are referred to but not relayed to the reader. Most notably, however, Kenner, in articulating his own thesis regarding *Ulysses*, allows for a broad range of interpretations, indicating that Joyce's text presents Dublin and modern society from numerous perspectives and that any given reader can grasp only a few of these trends. Hugh Kenner's precise reading of *Ulysses* elaborated on and extended the work of Levin and Kain, using the same techniques of close reading and analysis to both illuminate the subjects that the text discusses and to cast light on the elements the text avoids. Kenner's work also lays the groundwork for deconstructionist and poststructuralist readings of the text by opening the possibility of a multitude of possible interpretations and scenes and allowing for *Ulysses'* ability to draw a reader into his own theories and thoughts that complete the half-stated and half-started reflections of numerous characters.

The 1950s came to an end with the publication of William York Tindall's *A Reader's Guide to James Joyce* (New York: Noonday Press, 1959). Tindall's work, written from an academic perspective (Tindall had earlier published a book exploring in traditional academic terms Joyce's use of symbolism), is nonetheless directed to a nonacademic audience. Tindall attempts to make the themes and subtleties of Joyce's text available to the general reader. In his *Guide*, Tindall advances his view that *Ulysses* promotes charity while discouraging pride. Subsequently, Tindall traces his theme through an episode-by-episode close reading of the text, making particular note of major extratextual references and occasionally explicating passages beginning readers may find particularly difficult. In a further attempt to engage the general reader, Tindall occasionally comments on his personal reactions to certain episodes, sharing his frustration with the "Oxen of the Sun" and his joy with "Ithaca." Tindall seems most pleased with his reading of Molly that sees her, in part, as a sexual/sensual offering to the novel's various male figures. *A Reader's Guide to James Joyce* clarifies and simplifies the complexities of Joyce's work and of *Ulysses* with the aim of making his works more generally accessible to a nonacademic audience.

Other critics began to place Joyce firmly within the British literary tradition, and many critics began to explore the relationship between Shakespeare's work and *Ulysses*. Specifically, Edward Duncan examines in "Unsubstantial Father: A Study of the 'Hamlet' symbolism in Joyce's *Ulysses*" the connections between Shakepeare's play and Joyce's text. Arthur Heine's "Shakespeare in James Joyce" also traces the connections between the two authors. In addition, William Schutte's *Joyce and Shakespeare* (New Haven: Yale University Press, 1957) explores in detail the interconnections between *Ulysses* and Shakespeare's works, tracing out not simply the complex network of allusions and references in *Ulysses* but also how those references reinforce *Ulysses'* thematic subtleties. Specifically, Schutte reads Stephen's flaws into the character's misreadings, as Schutte sees them of Shakespeare's life and work. *Joyce and Shakespeare*, building on the work of earlier critics, is the first extended study of the couples' interconnections of Shakespeare's and Joyce's work.

Other notable studies of this period include R.P. Blackmur's "The Jew in Search of a Son" (*Eleven Essays in the European Novel* [New York: Harcourt, 1964] , which links the paternal themes to *Ulysses'* representation of moral decay. However, as the 1950s came to an end and even as Joyce's work began to solidify its position in the academic world, not all voices from the academy were optimistic about *Ulysses'* future in the Western literary cannon. F.R. Leavis, in *The Great Tradition* (London: Chatto and Windus, 1960), acknowledges the text's technical skill and literary craftsmanship yet argues that it is *Ulysses'* revolutionary and experimental qualities that would mark its demise in the future. Despite Leavis's objections, *Ulysses* would, in fact, go on to play a dominant role in literary criticism, with only the works of Shakespeare receiving more critical attention than the works of Joyce. The critical framework laid down by Levin, Kain, Kenner, and others in the 1940s and 1950s established *Ulysses* in academia and exposed the nuances and subtleties of Joyce's literary craftsmanship.

The 1960s saw an evolution in Joyce scholarship, from the early critical explorations of the text to a more elaborate critical examination of the details of Joyce's work. Scholars, essentially, began to examine the nuances of *Ulysses* rather than simply attempt to trace out its basic parameters.

The 1961 publication of S.L. Goldberg's *The Classical Temper: A Study of James Joyce's* Ulysses (London: Chatto and Windus, 1961) marked the first significant study of the decade. Goldberg traces the concept of humanistic subjectivity through Joyce's text, focusing on the evolution and development of Stephen Dedalus's creative aesthetic. Robert Martin Adams's *Surface and Symbol* (Oxford: Oxford University Press, 1962) builds on the work of earlier critics, discussing Joyce's use of factual materials in *Ulysses*. Adams explores not only Joyce's adherence to fact but also his blurring of fact in order to reinforce thematic issues. Arnold Goldman's *The Joyce Paradox: Form and Freedom in His Fiction* (London: Routledge, 1966) anticipates deconstuctive readings of the text. Goldman examines the ways in which *Ulysses* presents details and themes that offer possibly contradictory readings. In 1964, Stanley Sultan published *The Argument of* Ulysses (Columbus: OSU Press, 1965), which traces the development of narrative detail along symbolic and thematic lines. Sultan examines his themes utilizing a chapter-by-chapter approach, offing a valuable close reading of certain sections of the text. Harry Blamires's *The Bloomsday Book: A Guide through Joyce's* Ulysses (London: Methuen, 1966) also offers a chapter-by-chapter close reading of the narrative. Clive Hart's *James Joyce's* Ulysses (University Park: PSU Press, 1968) also offers a close reading of the narrative, offering, in addition, background information of various themes and other introductory material. Despite the obvious evolution in critical understanding of *Ulysses*, opposition appeared voicing concerns about the general critical trends in Joycean scholarship. Anthony Cronin in *A Question of Modernity* (London: Secker and Warburg, 1966) asks whether critical scrutiny that traces out themes and patterns in Joyce's text, with a design toward critical explication, does not necessarily distort an understanding of *Ulysses*. Cronin advocates what he understands to be the creative essence of Joyce's work, arguing for a greater appreciation for the creative product and not so much for its intricacies and influences. Cronin argues that critics, with their explications and thematic tracings, make *Ulysses* into something more like a traditional novel than it is or was ever intended to be. Cronin instead argues for Joyce's revolutionary designs and structure, creating a book that less closely resembles traditional forms and more closely resembles human life. Cronin's not so subtle subtext also suggests a visit to Dublin by various critics too preoccupied with the highly symbolic associations of places and symbols. If such critics were to come to Ireland, Cronin's article suggests, they might be surprised at the city's highly symbolic associations and symbols.

The work of these and other critics would not have been possible if it were not for the publication of two highly significant studies of Joyce's life and his composition practices. Specifically, in 1961, A. Walton Litz published *The Art of James Joyce: Method and Design in* Ulysses *and* Finnegans Wake (London: Oxford University Press, 1964), which explored Joyce's processes of composition and revision, granting insight into Joyce's works' use and development of themes and motifs. Litz argues that the composition history of the texts suggests that Joyce revised and updated his overall designs for each of the works at various stages of composition. The most significant event in Joycean scholarship of the era was Richard Ellmann's *James Joyce* (Oxford: Oxford University Press), published in 1959. Ellmann's biography carefully and in a detailed way explores Joyce's life, his influences, and his composition processes. It is a benchmark in Joycean criticism, offering a definitive account of the author's life and work and providing a stable source for a variety of critical interpretations. In the 1960s, Ellmann also supplemented Stuart Gilbert's single volume of Joyce's letters with the publication of two more volumes of letters, offering the scholarly community general access to important primary documents. Ellmann's work laid the foundation for the scholarly evolution of Joycean criticism.

In the 1970s, new theoretical approaches to literary study emerged, and many used Joyce's works, particularly *Ulysses* and *Finnegans Wake*, as proving grounds for their epistemological theories. Chapter 7 treats the major critical-theory schools' readings of *Ulysses*. Other critical trends focused further on textual explication and on the variety of influences and sources for Joyce's work.

Notably, David Hayman's *Ulysses: The Mechanics of Meaning* (Madison: University of Wisconsin Press, 1982) functions as a type of introductory text, exploring in detail Joyce's place within a variety of literary and cultural traditions. Erwin Steinberg's *The Stream of Consciousness and Beyond in Ulysses* (Pittsburgh: University of Pittsburgh Press, 1973) explores the literary history of the stream-of-consciousness narrative technique and also explores Joyce's particular adaptation and expansion of the device. Steinberg, utilizing manuscript and early draft material, explores the differences and development of Bloom's, Molly's, and Stephen's characters in light of their individual styles of stream-of-conscious thought. Louis Hyman's *The Jews of Ireland from the Earliest Times to 1910* (Shannon: Irish University Press, 1972) offers essential background for Leopold Bloom's character. Richard Ellmann's *Ulysses on the Liffey* (Oxford: Oxford University Press, 1979) takes a fresh look at the book. Ellmann's work makes little reference to *Ulysses* criticism and scholarship, which raised the wrath of the critical community. However, Ellmann's work did receive popular attention and garnered popular attention for *Ulysses*. His neglect of the critical history of Joycean scholarship and his reiteration of themes advanced and explored by other scholars may be explained by his potential audience. The book does not appear to be written for the scholarly community but rather for general readers of the text. In addition to volumes by individual authors, a variety of fiftieth-anniversary critical studies saw publication. Thomas Staley's volume of essays from various contributors, titled *Ulysses: Fifty Years* (Pittsburgh: University of Pittsburgh Press, 1970), offers a number of useful readings of the text, explicating details of individual episodes that had escaped scholarly scrutiny. Another collection of essays, titled *Ulysses: Critical Essays* (Berkeley: University of California Press, 1974) and edited by Clive Hart and David Hayman, offers an episode-by-episode reading of each chapter.

In addition to critical works, a variety of critical annotations and references also appeared in the 1970s. Don Gifford, with the help of Robert Seidman, traces out in detail *Ulysses'* various allusive references (Berkeley: University of California Press, 1988). Gifford's book, in its current revised form, offers an extremely valuable and indispensable tool for basic to more-advanced readings of the text. Zack Bowen added to an understanding of *Ulysses* with his *Musical Allusions in the Works of James Joyce* (Albany: SUNY Press, 1974), providing detailed and illuminating notes on Joyce's pervasive use of music in his works. However, *The James Joyce Archive* (New York: Garland, 1977–1979), arranged by Michael Groden, is the major critical tool published in the decade. It makes available facsimile copies of more than 25,000 pages of all extant note, manuscripts, typescripts, and drafts for all of Joyce's works. Essentially, it gathers much of the world's manuscript holdings of Joyce into a series of volumes, readily available to scholars.

The last twenty years of scholarship have witnessed a surge in attention to Joyce's works both in the fields of literary theory and in more traditional scholarship. Hugh Kenner's *Ulysses* (Baltimore: Johns Hopkins University Press, 1987) condenses and focuses the arguments of his previous works and functions as an ideal critical introduction to the novel. Kenner focuses on Joyce's rhetoric, his technique, and his use of Homeric parallels. In terms of rhetoric, Kenner notes how almost every scene in the book has at least two narrative points of view. Kenner also reiterates his "Uncle Charles principle," which states that a narrative voice mimics the perspective of the scene's character. Kenner also argues, in terms of *Ulysses'* use of the *Odyssey*, that Joyce's text uses Homer for both comic and thematic effect. In terms of technique, Kenner suggests that the style of *Ulysses* draws the reader into the text, making the reader a participant in the narrative.

Other useful books on *Ulysses* published in the last twenty years include Roy Gottfried's *The Art of Syntax in Joyce's* Ulysses (Athens: University of Georgia Press, 1980), which explores the book on a linguistic level. Cheryl Herr's *Joyce and the Anatomy of Culture* (Urbana: University of Illinois Press, 1986) examines *Ulysses'* use of popular and cultural influences. Seamus Deane in *Celtic Revivals* (London: Faber and Faber, 1985) explores Joyce within the context of the Irish Literary Revival. Declan Kiberd also explores Joyce within the context of Irish literary history and Irish political history in *Inventing Ireland* (London: Jonathan Cape, 1995) and in his introduction to his annotated student's edition of *Ulysses*. Kiberd sees Joyce's text as a transition narrative, bridging the gap between the language of colonialism and the language of liberation. Vincent Cheng in *Joyce, Race, and Empire* (Cambridge: Cambridge University Press, 1995) explores the racial implications of Irishness in the text. Maria Tymoczko's *The Irish Ulysses* (Berkeley: University of California Press, 1994) addresses the Irish context of the novel, examining Joyce's use of Irish traditions and stories in *Ulysses*. Most recently, John Rickard, in *Joyce's Book of Memory: The Mnemotechnic of 'Ulysses'* (Durham: Duke University Press, 1999), explores individual character's personal formations of memory and the implications of how those formations impact identity.

In terms of literary theory, there are two indispensable surveys of Joyce and critical theory: Margot Norris's *A Companion to James Joyce's* Ulysses and Alan Roughley's *James Joyce and Critical Theory: An Introduction*. Norris's book offers representative essays on *Ulysses* from a variety of critical theory perspectives, including deconstruction, reader response, feminist and gender theory, psychoanalytic criticism, and Marxist criticism. Roughley's book surveys significant articles and books, segregating them into various theoretical disciplines. Both texts offer excellent bibliographies. Students and general readers coming to *Ulysses* for the first time and wishing to review the thoughts of the variety of critical theoreticians on Joyce's text will discover in Roughly and Norris an easy-to-follow presentation of the major ideas of each theoretical school.

# Index

## About the Author

BERNARD MCKENNA is Associate Professor of Literature at Palm Beach Atlantic College. He is the author of numerous articles on Irish literature, culture, and art, which have appeared in such journals as *Eire-Ireland*, *Yeats: An Annual of Critical and Textual Studies*, and *Philological Quarterly*. He is also an Associate Editor of the *Dictionary of Irish Literature* (2nd ed., Greenwood, 1996).